Catholic Advocate of the Evangelical Truth

era trāslatio ſm hebraicā vitatem
u placētula frumēti: qō ppue ap
ſpē placētule frumēti verū corp̄
ſlatio chaldaica in q̄ vbi dr̄: In ſu
p̄ ſacerdotum. ⸿ In code ps. vbi
et nomen eius. ADDITIO.
oi dr̄: perm̄ āet nomē ei?: dicit hy
ignificatiōis cū hoc qō dr̄: perma
net: ſz ſignificat filiatio
nē: vn̄ Rabi abenhazra
in ſua gl. in B loco ſic dic

Catholic Advocate of the Evangelical Truth

Marcus Marulus (Marko Marulić) of Split (1450–1524)

FRANZ POSSET

Foreword by Bratislav Lučin

COLLECTED WORKS
VOLUME 5

WIPF & STOCK · Eugene, Oregon

CATHOLIC ADVOCATE OF THE EVANGELICAL TRUTH
Marcus Marulus (Marko Marulić) of Split (1450–1524)

Copyright © 2021 Franz Posset. All rights reserved. Except for brief quotations in critical publications or reviews, no part of this book may be reproduced in any manner without prior written permission from the publisher. Write: Permissions, Wipf and Stock Publishers, 199 W. 8th Ave., Suite 3, Eugene, OR 97401.

Explanation of image on book cover: First of the two eucharistic symbols (chalice and host) which Marulus entered in his *Biblia Latina*, on Psalm 71:16; next to Burgos' *ADDITIO*; *Biblia Latina*, volume 2; detail of folio 158.

Wipf & Stock
An Imprint of Wipf and Stock Publishers
199 W. 8th Ave., Suite 3
Eugene, OR 97401

www.wipfandstock.com

PAPERBACK ISBN: 978-1-5326-7870-7
HARDCOVER ISBN: 978-1-5326-7871-4
EBOOK ISBN: 978-1-5326-7872-1

04/12/21

Dedicated to
Zvonko Pandžić

Contents

Foreword by Bratislav Lučin		ix
Acknowledgments		xvii
Abbreviations		xix
Preface		xxi
Chapter 1	Marulus and Luther: What Do Marcus Marulus and Martin Luther Have in Common?	1
Chapter 2	Christ Speaking from the Cross: A Cistercian Monk as Editor of the *Carmen* of the Croatian Humanist Marcus Marulus	27
Chapter 3	The Empires: The Mouse, the Frog, and the Unidentified Flying Object: Metaphors for "Empires" in the Latin Works of the Croatian Humanist Marcus Marulus and of the German Humanist Ulrich von Hutten	40
Chapter 4	The Pope: Open Letter of a Croatian Lay Theologian to a "German" Pope	63
Chapter 5	The Bible: The Illustrated *Biblia cum comento* from the Library of the Father of Croatian Literature, with Samples of His Marginalia	86
Chapter 6	The "Rock": Marcus Marulus's Theological Patrimony Concerning the Interpretation of "You Are Peter and Upon This Rock I Will Build My Church"	113
Chapter 7	"The Tree of the Cross" and Other Early Christian Latin Poetry with the Marulus's Marginalia	130

Chapter 8 The Turks: Marulus on Christian-Muslim Relations	149
In Place of a Conclusion	183
Bibliography	187
Index of Personal Names	201
Index of Biblical References	209

Editorial Note:

The two forms of our subject's name (Marulus / Marulić) will be used in alternation throughout this volume. Contemporary Croatian authors and editors prefer Marko Marulić. The historical sources use the Latin version, Marcus Marulus.

Foreword

MARKO MARULIĆ (SPLIT, 1450–1524) is widely agreed to be the central figure of Croatian literature of the fifteenth and sixteenth centuries and a national classic. However, the basic characteristics of neither his work nor his life are easy to summarize. There is no surprise that this should be the case. This is an author who wrote on the cusp of two eras: he was a Christian moralist, but also a humanist poet and a citizen of the Renaissance. He wrote in Croatian, Latin, and Italian, and running inextricably through his work are strands of the old and the new, the local and European, the mundane and the eternal. The sheer volume of his oeuvre, its polyglotism, intricacy of theme and genre are the basic properties that are observed in any systematic approach to Marulić. To these may be added his capacity to internalize various literary inputs, a developed linguistic and literary competence, and authorial self-consciousness as a characteristic *signum temporis*.

Marulić acquired his basic education in the humanist school of his native town. There is no information about any studies he might have had outside Split, but the works that he wrote and the contents list of his personal library tell of his deep and heterogeneous learning. He was superlatively well versed in the Bible and patristics, but at the same time he was attentive in his reading of the Greek and Roman classics (the former in Latin translation). He copied and interpreted ancient epigraphs, wrote glosses on the verses of Catullus, read Petronius's *Satyricon*, and admired Erasmus of Rotterdam. He is best known as a writer of important moral and theological syntheses, the author of a Christian epic, and a concerned patriot, but he was also a master in the genre of the humanist elegy, of satirical, occasional, and even erotic epigrams.

Because of his works in Croatian, particularly the epic *Judith* (written in 1501, first printed 1521), Marulić in his home country obtained the title of honor of "father of Croatian literature"; thanks to his Latin works, which comprise by far the largest part of his oeuvre, he is perceived today as a representative of Christian humanism—of a particular spiritual and literary trend the characteristic of which is that it puts stylistic cultivation of expression and classical culture at the service of the promotion of a Christian worldview. It is perhaps in this very combination of Christianity, the classics, and style that one of the key reasons for the European success of his Latin works can be perceived. During the sixteenth and seventeenth centuries his three books *De institutione bene uiuendi per exempla sanctorum* ("Instruction on How to Lead a Virtuous Life Based on the Examples of Saints"), *Euangelistarium* ("Evangelistary"), and *Quinquaginta parabolę* ("Fifty Parables")—to mention just the most-read titles of his extensive oeuvre—were published more than eighty times, in both the Latin originals and in translations into many vernaculars (Italian, German, Portuguese, French, Spanish, Czech, partially Flemish, and even Icelandic).

Naturally, demand for the works of the Split humanist was to a great extent spurred by changes in religious relations in Europe. Recent research has shown that the religious and political ferments of the sixteenth century, the polarization between Catholicism and the Reformation while at the same time the conflict of Christianity and Islam was unfolding, are reflected in the exciting printing history of Marulić's books. Gradually being revealed is the web of contacts and influences that the work of the Croatian humanist wove all around the old continent, and even beyond its borders. Marulić was attentively read not only by theologians, saints, and clerics, such as St. Francis Xavier, St. Francis de Sales, Fra Luis de Granada, St. Peter Canisius, St. Philip Howard, Piotr Skarga and St. Charles Borromeo, but also by kings and politicians such as Henry VIII, Thomas More, and Charles V; by translators and compilers of manuals of Christian morality like Jacques de Billy and Pieter de Backere; by humanists and poets of the rank of Jan Dantyszek, Conrad Peutinger, and Francisco de Quevedo y Villegas; and finally scholars, publishers, lexicographers, and encyclopaedists such as Sebastian Münster and John Fowler, Johann Georg Schwandtner and Pierre Bayle. The involvement of Marulić's oeuvre in the generic programs, thematic preoccupations, and spiritual currents with which the finest spirits of his time were occupied (the biblical epic, the allegorical interpretation of the Bible, the return to patristics, the religious lyric, the renewal of lay piety, i.e., the *Devotio moderna* movement, the doctrinal disputes of Reformation and Counter-Reformation, humanist poetry, the study of ancient literature, history, architecture and epigraphy, the internecine wars of Christendom and the Ottoman threat).

A particular phenomenon is Marulić's epic in Croatian *Judith*. The epic treatment of the Old Testament book was in his time a singularity, for poets writing biblical epics at the turn of the fifteenth to sixteenth century regularly chose New Testament themes and figures. Thematically exceptional for its own time and poetically interesting today, *Judith* repeats as it were the bygone successes of Marulić's Latin writings. In recent decades it was translated into English, Hungarian, Italian, French, and Lithuanian, and partially into Spanish and German.

Systematic research into the Marulić bequest started thirty or so years back, coinciding with the publication of the first volumes of the *Marci Maruli Opera omnia*. Since 1992 regular conferences devoted to Marulić and the literature of Croatian Renaissance humanism have been held in Marulić's birthplace, Split, the papers being published in the annual *Colloquia Maruliana*. A whole branch of learned studies has arisen, taking the name of *Marulology*.

In addition to his incontestable position as national classic, in recent times Marulić has acquired the attributes of an important representative of Christian humanism and a Latin poet of European stature. The internationalisation of interest in his oeuvre can be ascribed precisely to its properties: dealing with Marulić, foreign researchers are at the same time dealing with their own cultural and literary history, in which Marulić has regularly been a feature in one way or other: their forbears printed and translated the works of Marulić, bought and read, celebrated and banned, quoted and censured, copied out and found inspiration in his thoughts, took his books on distant travels... There is no surprise then that at the conferences in Split, alongside many scholars from Croatia, some fifty participants from thirteen countries from both sides of the Atlantic have taken part. Some of them have returned several times, dedicating a good part of their scholarly activity to the study of Marulić's oeuvre and its reception. Among the most notable we should mention Charles Béné (Grenoble), Luciana Borsetto (Padova), Ruggero Cattaneo (Milan), Elisabeth von Erdmann (Bamberg), Francisco Javier Juéz Gálvez (Madrid), Franz Leschinkohl (Mainz), and István Lökös (Debrecen). The literature about Marulić, too, has become polyglot: there is today a very considerable bibliography of books and studies in English, French, German, Hungarian, Italian, and Spanish.

Among the most distinguished present-day Marulologists one must undoubtedly count the internationally known Catholic scholar Franz Posset, a specialist in Martin Luther, Johannes Reuchlin, and Johann von Staupitz, translator of St. Bernard of Clairvaux, estimable researcher into the spirituality of Catholicism and the Reformation, the history of the theology and cultural history of sixteenth-century Europe. When the areas of Posset's scholarly interests are known, it will be clear that it is practically a matter of course that in his work he was bound to come upon the name of Marko Marulić. But by no means a matter of course are the exceptional expertise, industry, and love that in the last fifteen years or so Franz Posset has put into the study of the Croatian lay theologian (this description of Marulić is actually owed to Posset). In his time, engaged in monastic humanism (*Klosterhumanismus*), more specifically the work of the Cistercian Henricus Urbanus and the humanist Conrad Mutianus, he came across an edition of the famed Marulić poem *Carmen de doctrina Domini nostri Iesu Christi pendentis in cruce* ("Poem About the Teaching of Our Lord Jesus Christ Hanging on the Cross"). The poem, which was originally the concluding part of Marulić's voluminous *De institutione bene uiuendi*, was published by Urbanus as a stand-alone, finely produced edition in Erfurt in 1514. A paper about this theme, printed in 2004, marked the beginning of his systematic approach to Marulić. Having acquired volumes of the *Opera omnia* and supplying himself with literature about Marulić in English and other languages, he set out on his own adventure in Marulology. Having discovered the many-sided activity of the Split humanist, he got to know him not only as a writer of numerous and diverse works in prose and verse, but also as a meticulous reader, who left his signs and comments on the margins of his books, for decades systematically recording excerpts from his reading; as a learned Catholic theologian who oriented his Christian thinking particularly in the direction of Christology, founding it only on the message of the Bible, without the weight of commentaries and scholastic analyses, without the involvement of contentious issues (such a simple approach is entirely in line with the *Sola scriptura* principle of Protestantism, i.e., that the Holy Writ is the sole spiritual authority, not the pope and not the doctors of the church). And finally, he discovered Marulić as a political thinker who vigorously kept up with events in Europe (particularly in the Apennine peninsula), who, like Erasmus, abhorred the fratricidal wars of the Christians and agonized over the power of the Ottomans, which had reached the very threshold of his own homeland. Not only did Marulić follow political, military, and ecclesiastical events, he also wrote of them in Croatian and Latin verses, in Latin prose. As a seventy-two-year-old he put in print an open letter to the newly elected pope, Adrian VI, a political memorandum "about present misfortunes and a call to union and peace of all Christians."

In this book of collected studies, the reader will find invaluable information about the causes and context of the celebrated edition of *Carmen de doctrina* of 1514; the first relevant reading and interpretation of Marulić's epigram *In discordiam principum Christianorum* ("Against Discord among the Christian Rulers") as political allegory; fresh considerations on the *Epistola ad Adrianum VI* ("Epistle to Pope Adrian VI") from the viewpoint of ecclesiastical history and historical theology; a pioneering study of Marulić's marginalia in the copy of his personal *Biblia latina* of 1489 (one of the twelve surviving volumes from his personal library; all of them are crammed with the owners' notes); two works are dedicated to the patristic heritage and christological themes (concerning the importance that Marulić attached to the word "rock" in Matt 16:18; on the role of marginal notes, particularly the drawings of the cross on a plinth, in Marulić's edition of *Early Christian Poets*). The volume is bookended with two synthesizing articles: at the beginning is a concise encyclopaedic note about Marulić, and at the end a lengthy, collaboratively written, compendious survey of the life of Marulić and his oeuvre in the perspective of Christian-Muslim relationships.

Perhaps it is not out of place to remind the reader that this is not the first book Posset has written about Marulić. From the paper about the marginalia in the Latin Bible came a specialized monograph, *Marcus Marulus and the Biblia Latina of 1489: An Approach to His Biblical Hermeneutics* (2013). In it Posset combined an uncommon breadth and depth of theological and historical knowledge with an admirable persistence in and concentration on the unriddling, classification, and contextualization of Marulić's marginal notes—contextualization equally relating to the annotated biblical text and to the echoes of the pertinent biblical places in the Marulić oeuvre. (How great is Posset's *cognitionis amor et scientiae* the present author found out first-hand in almost countless but always agreeable written contacts and in the alas few but unforgettable personal encounters and conversations.) The book *Marcus Marulus and the Biblia Latina of 1489* is an exceptionally valuable contribution to Marulić studies as well as to the knowledge of the ways in which Christian humanists read the biblical text. Posset's book was reviewed seven times in well-regarded Croatian and world periodicals (in order of publication: Zvonko Pandžić in *Vijenac*, Nicolina Trunte in *Südosteuropa-Forschungen*, Jadranka Neralić in *Colloquia Maruliana*, Anne Thayer in *Sehepunkte*, G. R. Evans in the *Journal of Theological Studies*, Luka Špoljarić in *Renaissance Quarterly*, Damir Benko in the *Journal of Croatian Studies*). A kind of oral review was the *laudatio* given by Zvonko Pandžić in presenting the book in April 2013 in Split.[1] Finally, the book was rewarded with the respectable prize *Dauidias*, awarded each year by the Croatian Writers' Association "for the best translation of a work from the Croatian literary heritage into a foreign language or the best book or study

---

1. Online at https://www.youtube.com/watch?v=W-vdFAvE_zY.

of a foreign scholar about the Croatian literary heritage." The statement of reasons for the award, compiled in the name of the commission by Ivan J. Bošković, was printed (in Croatian) in *Colloquia Maruliana* 24 (2015).

Marulić's work offers much more space for research. So far eighteen volumes of the *Opera omnia* have been released, and it is expected there will be three or perhaps four more. The completion of them faces the editors with serious tasks related to the critical establishment of the text, and the resolution of some quandaries with respect to attribution. In the last few decades, several lost works have been discovered; it is to be hoped that there will be more such discoveries, the more so in that some of their titles do exist. In spite of the huge work already undertaken, many themes in philology and literary history are still open to students. Some of the ways for future research have been charted by Franz Posset himself: there has to be more research on Marulić's connections with the literary and publication context, deeper investigation of the sources of and responses to his thinking in moral theology, analytical treatment of the marginal notes in other volumes from his household library and so on. The book that the reader holds in his or her hands vividly shows how fruitful such research can be and how much a writer and a national tradition are necessarily bound up in a universal context.

The lay theologian has found a lay theologian; a participant in the turmoil of the early sixteenth century has found a modern scholar excellently versed in that turmoil; a meticulous reader has found another meticulous reader. In short, in Franz Posset, Marko Marulić has found an ideal interpreter—if not for the whole of the oeuvre, then certainly for a significant part of it. The author of this book is due the thanks and congratulations of not only all those who are engaged with Marulić but also of those who would like to attain a more comprehensive knowledge of the European culture of the sixteenth century.

BRATISLAV LUČIN,
Head of *Marulianum*,
Split, Croatia

Fig. 0.1. The author and Dr. Bratislav Lučin (right) at the tomb of Marcus Marulus, who died in Split on January 5, 1524 and is buried in the church of St. Francis in Split.

Acknowledgments

THE ORIGINAL VERSIONS OF the chapters appeared in the following publications:

Chapter 1   *Opera Dei revelare honorificum est. Zbornik radova u čast Baziliju Pandžiću* [*Festschrift for Fr. Basil Stephen Pandžić on His 100th Birthday*] (Mostar; Grude: Hercegovačka Franjevačka Provincija Uznesenja, 2018), 159–82.

Chapter 2   *Cistercian Studies Quarterly* 39 (2004) 399–419. Occasionally cross-referenced as Posset 2008b.

Chapter 3   CM 17 (2008) 125–46.

Chapter 4   CM 18 (2009) 135–60.

Chapter 5   CM 19 (2010) 141–61.

Chapter 6   CM 23 (2014) 213–30.

Chapter 7   *Journal of Croatian Studies* 48 (2007; issued in 2013) 114–36.

Chapter 8   "Marko Marulić, Marko Pecinić, Marcus Marulus." In *Christian-Muslim Relations: A Bibliographic History*, vol. 7, *Central and Eastern Europe, Asia, Africa and South America (1500–1600)*, edited by David Thomas and John Chesworth with John Azumah, Stanislaw Grodź, Andrew Newman, Douglas Pratt, 90–125. Leiden: Brill, 2015.

I am most grateful to Dr. Bratislav Lučin of the Marulianum Institute in Split, Croatia, for patient support and for his foreword; to Zvonko Pandžić and Vladimir Bubrin for their careful reading of the final draft, helpful hints, and endorsements.

Abbreviations

CM   *Colloquia Maruliana*. Split.

Dossier   *Dossier: Marko Marulić*. Special issue of *Most / The Bridge Literary Magazine* 1–4 (1999) 3–171.

LMD   *Latinska manja djela*. Translated and edited by Branimir Glavičić. Split: Knjizevni Krug, 1992.

MM   Posset, Franz. *Marcus Marulus and the Biblia Latina of 1489: An Approach to His Biblical Hermeneutics*. Cologne: Böhlau, 2013.

MR   *The Marulić Reader*. Edited by Bratislav Lučin. Split: Marulianum, 2007.

MT   *Nobilis Domini Marci Maruli Testamentum*. CM 14 (2005) 28–71.

OO   Glavičić, Branimir, and Bratislav Lučin, eds. *Marci Maruli Opera omnia*. Vols. 1–16 edited by B. Glavičić, vols. 17– edited by B. Lučin. Split: Književni Krug, 1988–.

WA   *Weimarer Ausgabe. D. Martin Luthers Werke*. Kritische Gesamtausgabe. Weimar: Böhlau, 1883–2009.

Preface

With a Biographical Sketch of Marcus Marulus (1450–1524)

SEVERAL CONTRIBUTIONS TO THIS volume are slightly revised reprints, occasionally updated, of some of my presentations between 2008 and 2014 given at the annual Marcus Marulus Days in Split, Croatia. They were first printed in *Colloquia Maruliana*, a yearbook edited by the Marulić Institute (Marulianum) in Split, in memory of perhaps Croatia's greatest son, who had been given the honorary title of "Father of Croatian Literature." The first sixteen volumes of *Colloquia Maruliana* were actually devoted in their entirety to the study of his life and works. The director of the Marulianum in Split, Dr. Bratislav Lučin, provides the Foreword to this collection of my Marulus studies. I am most grateful to him for his *Geleitwort*. He has over the years tirelessly assisted me in my studies of "Marulology." This notion ("Marulology") appears to have been coined by Mirko Tomasović (1938–2017, professor of comparative literature in the Department of Comparative Literature of the Faculty of Humanities and Social Sciences in Zagreb, and a member of Croatian Academy of Sciences and Arts).[2] It was later utilized by the late German Marulus researcher Franz Leschinkohl, during his search for books by Marulus in libraries throughout Europe. He discovered that the Germanophone area (Germany, Austria, and the German-language part of Switzerland) was the most fertile ground for Marulus's books, as witnessed by the 807 works by Marulus that Leschinkohl managed to track down in that European region (Germany 515, Austria 179, Switzerland 113). He was able to trace a considerable dissemination of Marulus's books in the German-speaking areas, and according to his own words he "also managed,

---

2. I am grateful to Bratislav Lučin for this information.

outside this area, all around Europe, and even in America, to discover some 200 more of his books, and thus save over a thousand books from oblivion and bring them back under the wing of Marulology."[3]

Chapters 3–6 appeared first in *Colloquia Maruliana*. The other chapters came into existence on other occasions. An extended subtitle of my collection could very well read: "Marcus Marulus of Split at the Time of the Modern Devotion, Renaissance Humanism, and the Early Reformation," with which the scope of these articles is roughly delineated. My brief biographical entry in volume 3 of the *The Encyclopedia of Christian Civilization* (of 2011) on Marcus Marulus may serve as an initial short introduction in order to whet the appetite of those who are not familiar with this Renaissance man of Split (see below within this Preface: "A Biographical Sketch of Marcus Marulus (1450–1524)." It was important to me that Marulus's name and his homeland, Croatia/Dalmatia, were included in an encyclopedia of Christian civilization and that, therefore, it is incorporated in the present volume.

Equally important is the fact (which can easily be overlooked) that this Croatian lay theologian and spiritual reformer was a contemporary of the German reformer Martin Luther (1483–1546). Marulus, however, was a generation older than Luther. Marulus's most famous work, *Instruction on How to Lead a Virtuous Life Based on the Examples of Saints* (originally written in Latin), was translated into almost all of the European languages. Luther, however, apparently had never heard of this or any other of Marulus's works. Equally surprising is the fact that—according to our knowledge—nothing from Luther's pen ever became known to Marulus in Split. This observation makes one wonder about the claim that Luther's famous so-called 95 Theses, which supposedly sparked the Reformation, spread like "wildfire" all over Europe (I speak of the "so-called Theses" because Luther himself actually never referred to them as such, but wrote of them much less provocatively and in Latin as his *propositiones*).[4] Furthermore, such "wildfire" talk with respect to the spread of Luther's *propositiones* is a great exaggeration when one considers the following: The so-called Theses did not reach the place where Marulus lived, i.e., Split, which then was part of the powerful Republic of Venice, even though a humanistic sodality did exist in Split.[5] Apparently, this group to which Marulus belonged was not part of the European "humanist network" which channeled Luther's ideas.[6] Erasmus of Rotterdam (c. 1466–1536),

---

3. Leschinkohl 2001, abstract.
4. Posset 2011c.
5. MM, 25–34.
6. On this, see Rex 2017, 1:207. German and English editions, Berlin: De Gruyter, 2017. Italian edition, Bologna: Il Mulino, 2017.

however, was known in Split.⁷ Indeed, the so-called Theses and other works of Luther spread only or primarily through the "humanist network" of German cities (including Basel), but not to all of them. They did not reach, for instance, Johann Reuchlin (1455–1522) in Stuttgart or Pforzheim in southwestern Germany. In Reuchlin's correspondence (which is now available in the critical edition of four volumes, 1999–2013) no mention is made of Luther's "Theses."⁸

We are better informed about the dissemination of Luther's reformational ideas in Florence and other cities in Italy prior to 1524⁹ (the year Marulus died) and to other southeastern European regions, especially Hungary and Transylvania,¹⁰ and also to Spain, where Luther's books appeared since 1521.¹¹ His books were burned there between 1523 and 1525. Interestingly, they had been shipped via Venice to Granada in 1525,¹² but no information is available as to whether Lutheran books left Venice also in the direction of Dalmatia/Croatia, which as mentioned belonged to the Republic of Venice at that time.

So far no research has been done that would try to explain the reasons why reformational ideas did not spread, or could not have spread, to Marulus in Split during his lifetime. Was the religious milieu in Marulus's homeland so different from Luther's in Saxony that Luther's reform efforts were perhaps of no interest in Croatia/Dalmatia? Or did the rulers of the Republic of Venice successfully block any flow of reformational ideas into their *hinterland*? The research assembled here does not try to provide answers to such questions. Instead, it attempts to bring Marulus's religious thought to the attention of the historians of Christian piety, theology, and literature. And, my research results offer a few additional stones to the greater mosaic of the Renaissance and Reformation times in Europe.¹³ On the other hand, as noted above, Marulus's works in Latin found wide-spread attention in Europe, including Erfurt, Germany, where Marulus's poem was printed in 1514 at the press of Canappus.¹⁴ This city was home to one of the leading

---

7. Lučin 2004.

8. Reuchlin 1999–2013; Posset 2015a.

9. On the first known trial of Italian sympathizers of Luther, see Biasiori 2017; Biasiori mentions other early points of entry for Lutheran ideas in Italian cities, including Bologna.

10. Fata and Schindling 2017.

11. Hernán 2017.

12. Delgado 2017, 261–62.

13. The issue of the neglect of this region in academic research was raised by Bubrin 2013.

14. Posset 2005a, ch. 4.

universities where Luther began his academic studies. It was at Erfurt where Luther had studied and then entered the Order of St. Augustine in 1505.

In the collected works of Marulus, which have so far been issued in a critical edition,[15] no references are found to Luther or the Reformation. Even though Marulus and Luther probably never heard of each other, it is worthwhile pursuing the question: What may Marulus and Luther have in common? (chapter 1).

Chapter 2, features Marulus's most famous religious poem, about the teaching of our Lord Jesus Christ as he is hanging on the cross (*Carmen de doctrina domini nostri Jesu Christi pendentis in Cruce per modum dialogissmi Christi et Christiani*). This cross- and Christ-centered poem had come to the attention not of Luther himself, but of Luther's contemporary Henricus Urbanus (c. 1470–c. 1539), who was a monk of the Cistercian order in Thuringia. Urbanus published Marulus's poem in 1514 at the printing press of Canappus in Erfurt. The publication of that poem apparently did not catch Luther's attention, although early on he had developed a strong christocentrism in his own spirituality and theology under the influence of the superior of the reformed Augustinians in German-speaking lands.[16]

Centuries later, in 1998, Marulus's *Carmen* caught the attention of Pope John Paul II (1920–2005), who quoted from it in his speech during his apostolic visit to Solin in Croatia (see chapter 2). This very fact (the pope quoting from Marulus's *Carmen*) should have sent a signal to the present-day religious world about the forgotten author of Split. But it did not, and the pope's recollection fell into oblivion.

The relevance of Marulus's entire opus should be brought into renewed focus after the recent commemoration of the five-hundredth anniversary of Luther's Reformation in 2017. Marulus and Luther apparently shared a deep concern about the Evangelical Truth (*Evangelica veritas*), yet completely independent from each other, and in what appears to be two somewhat different cultural regions of Europe. It is now clear that the interest in the Evangelical Truth was not Luther's specific proprium.

By no means was Marulus an isolated figure in his time. He was part of the international Renaissance humanism.[17] He became the first Croatian writer of world repute. Croatian urban centers on the eastern coast of the Adriatic, such as Split, shared in the humanistic trends of the time— "back to the sources." There was an uninterrupted medieval Latin tradition that allowed Marulus and his cultural milieu to become part of Western

---

15. Glavičić and Lučin, eds, *Marci Maruli Opera omnia*, hereafter abbreviated OO.
16. Posset 2016b; Posset 2018.
17. MR, 7.

civilization. He was friends with Italian humanists while simultaneously he was also influenced by the Modern Devotion which originated in the Low Countries. He was the central figure of Croatian humanism in Split when this city and region was the bulwark of Western Christianity during the attacks by the Ottoman Turks.

Marulus was born at a time when his homeland had been ruled by Venice since 1420, which is touched upon in chapter 3. The reader interested in greater details about the historical-political context of Marulus in Venetian Split is well advised to consult the book by James D. Tracy.[18] For the better understanding of the wider context and background, the significance of the changes that were surging in German lands are to be taken into consideration, specifically Luther's influential view of the Turks.[19] Somewhat of a more elaborate updating was done in this chapter with respect to the notion "red Jews," which in recent years has caught some scholarly attention. My chapters 3, 4, and 8, on "The Empire," "The Pope," and "Christian-Muslim Relations," are to be read within that context. They provide insight into Marulus's and Split's precarious situation. In particular, chapter 4 shows the hopes which the lay theologian of Split nurtured with respect to the pope's role in the defense against the Turkish threat—in contrast to Luther, a fact which is often underexposed. Chapter 8 needs to be read with the political-military situation of Marulus's homeland in mind. This concluding chapter is encyclopedic in character due to the format in which it originally appeared, namely, as a segment which is titled "Works on Christian-Muslim Relations 1500–1600," within the larger topic, "Central and Eastern Europe, Asia, Africa and South America (1500–1600)." As such it belongs to the monumental project, *Christian-Muslim Relations: A Bibliographical History*.[20] My contribution includes ten texts by Marulus in which references are found to the Turks and the Ottoman Empire: 1) "A Prayer against the Turks"; 2) *Judith*; 3) "What Wonder of the Turkish Fury"; 4) "On the Humility and Glory of Christ"; 5) *Evangelistarium*; 6) "Lament of the City of Jerusalem," begging the pope to assemble Christian nobles and deliver it from pagan hands; 7) "On the French and the Spanish Fighting One Another; 8) "The Epistle of Lord Marko Marulić of Split to Pope Hadrian VI"; 9) "Against the Discord among Christian Rulers"; 10) "To Clement VII, Supreme Pontiff." Each of those ten subchapters of chapter 8 provides exhaustive bibliographies for further scholarly research. When that research piece was published, the bibliography

18. Tracy 2016.
19. On this, see Miller 2017.
20. Edited by David Thomas and John Chesworth with John Azumah, Stanisław Grodź, Andrew Newman, Douglas Pratt. See the updated version of my contribution in chapter 8.

covered the years up to 2015. In the now updated version (in my chapter 8) any recent research on this specific subject is incorporated, with the help of Branko Jozić (1960–) and Bratislav Lučin (1956–) of the Marulianum in Split. This biographical-bibliographical contribution could come into existence only with the extensive assistance of these two scholars at the Marulianum. The international bibliographies on Marulus are the results of their tireless efforts. Their names are, therefore, included in the heading of chapter 8.

Chapters 2, 5, 6, and 7 deal specifically with Marulus's spirituality, which is decisively inspired by his intensive studies of the Latin Bible. We learn of his interpretation of Matthew 16:18, "You are Peter and upon this rock I will build my church," and are introduced to more of his Latin religious poetry.

Occasional overlapping and inconsistencies in style are unavoidable due to the nature of the essays, which originally were individual research pieces for divergent publications. In all, these articles may serve as a companion volume to my book *Marcus Marulus and the Biblia Latina of 1489: An Approach to His Biblical Hermeneutics* (2013), which was published in the German series of "Building-Blocks for the Slavic Philology and Cultural History" (*Bausteine zur slavischen Philologie und Kulturgeschichte*); it is accompanied by a DVD of the four large volumes of Marulus's *Biblia Latina cum comento* with his handwritten marginalia. This book, together with the present collection of my studies, should open "the door to topics and shed light on areas that require much more investigation."[21] In that book I have laid out some areas of Marulology that deserve closer attention in the future, such as a revisiting of the biblical figure of Judith, who appears to have been primarily a liar for a good cause, and less the killer of a tyrant, in Marulus's thinking.[22]

Further research is recommended with respect to Marulus's concept of "heresy," which he occasionally applied to Islam ("the Turks") and Judaism,[23]

21. As per the words of a book reviewer (2017) of my *Marcus Marulus and the Biblia Latina*. The book has received several reviews:

(1) By Zvonko Pandžić, "Marulić—prvi hrvatski teoretičar književnosti. Prva knjiga o hermeneutici Marka Marulića: Franz Posset, Marcus Marulus and the Biblia Latina of 1489," in *Vijenac* 505 (July 11, 2013), online: https://www.matica.hr/vijenac/505/Maruli%C4%87%20%E2%80%93%20prvi%20hrvatski%20teoreti%C4%8Dar%20knji%C5%BEevnosti/.

(2) By Nicolina Trunte in *Südosteuropa-Forschungen* 72 (2013) 614–17.

(3) By Jadranka Neralić; Institut za povijest HAZU, Zagreb, in CM 23 (2014) 271–77.

(4) By Anne Thayer in *Sehpunkte* 15 (2015) no. 9.

(5) By G. R. Evans in *Journal of Theological Studies* 67, n.s. (2016) 356–58.

(6) By Luka Špoljarić in *Renaissance Quarterly* 69 (2016) 323–24.

(7) By Damir Benko in *Journal of Croatian Studies* 49 (2017) 143–48.

22. MM, 205–6.

23. MM, 200.

although, strictly speaking, "heresy" may occur only within Christianity. In this connection, the challenging desideratum needs to be repeated concerning Marulus's view of the relationship between Christians and Jews, and also his thoughts about the "sons of Israel" according to Ecclesiasticus (which Marulus encountered in volume 2 of his *Biblia latina*). A further, worthwhile object of study would be his notion of a "church of Jews and Gentiles" and the idea of one church from the time of Abel (*ecclesia ab Abel*).[24]

For a recent, select bibliography, see "Main Sources of Information" in chapter 8 and my entry "Marulus, Marcus" in *Biographisch-Bibliographisches Kirchenlexikon*.[25]

RESEARCH CONTINUES

One of the esteemed scholars at the Marulianum in Split, Branko Jozić, in one of his most recent studies, pursued the issue of a papal response to Marulić's open letter: "Nepoznato pismo pape Hadrijana VI. Marku Maruliću" (CM 25 (2016) 149–56). The English summary, "An Unknown Letter of Pope Adrian VI to Marko Marulić," is reprinted here:

> Even during his lifetime, Marulić was a writer with a worldwide reputation, and was often cited as an authority. It was probably for this reason that the Dominican preacher Dominik Buća asked him to lay before the pope the fraught condition of the Christians and the perils that, particularly after the fall of Belgrade in 1521, threatened the whole of Europe. Acceding to his request, the Split writer addressed the newly elected Pope Adrian VI in a letter that was printed in Rome on April 30, 1522, even before the new pope's enthronement. Ascending the papal throne, in the tangled ecclesiastical, social and political conditions of the time the pope took various steps (in line with those that Marulić had urged), but it has been unclear so far whether he personally replied to the Split humanist. In this paper a newly found bibliographic item is discussed suggesting that such a reply really did exist.
>
> This clue is found in the second (H–M) volume of the bio-bibliographic lexicon of Antonio Possevino *Apparatus sacer ad scriptores Veteris & Novi Testamenti, eorum interpretes*, [. . .] *poetas sacros, libros pios, quocumque idiomate conscriptos* (Venice, 1606). In this volume alone, more than two and a half thousand authors are discussed, among them, on pp. 385–386,

---

24. MM, 209–10; see also 124–32.
25. Posset 2011b.

Marko Marulić. Possevino knows nothing of his life, but cites the fifteen editions of the De institutione, Evangelistarium, Quinquaginta parabolae. At the very beginning of this volume there is an article about Adrian VI: on p. 2, in the list of his works, Possevino among other things notes: Praeter alias vero insignes eius epistolas extant eae, quas scripsit ad Senatum Ciuitatis Bambergensis, atque ad singulos quosque Principes, & Ecclesiasticos Laicos eiusdem argumenti, sed praesertim ad Ducem Saxoniae Fredericum, in cuius ditione viuebat Germanici incendij fax Lutherus. Et aliam ad Marcum Marulum virum optimum, atque doctissimum plenam honoris, & erga illum beneuolentiae. Romae quoqe impressam. This information was repeated several times (with certain variations) in similar bio-bibliographic surveys (Henri-Louis de Chasteigner de la Rocheposay, Louis Jacob de Saint-Charles, Giovanni Palazzi).

Naturally, it might be thought that Possevino knew of Marulić's letter to Adrian, but was confused as to who was sender and who was recipient. But the actual formulation of Possevino—the pope sent a letter to »the excellent and very learned man,« a letter »full of respect and benevolence for him«—would tend to suggest rather that the compiler of the lexicon was well informed (perhaps that he had the pope's letter in his hands). The information that the letter to Marulić was printed, in Rome itself (Romae quoque impressam), even aroused hope that an extant copy might be found. But unfortunately, research to date has not been productive.

Pope Adrian VI probably knew of Marulić. He could well have found out about the Split writer not only from his books but also from Thomas Niger, Marulić's close friend. After the fall of Belgrade in 1521 the pope of the time, Leo X, had sent Niger to the court of Charles V, as a person of the highest rank in the European diplomatic world, to lobby for an anti-Ottoman war. Niger acquainted the newly elected and still unthroned Pope Adrian VI of the losses being suffered by the Christian people and the perils that loomed over the whole of Europe. It is perhaps for this mission that Marulić's letter to Adrian VI was in great haste prepared and printed.

[This much about the open letter.]

In Spring of 2019 Zvonko Pandžić alerted the scholarly world of his new finds of numerous volumes from Marulus's library with traces from his pen in Latin written in the margins. Pandžić retrieved them at monastic libraries in Croatia. He also provided an initial study, based on his findings of Marulus's Croatian manuscripts, in "'Magnificat Anima Mea Dominum'.

Croatian Translation und Exegesis of Marko Marulić."[26] Further interest in Marulus and his achievements will undoubtedly increase and be fostered now and during the preparations for the celebration of the five-hundredth anniversary of his death in 2024.

A BIOGRAPHICAL SKETCH OF MARCUS MARULUS (1450–1524)

Marko Marulić, or Marulich, or Pecinić. Croatian. Born in Split, Croatia, on August 18, 1450. to a noble family. Split then belonged to the Republic of Venice. He attended the local school led by humanist laymen and may have had some training in law as he performed some administrative work in the community while mostly writing historical and religious works in Latin. As a bachelor he lived most of his life at the family estate. He was friends with Italian humanists and was influenced also by the *Devotio moderna*. He translated the *Imitation of Christ* (attributed to Thomas à Kempis) into Croatian. As a theological autodidact prior to 1500 he worked on his *Repertorium*, a large collection of excerpts from classical authors, the Bible, and early Christian writers. From 1496 to 1499 he worked on the *Instruction on How to Lead a Virtuous Life Based on the Examples of Saints*, published in Latin in 1507. This work established his fame throughout Europe as it was translated into Italian, German, Portuguese, French, and Czech, all prior to 1686. St. Francis Xavier carried this book with him on his mission journeys to the Far East. Further research will have to determine whether excerpts were translated into Japanese by Paulo Yôhô-ken (1510–1599) and his son in the book *Sanctos no go-sagyô no uchi nukigakkan dai-ichi* ("Extracts from the Acts of the Saints," vol. 1), published by the Jesuit Mission Press in Japan in 1591.

His Latin *Carmen about the Teaching of Our Lord Jesus Christ* (usually part of the *Instruction*) was edited separately at Erfurt, Germany, in 1514. In 1510 he wrote *The Deeds of the Kings of Dalmatia and Croatia*, and *Fifty Parables*, and in 1513 *The Life of St. Jerome*. His *Evangelistarium*, a moral-theological compendium of biblical texts, is known in a print from 1516. The five-hundredth anniversary of the first edition of the opus was celebrated in 2016 with an exhibition in Split.[27] The *Evangelistarium* was re-edited in 1519 by the German humanist friar Sebastian Münster. The opus was used by Thomas Morus and King Henry VIII (see chapter 1).

---

26. See Pandžić 2019.
27. Catalogue (in Croatian): Jozić and Lučin 2016.

In 1518 he wrote *On the Humility and Glory of Christ* and *An Account of Illustrious Men of the Old Testament,* and in 1520–1521 on *The Last Judgment of Christ.* For his epic *Judith* of 1521, written in Croatian, he will earn the honorific title "Father of Croatian Literature" in a later century. Marulus called upon Pope Adrian VI for help against the Ottoman armies. His *Davidias* tells the story of the biblical David in verse form, first edited in 1954. His *Praise of Hercules* was published posthumously in 1524. In it he lets the followers of Hercules compete with the followers of Christ. He was interested in local and national history, being a collector of inscriptions from cities in Italy and Croatia. His overall goal remained the renewal of Christianity, as he admired Erasmus of Rotterdam. As a lay theologian he became one of the great figures of European Renaissance humanism. He died in Split on January 5, 1524 and is buried in the church of St. Francis in downtown Split.

Chapter 1

Marulus and Luther

What Do Marcus Marulus and Martin Luther Have in Common?

Observations on the 500th Anniversary of the Reformation in Europe[1]
Dedicated to Fr. Basil Stephen Pandžić on His 100th Birthday on January 30, 2018

FR. BASIL PANDŽIĆ SHARES the cultural and religious heritage of Marko Marulić (Marcus Marulus, 1450–1524) of Split and he lives among us at a time when the five-hundredth anniversary of Martin Luther's (1483–1546) Reformation is commemorated and celebrated. With the year 2017 a decade of commemoration of Luther's Reformation came to a climax (a commemoration that started in 2007). Luther is celebrated globally. Marulić is celebrated locally,[2] but increasingly he is also recognized for his and Croatia's

---

1. This contribution is a revised version of the presentation given at the Marulić Conference, April 21–22, 2017, in Split.
2. Annually, the Colloquia Maruliana Days are celebrated in Split. For an introduction to Marulić in English, see MR. The critical edition of Marulić's works is still in the making: *Marci Maruli Opera omnia* (hereafter abbreviated as OO), edited by Branimir Glavičić (vols. 1–16) and Bratislav Lučin (vols. 17–) (Split: Književni Krug, 1988–). All bibliographical information concerning Marulić can be found in Jozić and Lučin 1998.

role in the history of Christian civilization altogether.[3] In the following, I want to compare the Croatian Marulić with the German Luther.

Under the influence of Lutheran historiography, the year 1517 was made the historical focal point, when Augustinian friar Martin Luther allegedly "hammered" his so-called "95 Theses on the Power of Indulgences" on the church door at Wittenberg. However, there is no reliable proof that he actually nailed them down. There are no eyewitnesses and Luther never mentioned any such act with a hammer anywhere in his works. Since the 1960s Catholic historiographers dispute the nailing of the 95 Theses.[4] But Luther did write those so-called 95 Theses, even though he never called them "theses." The earliest prints of late 1517 use the Latin notion *propositiones*.[5]

What Marulić and Luther have in common is, first of all, that they are contemporaries. Marulić was more than a generation older than Luther. Both men had to cope with the Turkish threat to Western Christianity in their times (a topic which cannot be covered here).[6] They also have in common a Swiss publisher, Adam Petri (1454–1527), who printed some of their works in Basel, as we shall see.

Marulić is known to some as the "Father of Croatian Literature," at least since the nineteenth century, whereas Luther is known as the "Father of the German Reformation" and of Lutheranism since the sixteenth century. Luther's theology is best known for its maxims of exclusivity, such as "Scripture alone" and "Christ alone." Those two maxims are not Luther's inventions, as evidenced by what can be found in medieval thought.[7] Marulić put into his biblical works much of what Luther polemically advocated with his "Scripture alone."

It is safe to say that Marulić is not well known in German-speaking lands or in the Anglo-Saxon world.[8] It is also safe to say that, all in all, Marulić was more famous in the sixteenth than he is in the twenty-first century due to the fact that he wrote much of his opus in Latin,[9] the *lingua franca* of the time. A comparison of the two will touch upon some fundamental historical-theological concepts. In terms of an approximate *terminus ad quem*, it should be noted that the year 1524, when Luther was still an Augustinian

---

3. Posset 2011a, 1435–36.
4. Iserloh 1966; Ott and Treu 2008.
5. Posset 2011c, 12–21.
6. On Luther and the Turks, see Francisco 2015; on Marulić and the Turks, see Posset and Lučin 2015, now chapter 8 in the present collection.
7. With respect to "Scripture alone," see Posset 2006.
8. Erdmann 2009; Bubrin 2013.
9. Ramminger 2010.

friar, was also the year when Luther's very supportive former superior in the Augustinian order, Johann von Staupitz (c. 1465–1524), died.[10] Luther got married in the following year, 1525.The superior Staupitz comes into play here mainly because Luther considered himself a life-long Staupitzian,[11] yet Staupitz died as the abbot of the Benedictine abbey in Salzburg.

MARULIĆ AND LUTHER SHARED A COMMON SPIRITUAL, INTELLECTUAL, AND THEOLOGICAL MATRIX

There are three components of that spiritual-theological matrix: (1) The retrieval of biblical and patristic theology is part of the wider picture of the *Devotio Moderna*, a movement for religious reform, calling for apostolic renewal through the return to genuine pious practices and simplicity of life; a movement which was coming out of the Low Countries since the fourteenth century.[12] (2) Such retrieval is also part of Renaissance humanism, which was coming from Italy. (3) Both men's theological thinking may be characterized with what in recent years is called a "theology-for-piety" (*Frömmigkeitstheologie*)[13] in the fifteenth and early sixteenth centuries. The "modern devout" or the "new devout" (*moderni devoti*) appeared first in contrast to the religious practices of the past (*antiquae consuetudines*) in the perspective of the medieval spiritual writer Henry Suso (c. 1300–1366); he wrote about it in his *Horologium Sapientiae*,[14] a book which could have been available to Marulić from the book market in Venice since 1492 (but he never quoted from it explicitly).[15]

Both Marulić in Venetian Croatia and Luther in Saxony grew up in a milieu influenced by those international, spiritual and theological movements. In 1500 Marulić had finished his Croatian translation of the principal work of the Modern Devotion, the *Imitation of Christ* (attributed to Thomas à Kempis, 1380–1471); but Marulić's work was first printed only in

10. Posset 2003b.
11. Posset 2016b; Posset 2017b.
12. See Van Engen 1988.
13. Hamm 1982.
14. Künzle 1977, 408. The historical-theological concept "devotio moderna" is likely derived from—or influenced by—Suso's designation "moderni devoti." In the fifteenth century it became prominent through Henricus Pomerius with his short history of his religious house near Brussels, together with an account of its most known resident, John of Ruusbroec (d. 1381); see Van Engen 1988, 7.
15. Printed by Petrus de Quarengiis; MM, 20–21.

the twentieth century (1989). Apparently Marulić also wrote his own *Imitatio Christi*, in Latin, dedicated to the Archbishop of Split, Bernardo Zane (c. 1450–1527), but the manuscript is lost.[16] Martin Luther, at the end of the fifteenth century (in 1496/1497), before he began his university studies at Erfurt, was a pupil at a boarding house of the Brethren of the Common Life in Magdeburg, a place influenced by the *Devotio Moderna* with its emphasis on Bible studies.[17]

Further common ground is the European Renaissance humanism. Both Marulić and Luther were open to humanistic ideas which included the promotion of the study of the ancient languages, especially Greek and Hebrew, for the better understanding of the Sacred Scriptures (we call this "biblical humanism"[18]). Marulić had some inkling of Greek,[19] but did not advance to proficiency in it. He actually wrote a few words in Greek letters into his *Biblia Latina* as he clumsily tried to extract two already transliterated words from chapter 4 of Jerome's *Prologue* to the Latin Bible. He entered them in the margin: ΔυΔασκοί Τευ (*sic*; lower left margin); his first christogram (XC, or Xς) with a curly vertical line, and the word λογοσ (right margin) (see fig 1.1).[20]

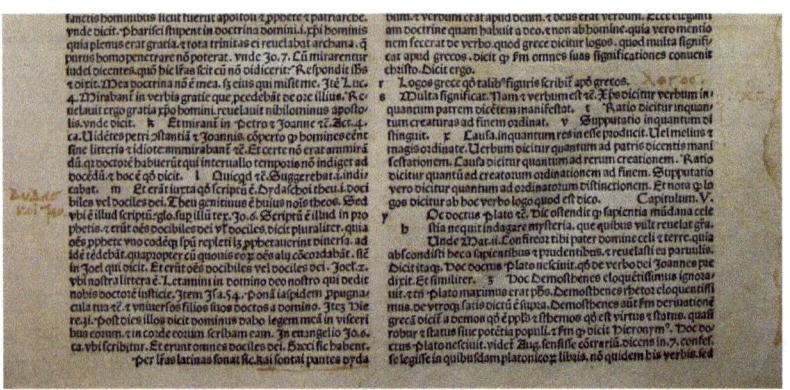

Fig. 1.1. Left: Jerome's *Prologue* in the copy of Marulić's *Biblia Latina*: *Dydaschoi theu*. Marulić's Greek spelling in the left margin: ΔυΔασκοί Τευ (folio 6r).
Right: Jerome: *logos* (spelled in Latin letters)
Marulić's Greek spelling: λογοσ (*sic*) and Christogram (folio 6r).

16. MR, 29, 277–78. On Marulić's intellectual connections, see Šanjek 1999.
17. Junghans 1984, 27–29.
18. Augustijn 2003; Rummel 2008.
19. Marulić's teacher of Greek was Hieronymus Genesius Picentinus; MM, 20.
20. See chapter 5; MM, 66–67.

The third example of Marulić writing original Greek letters is found in the abbreviation of "Christ" for the phrase *Resurrectio* χρι, next to his curly vertical line, for a passage of the Acts of the Apostles (*Biblia*, vol. 4, f. 207v). Usually, he simply copied any transliterated Greek or Hebrew words as he found them in the commentary sections of his *Biblia*.[21]

Compared to Marulić, Luther had a much better grasp of Greek and also of Hebrew. Luther made ample use of Johann Reuchlin's (1455–1522) Hebrew grammar, *De rudimentis hebraicis*, of 1506 and of Reuchlin's bilingual edition (Hebrew/Latin) of the Seven Penitential Psalms of 1512.[22] Marulić did not use any of Reuchlin's works. Luther in his later years still had to admit (in a Table Talk of 1532) that if he were younger, he would study Hebrew a lot more thoroughly:

> If I were younger, I would want to learn this language [Hebrew] better, because without it one can never understand Sacred Scripture. For the New Testament, even though it is written in Greek, is full of Hebraisms and of the Hebrew way of speaking. For that reason they are correct who say: "The Hebrews drink from the source, the Greeks from the rills that are flowing from the source, and the Latin people [drink] from the puddle."[23]

Marulić had no knowledge of Hebrew. Yet, he was sensitive to the "Hebrew Truth" (*Hebraica veritas*) when reading his Latin Bible. The concept of the "Hebrew Truth" was known from the time of the church father Jerome, who may have coined this expression, and about whom Marulić wrote a biography in 1507.[24] When studying his *Biblia*, Marulić took note of passages about the "Hebrew Truth" which the medieval Bible commentator Nicholas of Lyra (c. 1270–1349), had mentioned. This Franciscan scholar was respected by Marulić and by Luther. What is true for Luther is true also

---

21. MM, 203.

22. On Reuchlin's study of the seven Penitential Psalms, see Posset 2015a, 434–39. Luther on these psalms in WA 1:158–220. WA is the abbreviation used for *Weimarer Ausgabe*, which is the critical, standard edition of Luther's works; WA.TR (*Tischreden*) refers to the volumes on Table Talk. When quoting from Luther's Table Talk one must be cautious because Table Talk might not always represent Luther's original sayings. WA.DB (*Deutsche Bibel*) refers to the volumes on Luther's Bible. On Luther's use of Reuchlin's study, see Posset 2011c, 82 with n. 153.

23. WA.TR 1:525, 15–20 (no. 1040). On this Table Talk, see Posset 2015c; Posset 2017a.

24. The full title of Marulić's codex reads: "The Life of Saint Jerome Presbyter Composed by Marko Marulić; with the Miracles which Cyril, the Bishop of Nazareth, narrated about him, Added in Abbreviated Form" (*Vita diui Hieronymi Presbiteri a Marco Marulo edita: adiectis miraculis que de illo Cyrillus Nazarethi episcopus commemorat in summamque redactis breuiorem*); Novaković 1994, with the *editio princeps*.

for Marulić: "Had Lyra not played his lyre, Marulić / Luther would not have danced" (*Si Lyra non lyrasset Marulić [Lutherus] non saltasset*). This version of the Latin couplet is the rewording of what in their days was said about this Franciscan: "If Lyra had not played the lyre," i.e., had he not presented his biblical commentaries, none of the subsequent Bible scholars would have danced, i.e., profited from his labors.[25]

Marulić underlined in Lyra's comment the Hebrew word for God, *Elohim*, in the Latin spelling of it, *Heloym*, which he copied into the margin. On the following folio (f. 169) he entered the expression *Tetragrammaton*, where Lyra wrote about the ineffable name of God (*Yahweh/Yehova*).[26] Evidently, Marulić cherished Lyra's influential views, as did Luther, who once said: "Lyra is very good,"[27] and without Lyra we would neither understand the New or the Old Testament.

At one point when studying Gen 22 in his *Biblia Latina* on the sacrifice of Isaac, Marulić noticed Lyra's mention of the "Hebrew Truth" in the commentary section, and also the christological interpretation of Isaac's sacrifice in this very context. Marulić underlined the comments and marked them with his characteristic curly vertical line in the margin.[28]

In short, both Marulić and Luther shared an interest in the sources (*ad fontes*), in the *Hebraica veritas* of the Bible, and in the exegetical comments by Lyra. But Luther investigated the Hebrew Bible in the original much more intensively.[29] He even discovered Hebraisms in the New Testament (as mentioned above with respect to the Table Talk of 1532: "For the New Testament, even though it is written in Greek, is full of Hebraisms and of the Hebrew way of speaking").

MARULIĆ AND LUTHER SHARE A GREAT INTEREST IN BIBLICAL THEOLOGY

Both Marulić and Luther were theologians. Friar Martin was trained in theology within his Augustinian order, while the nobleman Marulić was an

---

25. The original version may have been: *Si Lyra non lyrasset, totus mundus delirasset* ("Had Lyra not played the lyre, the whole world would have gone hay-wire [malfunctioned; gone crazy, delirious]"); MM, 13–17.

26. MM, 198. On Lyra, see Geiger 2011.

27. *Lira ist sehr gut*; WA 48:691 (no. 7118).

28. MM, 76; see also p. 105 with respect to *ad veritatem litterae hebraicae*, on *Biblia* folio 84.

29. Raeder 1961; Raeder 1967.

autodidact in theology, a lay theologian.[30] Both Marulić and Luther were scholars with a clear focus on the Bible. But it was only Luther who aggressively advocated *sola Scriptura*.

Some of their Scripture-related publications actually were printed by the same printer, Adam Petri in Basel, at one occasion with the very same graphic design by Vrs Graf (c. 1485–1528). His initials VG (= Vrs [Urs] Graf) are shown with the year of publication at the bottom of the pages: 15VG13 / 15VG19 for their title pages: Marulić's *De institutione bene vivendi* of 1513[31] and Luther's sermon about the Most Holy Sacrament of 1519[32] (figs. 1.2 and 1.3).

Fig. 1.2. Marulić's *De institutione* (*Instruction*) (Basel: Adam Petri, 1513); with the same graphic design as in fig. 1.3.

30. See the chapter "The Biblical Scholar in Cultural Context," in MM, 20–62.

31. Online: http://www.croatia.org/crown/articles/9770/2/bratislav-lucin-leading-expert-for-croatian-renaissance-classic-marko-marulic (see fig. 1.2).

32. *Ein gut trostliche predig von der wyrdigen bereytung zu dem hochwirdige sacrame[n]t Doctor Martini Luther Augustiner zu Wittenberg. Item wie das leyde Christi betrachtet sol werden* (Basel: Adam Petri, 1519). Online: http://daten.digitale-sammlungen.de/~db/0008/bsb00089454/images/index.html?id=00089454&groesser=&fip=sdasxssdaseayaeayayztseayaxdsydxdsydyzts&no=3&seite=5 (see fig. 1.3).

Fig. 1.3. Luther's *Sermon on the Most Holy Sacrament* (Basel: Adam Petri, 1519).

Instruction on How to Lead a Virtuous Life

When Marulić was in his forties he worked on the topic of Christian morality (1496–1499) which resulted in the book *Instruction on How to Lead a Virtuous Life Based on the Examples of Saints* (*De institutione bene vivendi per exempla sanctorum*). It was first published in Latin in 1507 in Venice (1506 *more Veneto*).[33] In it he writes of the "evangelical virtues" (*euangelicae virtutes*)[34] and of the "examples of the Gospel" (*euangelii exempla*).[35] His main sources are the biblical stories of both Testaments. Or, when he drew from the New Testament, he referred to them as "examples of the evangelical instruction."[36]

---

33. *De institutione bene vivendi per exempla sanctorum*. The first known edition, which is not extant, is dated *more Veneto*, February 10, 1506, which corresponds to the same date in 1507 in our calendar.

34. OO, 6:283.

35. OO, 7:508.

36. *Euangelicę institutionis exempla*; OO, 8:376. Besides the numerous scriptural stories and quotations, Marulić ladled from various patristic and medieval legends of the saints such as *The Golden Legend*. He usually divided his presentations into two sections, first the examples of men, then those of women. For example, he makes the transition by

With this *Instruction on How to Lead a Virtuous Life* (in Latin) he became known in German-speaking lands when the book was reprinted by Adam Petri in Basel in 1513. This book established Marulić's fame throughout Europe. It was translated in later years into German, Italian, Portuguese, French and Czech, all prior to 1686. Saint Francis Xavier (1506–1552) carried this book with him on his mission journeys to the Far East. Further research will have to be done to determine whether excerpts were translated also into Japanese by two Japanese Christians, Paulo Yôhô-ken (1510–1599) and his son, in their book *Sanctos no go-sagyô no uchi nukigakkan dai-ichi* ("Extracts from the Acts of the Saints," vol. 1), published by the Jesuit mission press in Japan in 1591.[37]

Song about the Teaching of Our Lord Jesus Christ Hanging on the Cross

In 1514 (when Luther was in his second year as a young Bible professor at Wittenberg), Marulić composed the *Carmen de doctrina Domini nostri Iesu Christi pendentis in cruce*[38] which was printed in what is now a "Luther City," i.e., Erfurt, Germany[39] (see fig. 1.4).

Fig. 1.4. Erfurt, "Luther City."[40]

---

writing: *Promamus aliqua etiam hoc in genere foeminarum exempla*; OO, 7:502.

37. MR, 13; MM, 21.

38. Béné 1994, with title page shown: I.1.3.2.

39. Posset 2004, with the reproduction of the title page on p. 413.

40. Online: http://www.erfurt-web.de/Lutherstadt_Erfurt.

In that same city of Erfurt Luther had entered the Reformed Order of Saint Augustine in 1505, and from there he was transferred to Wittenberg in 1512 to become professor of biblical theology (*lectura in biblia*), succeeding his superior, Johann von Staupitz. Luther could have taken notice of Marulić's *Carmen* as it was coming off the Erfurt press, but no mention is made of it in any of Luther's numerous works. Marulić's *Carmen* became most famous since Pope John Paul II quoted from it in a speech at Solin, Croatia, on October 4, 1998).[41]

Account (Commentary) of the Illustrious Men of the Old Testament

In the year 1517—which in ecclesiastical historiography is considered the spark for the Reformation in Germany—Marulić began to write another biblical book, *De Veteris Instrumenti uiris illustribus commentarium*. One may see in it an abridged narrative of the Old Testament, compiled as a series of biographies of the most prominent characters. However, we know of no edition that would have been issued in the sixteenth century (first published in Zagreb in 1979).

---

41. The quotation is the penultimate verse (77) of Marulus's *Carmen*. The pope interpreted this verse as follows: "One of your poets has written: *Felix qui semper vitae bene computat usum* ["Happy is the one who always puts his life to good use"]. It is vital to choose true values, not those which pass, to choose genuine truth, not half-truths and pseudo-truths. Do not trust those who promise you easy solutions. Nothing great can be built without sacrifice." The English edition of the pope's speech does not give the translation of the Latin verse 77. Online: http://www.fjp2.com/us/john-paul-ii/travels/240—apostolic-journey-to-croatia-october-2-4-1998-/19229-speech-to-cathechists-and-ecclesial-movements-4-october-1998.

Christ's Humility and Glory

Fig. 1.5 *De humilitate*, printed in 1519 and 1522.

Marulić issued *De humilitate et gloria Christi* in 1519 which was printed again in 1522.[42] In it he wrote, in a non-polemical way, the following: "Christ then is the Rock upon which the house is built which will stay stable even when it suffers from the winds and floods of temptations."[43] To both Marulić and Luther Christ is the Rock—not Saint Peter.[44] They shared the same patristic and medieval Catholic interpretation of Matt 16:18, "You are Peter and upon this rock I build my Church," in a Christ-centered way.[45] The same conviction is found in the thinking of Luther's fatherly friend, Staupitz. He

42. Image of title page (see fig. 1.5) found online: http://blogs.bl.uk/european/2014/06/marko-maruli%C4%87-and-the-croatian-latin-heritage.html.

43. *De humilitate*, in OO, 9:413–598, here 554–55; Posset 2014.

44. There are basically three options for interpreting the "rock": (1) the person of Peter, (2) the faith of Peter representing the church, or (3) Christ as the rock.

45. Posset 2001; see below chapter 6.

quite provocatively proclaimed in 1512, still as an Augustinian friar: "One may see and recognize that one needs to build upon Christ alone as the rock, and on nobody else."[46] Luther followed Staupitz when he said in 1521 that "the Church is built in the Spirit upon Christ the Rock, not upon the pope nor on the Roman Church."[47] In 1520 the Basel printer Adam Petri published Luther's *Commentary on Galatians* (see fig. 1.6),[48] in which Luther explained (on Gal 5:7) that the Lord's word in Matt 16:18 does not mean earthly power, but that the church is built on the solidity of the faith in Christ.[49]

Fig. 1.6. Luther's *Commentary on Galatians* (Basel: Adam Petri, 1520).

Luther's christocentrism is heavily influenced by Staupitz, who admonished Luther to always look at Christ crucified. Luther became an effective affective christocentrist.[50] Both he and Marulić interpreted the Old

46. Sermon 5, in: *Johann von Staupitz: Salzburger Predigten 1512: Eine textkritische Edition* (Tübingen: Neuphilologische Fakultät, 1990), 64.

47. WA 7:709, 25–28 (*Against Prierias*).

48. Online: http://www.europeana.eu/portal/ro/record/9200332/BibliographicResource_3000123599960.html.

49. WA 2:568, 24–33.

50. With respect to Luther's affective christocentrism in dependence upon Bernard of Clairvaux, see Posset 2016a.

Testament from a christological point of view. (It is not possible here to elaborate on Luther in this regard.[51])

As to Marulić, we know of his christological interpretation of the Hebrew Bible (Old Testament) from his hand-written christograms and small crosses on a socle which he entered on a regular basis into the margins of his desk copy of the Latin Bible, in particular while he was studying the Old Testament.[52] He entered his christogram in the book of Habakkuk (fig. 1.7) which we see at the top of the left margin and the cross on a socle at the bottom (vol. 3, f. 198v):[53]

He was always on the lookout for whatever promotes Christ in the Hebrew Bible.[54] Both Marulić and Luther promoted a Christ-centered religion and spirituality which Luther succinctly expressed in his famous slogan: *Was Christum treibet* ("Whatever promotes Christ").[55] Or, "Take Christ out of the Scriptures, what more then would you find in them?"[56]

---

51. "Kennzeichnend für Luther ist seine christozentrische Deutung der gesamten Bibel"; Seiler 2014, 56.

52. MM, Appendix I (Overview of Marulus's Christograms), 219-23.

53. Posset 2010, fig. 10.

54. MM, 18.

55. Luther's preface to the Letters of James and Jude; WA.DB 7:384, 27 and 385, 25-32 (1522).

56. *Tolle Christum e scripturis, quid amplius in illis invenies?* WA 18:606, 29; see also: *Die schrifft auff Christum allein ist gericht[et]*, WA 10-II:73, 16.

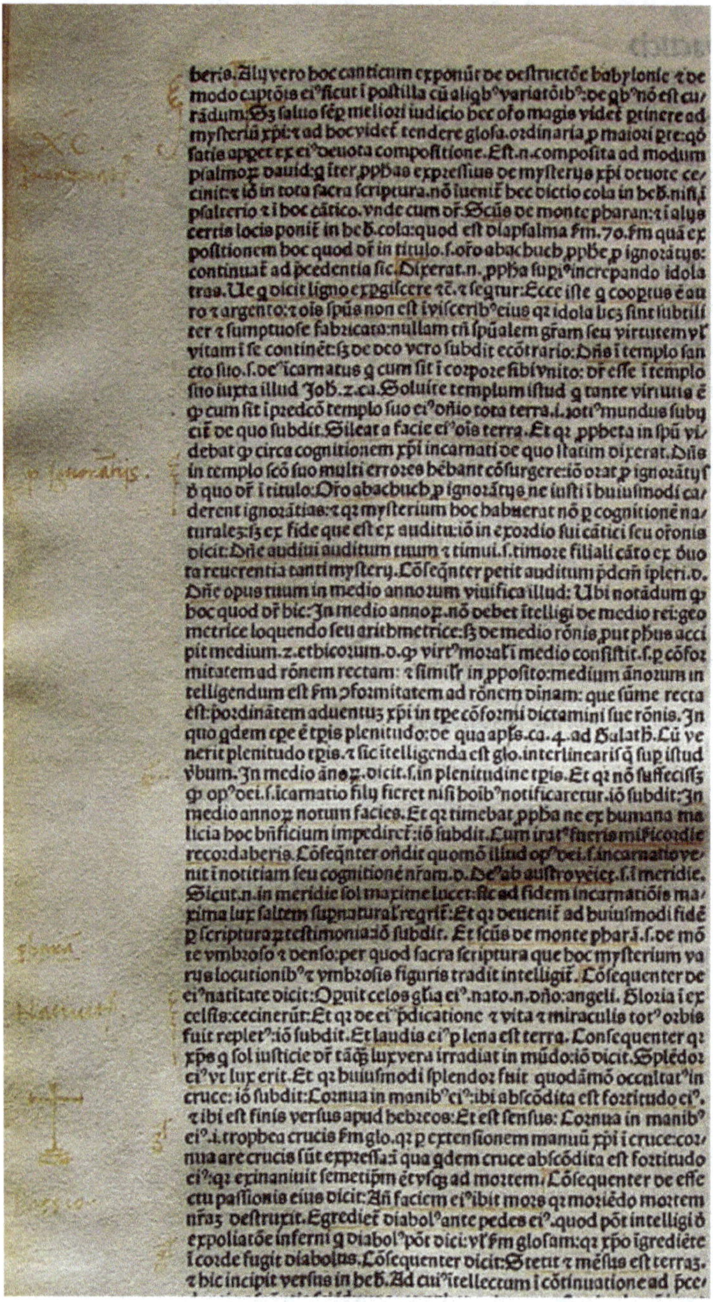

Fig. 1.7. Marginalia in Marulić's *Biblia Latina on Habakkuk*.

BOTH ARE ADVOCATES OF THE EVANGELICAL TRUTH

On the Last Judgment of Christ

In 1520 Marulić wrote On the Last Judgment of Christ (De ultimo Christi iudicio). It was not edited until 1901 in Zagreb.[57] Marulić called his booklet a sermo. It is his only work classified in this way, whereas Luther delivered many sermons—on average, three to four times a week—and he published many of them; more than two thousand sermons came down to us, often as notes taken by listeners.[58] Between 1518 and 1525, over eight hundred vernacular works of Luther, including reprints, were published; two of every five were sermons; approximately 2,300 printed sermons.[59] In advocating for the Evangelical Truth, Luther again followed Staupitz. Yet, most people in those years admired primarily Luther for standing up for the *evangelica veritas*.[60] But already with Staupitz we find the acerbated use of the concept, now also in German. When he delivered German Lenten sermons in 1520 in Salzburg, he explicitly used the expression "Gospel Truth"; in Early New High German: *Ewangelische warhait*. Apparently, Staupitz, like Marulić and Luther, was influenced by the Modern Devotion. Staupitz, too, preached about the imitation of Christ, but with combative words like these:

> If we stand up for the evangelical truth, then we have to fear neither force, nor beatings, nor death. We shall boldly insist upon the truth, with that we overcome and strike down our enemy before he can grab the sword.[61]

Marulić, too, was an advocate of the Evangelical Truth, but made no ruckus about it. Yet, the Evangelical Truth is definitely the common ground of both. Although both rose from that matrix, they each went in different directions, mainly when Luther employed the concept in a polemical, anti-papal way. Luther saw his publications in terms of a "victory run of the Gospel" (*Siegeslauf des Evangeliums*).[62] By 1524 Luther simply equated the terms "Lutheran" and "Evangelical."[63]

Marulić's printed *sermo* comprises more than fifty pages. This "sermon" most likely was not delivered from a pulpit in a church (Marulić was

---

57. Jozić and Lučin 1998, 111 (no. 219).
58. Beutel 2014, 559.
59. Kreitzer 2001, 35, 40; Hagen 2016, 241.
60. Posset 2015b.
61. Translation according to Markwald 1990, 56.
62. Kaufmann 2017, 220.
63. WA 15:111, 23–24. See Köpf 2015, 17.

not an ordained priest), but a sermon which was to be read at home (in German it is called a *Lesepredigt*). The lay theologian "preached" in it on the Gospel Truth to his imagined "most beloved brethren" (*fratres charissimi*).[64] There are four instances where he used the concept of Gospel Truth: First, it emerges in part 1, in the context of sermonizing on the Antichrist who is faced with the success of the preaching of the Gospel Truth that leads to professing Christ.[65] The Gospel Truth is used twice in part 2 of the *sermo*, first in a passage about the final coming of Christ and the resurrection of some to eternal life and of others to permanent disgrace (*opprobrium*). In any case, it is "the Gospel Truth [that] loudly shouts into the ears of all."[66] Here, as elsewhere with Marulić, the Gospel Truth is personified and is acting like a messenger, and from what follows it is apparent that it is Christ himself who is the *Evangelica Veritas* who is arguing with the Sadducees who deny any resurrection.[67] At the second instance within part 2,[68] the notion surfaces within Marulić's reflection about the general resurrection of the faithful into heaven, i.e., of those who have died and of those "who are alive, who are left until the coming of the Lord" (1 Thess 4:15–18).[69] Marulić is speaking with Paul in the first-person plural. What happens to us who are left behind and still living (*qui vivimus, qui relinquimur*)? In short: We are provided with the Gospel Truth (with its consoling promise of eternal life). In his attempt of interpreting the passage of 1 Thess 4:15–18 concerning those of us who are still living, Marulić sees us as the ones: (a) who are living and having been redeemed already by Christ; (b) who are freed of the obligation of old (*a uetustatis obligatione soluti*), by which Marulić means those who lived under the Law (*qui sub lege erant*); and (c) who are "left behind" for the Gospel Truth, or as one may translate the Latin *relinquimur* also with "we are bequeathed" with the Gospel Truth (*Euangelicę relinquimur ueritati*).[70] We received the inheritance of the Gospel Truth, which here

64. OO, 11:229.

65. OO, 11:241.

66. *Euangelica Veritas ad aures omnium clamiet . . .*; OO, 11:250.

67. OO, 11:251.

68. OO, 11:257.

69. *Hoc enim vobis dicimus in verbo Domini, quia nos, qui vivimus, qui residui sumus in adventum Domini, non praeveniemus eos, qui dormierunt. Quoniam ipse Dominus in iussu, et in voce Archangeli, et in tuba Dei descendet de caelo: et mortui, qui in Christo sunt, resurgent primi. Deinde nos qui vivimus, qui relinquimur, simul rapiemur cum illis in nubibus obviam Christo in aera, et sic semper cum Domino erimus. Itaque consolamini invicem in verbis istis* (Vulgate version of 1 Thess 4:15–18). The edited text of Marulus's *sermo* does not mark the biblical reference to 1 Thess 4:17 as it should, namely: "*Deinde nos*" inquit, "*qui uiuimus qui relinquimur*."

70. OO, 11:257. *Euangelicę ueritati* is the dative case.

means the comforting teaching of Saint Paul about the resurrection of those who are at the right hand of the Judge (Matt 25). The others who are forced to stand on the left are the "incredulous Jews," ill-believing heretics, and Christians lost in their sins.[71]

In part 3 of his *sermo* Marulić uses the notion for the fourth time, and here again in terms of his idiosyncratic personification of the *Euangelica ueritas* as Christ is its announcer, here with the words in John 4:14. Marulić explains in christological terms what "the watered garden" of Jer 31:12 means (*eritque anima eorum quasi hortus irriguus et ultra non esurient*):

> Jeremiah (XXXI): Their soul shall be like a watered garden, and never again shall they languish. Indeed, also the Gospel Truth, Christ the Lord, says: "Who ever drinks the water I shall give will never thirst; the water I shall give will become in him a spring of water welling up to eternal life" [John 4:14].[72]

Evangelistarium

As we deal with the Gospel Truth, we need to mention briefly Marulić's *Evangelistarium*, which is a moral-theological compendium of biblical texts, but taken not only from the Gospels, but also from the Law (the Old Testament). By giving his book this specific title, Marulić wants to point out the close relation of its content to biblical teaching.[73] His book has been printed since 1487 (Reggio Emilia, 1487; Venice, 1500). In 1515 the Jewish book publisher Gershom Soncino (Iheronimus Soccino, died in Turkey in 1534) published it in Pisa;[74] it is the same printer who in 1488 edited the *Biblia Hebraica*—all in Hebrew letters, which makes it the oldest edition of the whole Hebrew Scriptures that was ever printed. We know that some of Soncino's prints found their way into German lands because the German Catholic Hebraist Johann Reuchlin purchased a copy in the fall of 1492.[75] However,

---

71. OO, 11:257–58.

72. *Et Hieremias (XXXI): Erit, inquit anima eorum quasi hortus irriguus, et ultra non esurient. Quin et Euangelica ueritas Christus Dominus ait: Qui biberit ex aqua, quam ego dabo ei, non sitiet in ęternum; sed aqua, quam ego dabo ei, fiet in eo fons aquę salientis in uitam ęternam*; OO, 11 :273.

73. An "evangelistary" in the proper sense was a book of gospel readings. Marulić's use of it in the wider sense constitutes a medievalism according to Ramminger 2010, 132.

74. Runje 1994; Jozić and Lučin 1998, 38 (no. 18).

75. Posset 2015a, 117.

the 1515 print of Marulić's *Evangelistarium* by this Jewish publisher is lost. The earliest extant print of the *Evangelistarium* is that of Venice, 1516.

Marulić's *Evangelistarium* was read in England by Thomas Morus (1477/1478–1535) and also by King Henry VIII (1491–1547) whose own marginal notes were found in his personal copy (see figs. 1.8a and 1.8b) as he was writing his anti-Lutheran *Assertio septem sacramentorum* ("Defense of the Seven Sacraments").[76]

Fig. 1.8a. Pages in Marulus's *Evangelistarium* annotated personally by King Henry VIII, kept in the British Library (843 K 13).

76. MR, 15.

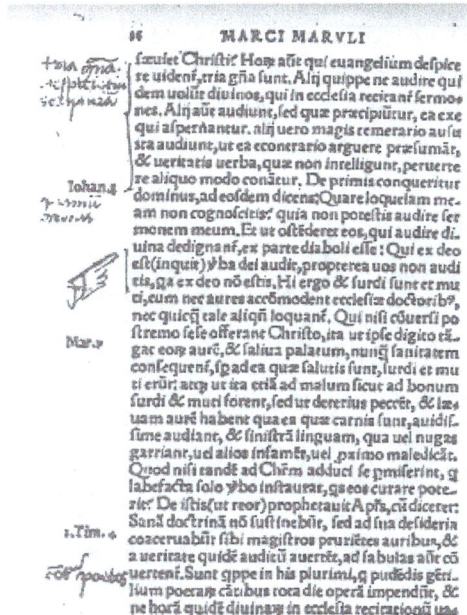

Fig. 1.8b. A page of Marulus's *Evangelistarium* annotated personally by King Henry VIII, kept in the British Library (843 K 13).[77]

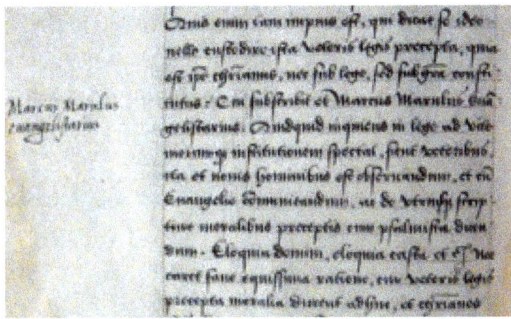

Fig. 1.8c. Detail from manuscript of "Gravissimae academiarum censurae" (with arguments for the king's rights to divorce). The entry on the left margin reads: *Marcus Marulus evangelistarium* [sic], kept in the British Library (MS Harley 1338), Clarke 2011 with Fig. 8. Detail view from *Katalog* (in Croatian), *Pet stoljeća Marulićeva Evanđelistara* (1516–2016) at https://drive.google.com/file/d/10Fd2sylkF3bQCi6UJSIIC-x5F_UXVWPA/view [page 22].

77. Béné 1994, 51. Image shown online: http://www.croatia.org/crown/articles/9770/2/bratislav-lucin-leading-expert-for-croatian-renaissance-classic-marko-marulichttp.

In 1519 the *Evangelistarium* was reissued by Sebastian Münster (1488–1552), the German Franciscan friar and humanist, also a Hebraist, who later married the widow of the Basel printer Adam Petri (who died in 1527).[78] How important he was in the cultural history of Germany can be deduced from the fact that his portrait appeared on a German bank note:

Fig. 1.9. Sebastian Münster depicted on a German bank note.

Marulić's edition of the *Evangelistarium* in 1519 (see fig. 1.11) was issued by Sebastian Münster, early on; he also edited or reprinted numerous works by Martin Luther for that same Basel printer.[79] Marulić's *Evangelistarium* was intended for the German market, printed in this important city at the German-Swiss border, as it came off the press of Adam Petri (see fig. 1.10). This happened in 1518, shortly after the same printer had published Luther's now very famous so-called "95 Theses on the Virtue of Indulgences."

---

78. He accepted an appointment at the University of Basel in 1529. He is best known as cartographer and cosmographer through his *Cosmographia*, which was one of the most successful and popular books of the sixteenth century.

79. British Museum 1894.

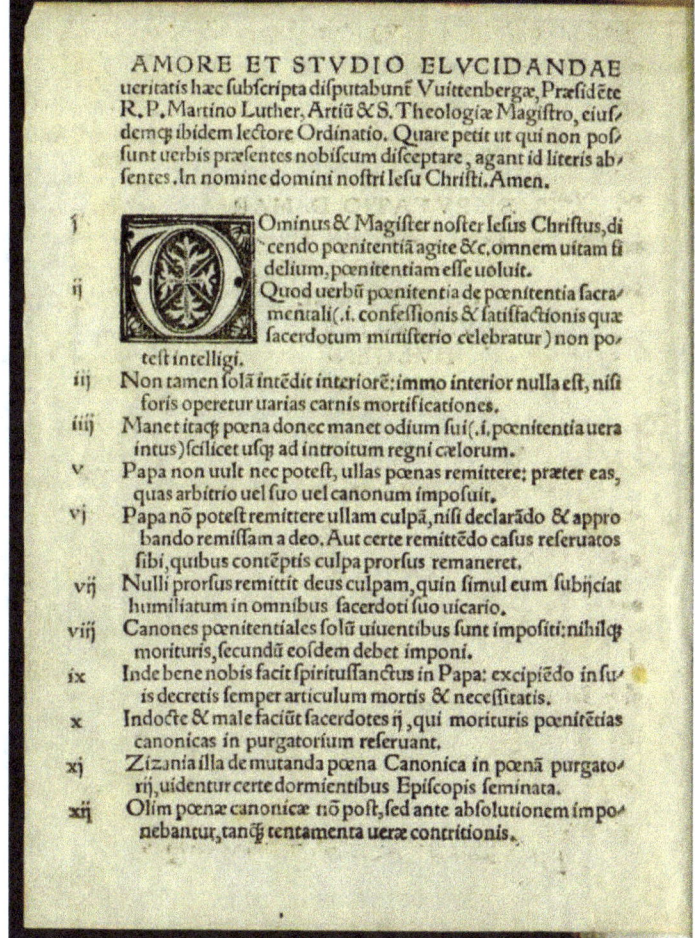

Fig. 1.10. Luther's 95 Theses (Basel: Adam Petri, 1518), showing the first page of the print of Luther's Latin Theses by using the format of a pamphlet.[80]

The 95 Theses were entered in 2015 into the records of the World Heritage of the United Nations Educational, Scientific, and Cultural Organization (UNESCO).[81]

Remarkably, the two earliest prints of Luther's 95 Theses which we know are not from a Wittenberg printer, but from Nuremberg and from

80. Shown online: https://luther.wursten.be/wp-content/uploads/2016/12/lutherthesen_Basel_07-751x1024.jpg.

81. UNESCO awards Memory of the World status for fourteen Luther manuscripts, March 18, 2016. Online: http://www.dw.com/de/unesco-ernennt-luther-schriften-zum-welterbe/a-19122767.

Basel. Petri's print of Luther's 95 Theses at Basel is the second oldest print. Petri also reprinted, for instance, Luther's *Exposition of the Lord's Prayer* in 1519 and in 1520 Luther's *To the Christian Nobility of the German Nation* (*An den christlichen Adel deutscher Nation*) and also Luther's *The Babylonian Captivity of the Church* (*De captivitate Babylonica Ecclesiae*). And it was this printer, Adam Petri, who had published also some of Marulić's works.

Fig. 1.11. Basel edition, 1519.[82]

82. Online: https://new.liveauctioneers.com/item/5046065_656-marulic-marulus-marko-evangelistarium-marci-.

Fig. 1.12. Cologne edition, 1529.[83]

The title page of the *Evangelistarium* of the Basel edition advertised its author, Marulić, as a most eloquent man (*vir disertissimus*); his book was praised and marketed as a "truly evangelical opus" (*opus uere euangelicum*). The Cologne edition of 1529 retained this text in its title page (fig. 1.12).

It remains inexplicable that Luther's early works did not become known to Marulić. And, on the other hand, it is even more amazing that

83. Online: http://britishlibrary.typepad.co.uk/.a/6a00d8341c464853ef01a73ddof4 03970d-.

Marulić's *Evangelistarium* did not catch Luther's attention. This fact is puzzling especially when one observes that Luther's German sermon *On the Ten Commandments* was edited in the following year, 1520, by the same editor, Sebastian Münster, and printed by the same printer, Adam Petri, in Basel.[84] Petri played a key role in the dissemination of the works of the author in Split and of the Reformer in Wittenberg. Petri in Basel printed some of Marulic's and some of Luther's works as can be seen from this overview:

1513: Marulić's *De institutione bene vivendi per exempla sanctorum*

("Instruction on How to Lead a Virtuous Life")

1518: *Luther's 95 Theses on the Power of Indulgences* of 1517 (in Latin)

1519: Luther's *Sermon on the Most Holy Sacrament* (in German)

1519: Marulić's *Evangelistarium*

1520: Luther's *Commentary on the Letter to the Galatians* (in Latin)

1522: Luther's New Testament translation (in German, reprint)

Whereas the sale of the indulgences became a problem in German lands, we know nothing about problems with any sale of indulgences around 1500 in Marulić's hometown or discussions about them.[85] Was this a problem at all in Venetian Dalmatia and Croatia? More studies are needed as to this issue and as to the question of *indulgentia* in Marulić's works.

---

84. *Der .x. [sic] gebot ein nutzliche erklerung Durch den hochgelerten .D. Martinum Luther Augustiner ordens beschriben und gepredigt, geistlichen und weltlichen dienende. Item ein schöne predig von den. vij. todsünden, auch durch in beschriben* (original in Latin of 1518: *Decem praecepta Wittenbergensi praedicata populo*).

85. A recent conference in Rome was dedicated to the problem with indulgences in the Late Middle Ages: Rehberg 2017. The Republic of Venice which at that time included Split was not part of the considerations at this conference; it focused on German lands, France, Bohemia, rural Italy, and Northern Europe.

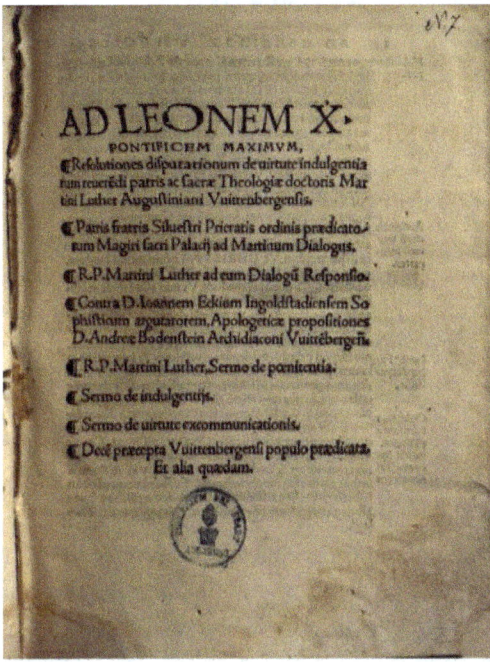

Fig.1.13. Collection of Luther's works, edited by Froben at Basel, 1518.

Another printer at Basel who had shown interest in Luther's writings was Johannes Froben (c. 1460–1527). He published Erasmus's Greek New Testament. He also reissued some of Luther's works (see fig. 1.13) and proudly reported to Luther on February 14, 1519 that his reprint of six hundred copies were sent to France, Spain, Brabant and England and to Pavia in northern Italy. All but ten copies were shipped out. This had never happened before with any of the books from his press.[86] Luther appears to have become known almost everywhere in Europe,[87] except in much of what today is Italy and Croatia.

---

86. WA (*Briefe*) 1:332–33; Froben's collection of 1518 is known under the title: *Ad Leonem X. Pontificem Maximum, Resolutiones disputationum de virtute indulgentiarum revere[n]di patris ac sacrae Theologiae doctoris Martini Luther Augustiniani Wittenbergensis* [. . .]. Munich Digitalisation Zentrum, online: http://reader.digitale-sammlungen.de/de/fs1/object/display/bsb11230139_00009.html (see fig. 13).

87. Dingel 2017.

CONCLUSION

The five-hundredth anniversaries of Luther's Reformation and of the first printing of Marulić's *Evangelistarium* offered us the opportunity to ask what Luther and Marulić may have in common. This question led to the observation that there was common ground, but that there were also major differences, mostly in regards to ecclesiastical issues surrounding the papacy. The layman at Split remained loyal to the papacy, whereas the friar and ex-friar at Wittenberg did not. Marulić and Luther shared a common matrix of the Modern Devotion and Renaissance humanism. Both men were representatives of the *Evangelica Veritas* and of a "theology-for-piety." Works by both were featured by the printer Adam Petri in Basel. Yet, Marulić probably would never had said anything close to what Luther said in identifying himself with the Gospel as such: "Praise God, I have more reformed 'with my Gospel' [*mit meinem Euangelio*] than they may have done with five Councils."[88]

The classical notion "Gospel Truth" is a general Catholic theological concept throughout the centuries, used in controversies with heretics, but not exclusively. In contrast to the situation in German-speaking territories around 1500, Marulić amply employed the concept in his own irenic ways, untouched by Luther's movement under the banner of the Gospel Truth. The concept was used also by Luther's Catholic friends, who remained with the "old church," as well as by those who turned Lutheran. They all saw in Luther the excellent exemplar of a teacher of the Gospel Truth. On the eve of the Reformation, Marulić in the hinterland of the Republic of Venice, and as of the Roman Catholic faith, primarily employed the notion in non-polemical ways. Yet, as a Christ-centered lay theologian he, too, with his biblical writings, is to be counted among the teachers of the Gospel Truth.

---

88. WA 38:271, 1–4.

Chapter 2

Christ Speaking from the Cross

A Cistercian Monk as Editor of the Carmen *of the Croatian Humanist Marcus Marulus*

The German Humanist Henricus Urbanus, O. Cist. (Died 1538)

IN A SPEECH IN 1998 on the occasion of his visit to Solin in Croatia, Pope John Paul II quoted from a poem of the Croatian layman and humanist Marcus Marulus. The quotation is the penultimate verse (77) of Marulus's *Carmen de doctrina domini nostri Jesu Christi pende[n]tis in Cruce* ("Poem About the Teaching of Our Lord Jesus Christ as He Is Hanging on the Cross").[1] The pope interpreted this verse as follows:

> One of your poets has written: *Felix qui semper vitae bene computat usum* ["Happy is the one who always puts his life to good use"]. It is vital to choose true values, not those which pass, to choose genuine truth, not half-truths and pseudo-truths. Do not trust those who promise you easy solutions. Nothing great can be built without sacrifice.[2]

---

1. See below, pp. 37-39.

2. The English edition of the pope's speech on October 4, 1998 does not give the translation of the Latin verse 77; see http:// www.papa.hr/pope/english/news/govor/ esolin.html.

It is worthwhile to illuminate the historical context of this quotation cited by the Holy Father and learn more about its author and editor: What is the literary-historical context of this poem? Who is Henricus Urbanus, O.Cist., the editor of the poem in Erfurt, Germany? Who is Marcus Marulus? What is the poem all about?

THE QUOTED POEM IN THE LITERARY "CONTEXT" OF SIMILAR PASSION POETRY

Humanist poems about Christ were not uncommon at that time. The Swiss humanist, physician, and Cistercian monk Nicolaus Salicetus (died 1494) edited the Pseudo-Bernardine *Oratio rhytmica* (Strasbourg: Johann Grüninger, 1489),[3] in the prayer book *Antidotarius animae*,[4] with meditations and prayers that function as antidotes for the soul, of which more than twenty editions are known from 1489 to 1513. In his introduction, Salicetus pointed out that he offers "spiritual medicine" for the soul. And since there are certain medicinal categories, he offers the corresponding spiritual medication, namely, "digestive" meditations and prayers that prepare for cleaning out the system and evoke repentance, "purgative" prayers that are meant for the time of confession, and, for receiving Holy Communion, "opiate" prayers that quiet and heal the soul. Other prayers aim at the meditation of Christ's passion; they are the most efficient antidotes.[5]

In 1501/1502 the Venetian printer Aldus Manutius had printed an anthology of ancient and modern poems, *Poetae Christiani veteres*, which included the poem on Christ's passion attributed[6] to Lactantius.[7] In 1510 the Benedictine monk Benedictus Chelidonius (died 1521) in Vienna compiled poems on the Life and Passion of Christ from contemporary editions of the works of Jerome of Padua (Hieronimus de Vallibus Paduanus, 1443),[8]

---

3. *Patrologia latina* 184:1319ff.; see Posset 1998, 295ff. Sheryl Frances Chen provided an English translation in Chen 1994, 25–40.

4. Full title: *Liber meditationum ac orationum devotatum qui anthidotarius animae dicitur*. See Pfleger 1901.

5. See Pfleger 1901, 594f.

6. See *Patrologia latina* 7:283–86; Denk 1906, 382–83.

7. (Lactantius:) *De passione Domini*; see Béné 1994, 92. I am grateful to Tinka Katic, Zagreb, for providing me with this book. The *Poetae Christiani veteres* included also works by Homer, Vergil, Sedulius, and for example the *Opusculum ad Annuntiationem beatissimae Virginis* (in a Greek-Latin version).

8. His book *Iesuida seu De passione Christi* was printed by Jacob Thanner (Leipzig, 1500).

Dominicus Mancinus,[9] Baptista Mantuanus,[10] and the ancient Coelius Sedulius.[11] Chelidonius's text selections were published together with illustrations by Albrecht Dürer (1471–1528) and became known as the *Large Passion*.[12]

Probably before 1513, the Benedictine Abbot Angelus Rumpler (died 1513) wrote his *Carmen de passione Christi* (a fragment).[13] In 1514, the Cistercian monk and preacher, later abbot of Aldersbach in Bavaria, Bolfgangus Marius (died 1544), recreated the life of Christ in the literary form of a hero's epic with his booklet *Christi Fasciculus Florido Heroici poematis charactere digestus*, which one may translate as something like "A Fascicle on Christ in the Flourishing Heroic Epic Style." It was dedicated to his former college friend, Abbot Conrad Reuter of the Cistercian abbey of Kaisheim, with the date of May 3, 1514. In his dedication he revealed that in a sudden, happy moment he was inspired to write this song on the life and death of Christ, and since it is so short (that is, about sixteen pages), he called it a "fascicle on Christ."[14] It was printed by the priest Johannes Weyssenburger (died c. 1536) at Landshut, Germany, in 1515.[15] Later, in 1580, a translation into German was produced at the Bavarian monastery of Tegernsee, entitled *Passio Jesu Christi aus den vier Evangelien*

---

9. His book *Carmen de Passione* was printed by Baligault (Paris, no date, perhaps 1478–91).

10. Selections were taken from his *Parthenice* and *Libri tres de calamitatibus temporum*, of which several editions were available.

11. The principal work of Sedulius (fifth century) is a poem in five books called *Carmen paschale*. The first book contains an overview of the Old Testament, the four others a summary of the New Testament.

12. *Passio Domini nostri Jesu ex Hieronymo Paduano, Dominico Mancino, Sedulio, et Baptista Mantuano per fratrem Chelidonium collecta. Cum figuris Alberti Dureri Norici Pictoris*; see Posset 2002, 430–32.

13. See Worstbrock 1981, 493 and 497. Abbot Rumpler also wrote poems on Christ's birth and on his resurrection.

14. The Latin text is printed in Gloning 1912, here 489f. Marius included this *fasciculus* in his 1526 collection of poems. Marius sent a copy to the student Wolfgang Seidel (1492–1562), who later became known as the Benedictine humanist Sedelius at the monastery of Tegernsee. Sedelius may have been instrumental in the printing of this work. Its full title reads as follows: *Fratris Wolfgangi Mayer* [Bolfgangus Marius] *Abbatis Alderspacensis, liberalium arcium Magistri divine cultoris Sophieque studiosissimi: Christi Fasciculus Florido Heroyci poematis charactere digestus. Impressum Landshut per venerabilem virum Joannem Weyssenburger caleographum sacerdocii professorem accuratissimum. Anno M. D. VX* (printing mistake for the correct XV, i.e., 1515). See Oswald 1964/65, 315.

15. In the same year, 1515, this printer edited a book of woodcuts on the lives of the saints; see Bleibrunner 1967. Also known from this printing press is the *Ars moriendi: Ex variis sententiis collecta cum figuris ad resistendum in mortis agone dyabolice suggestioni valens cuilibet Christifideli utilis ac multum necessaria* (Landshut: Weyssenburger, 1514).

zusammengezogen und in Gesangsweis dargestellt.[16] This German title indicates that Marius based his work on the four gospels. Similar to the Benedictine Chelidonius, the Cistercian Marius articulated the passion story of Christ in a style and form that was appealing to contemporary humanists. One may see his efforts as a sophisticated type of evangelization of the humanists, using means to which they were accustomed. This heroic epic demonstrates not only his rhetorical skills but also his deep Christian spirituality. The *Christi Fasciculus* shows that its author was a Christ-centered biblical humanist and theologian. In return, Marius himself received a poem from his friend Abbot Conrad Reuter.[17] This may suffice for a review of the literary-historical context of the *Carmen*.

HENRICUS URBANUS, O.CIST.

The *Carmen*, from which the pope quoted, has sometimes been ascribed to the Cistercian monk Henricus Urbanus, who probably died in October 1538. The last trace of his life suggests this year of his death. His monastery, Georgenthal, near Gotha/Erfurt, Germany, had been devastated in the 1520s during the Peasants' War.[18] Urbanus is known mostly as a monastic supporter of the Christian Hebraist Johann Reuchlin (1455–1522) against his Scholastic attackers.[19] His letters of support for Reuchlin, written sometime before August 22, 1513 and of October 15, 1513, are extant.[20]

---

16. See Paulus 1894, 579.

17. Partly edited in Gloning 1912, 489. The poem is included in Reuter's *Mortilogus F. Conradi Reitterii Nordlingensis, Prioris Monasterii Caesariensis, Epigrammata ad eruditissimos uaticolas* [sic] (Augsburg: Erhard Owglin and Georg Nadler, 1508; with woodcuts); the title *Mortilogus* may mean something like "the dance of death," *dance macabre*; see Gloning 1912, 487–89.

18. We have the exact date of neither his birth nor his death. Krause 1885, x. The other edition, Gillert 1890, was not available to me. The same date of Urbanus's death is given in Dall'Asta and Dörner 2003, 403 n. 2. A brief biographical sketch of Urbanus is included by Erich Kleineidam, "Henricus Urbanus."

19. On the Reuchlin Controversy, see Rummel 2002; however, without mention of the monastic humanist Urbanus as Reuchlin's supporter.

20. Edited in Dall'Asta and Dörner 2000–11, 2:401–5 and 449–51.

Fig. 2.1. Granary of the Monastery of Georgenthal, the only building that survived the Peasants' War in 1525. Photo from c. 1902 (private possession of the author).

Carl Krause, the editor of the correspondence of Mutianus Rufus, thought that this poem was written by his friend, the Cistercian Henricus Urbanus, to whom Mutianus wrote about it on May 28, 1513,[21] as he took the words *Vidi Marulum tuum* to mean Urbanus's own work ("I have seen your Marulus").[22] However, Mutianus really may have meant: "I have seen the book by Marulus that you possess" or "that you lent to me." Mutianus mentioned the poem and the *exempla* again in his letter to Urbanus (June 15, 1513), asking him to arrange for this work to be reprinted.[23] Mutianus had the entire work (*Institvtio bene vivendi per exempla sanctorum* and *Carmen*, "Instruction on How to Lead a Virtuous Life, Based on Exempla of the Saints") in mind, but only the *Carmen* was actually reprinted at Erfurt the following year. Perhaps Mutianus wished Urbanus's find to be better promoted in Germany from among the humanists' books (coming from Venice), especially because the *Carmen* was not included in recent collections of religious poems on the Passion of Christ such as those by Chelidonius/ Dürer.

21. *Nunc ad hilariora veniamus, ut dulce amarumque una misceatur. Vidi Marulum tuum. Carptim legi. Totus est christianus*; Krause 1885, 308f (Letter 250) with n. 5.

22. Bietenholz and Deutscher 1985–1987, 3:355f.

23. *Paucis ante diebus admonui, ut opus novum exemplorum investires*; Krause 1885, 314 (letter 255).

In general, the great significance of our Cistercian monk lies with the fact that he collected the correspondence of the leader of the humanist circle at Erfurt/Gotha, Mutianus, a collection that has facilitated the historiography of German humanism; without Urbanus's foresight one would have very few sources about Mutianus. Because of Urbanus's efforts in collecting the epistolary literature, the poems Mutianus had sent him were also preserved. These poems had been written by other humanists on the occasion of the death of the German arch-humanist Conrad Celtis, in 1508.[24]

The *Carmen* was to be published with Mutianus's blessing, but it is definitely not Urbanus's own work. It was written by the Croatian layman and humanist Marcus Marulus, and it is known in a print of 1506/1507 from Venice, as an epilogue to Marulus's other work, *Institvtio bene vivendi per exempla sanctorum*. It was the standard practice of humanist writers and poets at that time to conclude a book with a poem.[25] Since Mutianus called this text "totally Christian" already in May 1513, he could not have referred to its 1514 edition, but only to the 1506 or 1509 editions, both edited by the priest Franciscus Lucensis, at Venice,[26] or to the Basel edition of 1513 (see below). Mutianus evidently meant the smaller part of the two-part edition (*Institvtio* and *Carmen*) since he explains that he read the works "in pieces" (*carptim*) by selecting certain *exempla* from the lives of the saints at different times, that is, from the many sorts of pious stories which, as Mutianus wrote, the author produced in abundance. Mutianus thought these stories of the saints to be beneficial to Urbanus as a preacher.[27] Marulus's edition in Venice (his *Institvtio* with the *Carmen*, 1506 and 1509) was reprinted by Adamus Petrus de Langendorff at Basel in 1513 and 1518.[28]

Perhaps Mutianus did not know at the time that he urged Urbanus to arrange for a print at Erfurt that a new Marulus edition was being published in Basel that same year. Since the edition had appeared in 1513, it appears that Mutianus and Urbanus judged that at least the short *Carmen* by itself was worthy of a reprint. It was in fact printed by Canappus (Hans Knappe the Elder) at Erfurt in 1514. This edition was the first one for north-central Germany, and thus Mutianus and Urbanus contributed to the spread of Marulus's fame in German-speaking lands.[29]

24. See Rupprich 1934, 614–16.
25. See Béné 1994, 91.
26. See Béné 1994, 98.
27. *Vidi Marulum tuum . . . utilis tibi contionaturo*; Krause 1885, 309 (Letter 250).
28. See Béné 1994, 98f. The exact publication date of the 1513 edition is not given. If it was printed in early spring of 1513, Mutianus may have had knowledge of it when writing his letter on May 28, 1513.
29. Later sixteenth-century editions came out in Cologne in 1530 and 1531 and in

Mutianus had suggested already in his letter of April 15, 1506 (Letter 59) that Urbanus's edition of the *Carmen* should be graced with at least one illustration. (The plan to republish Marulus's entire work had apparently been dropped). Evidently, illustrated publications of Christ-centered poetry by humanists became very popular at that time. In order perhaps to make it even more marketable, Mutianus recommended to Urbanus once more, in June 1513, that he should "clothe the prints of Marulus well from the feet to the hip, yes all the way from head to feet. It is a useful work."[30] Urbanus's edition was in fact published with one illustration depicting the crucifixion (see illustration below).

Rarely has a connection been made between Mutianus's remarks in his correspondence with his Cistercian humanist friend, Urbanus, and the poem of the Croatian layman and humanist, Marulus. The connection lies with Urbanus's sponsorship (maybe funding?) of the Erfurt printing of Marulus's *Carmen* in 1514. The *Carmen* with illustration could apparently stand as a booklet on its own, even though it was originally meant to be "an integral part of the work [*Institvtio*] itself."[31]

MARCUS MARULUS (MARKO MARULIĆ, OR MARUL, OR PEČINIĆ)

Marulus was a layman from Croatia, born on August 18, 1450 in Split of distinguished noble parents.[32] He was one of the great figures of European Renaissance humanism, a leader in his native city Split, at the center of a circle of humanists there. He was the first child of seven in his family. His Italian mother was Dobrica de Albertis. In the 1460s he went to the lay-led school in Split (under lay, not clerical, direction), at the time when the Italian humanist Tideo Acciarini (1430-1490) was its principal. His schooling included Greek under the instructor Hieronymus Genesius Picentinus. In Marulus's library are found the textbook for Greek *Erotemata cum interpretatione latina* ("Questions with Latin Translation") by the Greek scholar living

---

Solingen (north of Cologne) in 1540; see Béné 1994, 97. Béné suspects that the Erfurt edition of 1514 may have been an "impetus for adaptations and translations in Luther's Germany, which remain to be discovered" (Béné 99). Still later editions of the *Carmen* were published in Antwerp (1577, 1584, 1593, 1601), in Paris (1586), and again in Cologne (1609 and 1686).

30. Mutianus's letter of June 1513 to Urbanus; Krause 1885, 313 (letter 254).

31. Béné 1994, 91.

32. See the biographical studies of Cronia 1953; Tomasovic 1966; Furthermore, Erdmann 1999; Pontificium consilium de cultura 2000. See also the recent exposition in Spain: Marko Marulic y la Europa Humanista, March 23 to April 14, 2002.

in Milan, Italy, Constantine Lascaris (died 1493 or 1500) and a volume titled *Vocabula de graeco derivata*. His knowledge of Greek, however, was limited, for he only occasionally used a Greek word.[33] Later in life Marulus was friends with numerous Italian humanists. He practiced law while writing his historical and religious books.[34] For most of his life he lived in his study at the family estate like a strict monk in "prayer and work" (*ora et labora*) according to the Rule of Saint Benedict, without eating any meat.[35] He died on January 5/8, 1524, in Split after a short illness and was buried in the Church of Saint Francis outside the walls (on the seafront), in the grave of his ancestors.[36]

Marulus was a prolific writer. In 1496/99 he worked on the *Institvtio*, which may be dependent upon the work of his teacher Acciarini, *De animorum medicamentis*.[37] The *Institvtio* and the *Carmen* were published in 1506/7 and 1509. He had already translated the *Imitation of Christ* of Thomas à Kempis into Croatian in 1500. In 1507 he finished a *Vita divi Hieronymi* ("Life of Saint Jerome"), which was published in 1513 with a versified "Prayer for the Holy Father Leo X" as its preface. In summer 1510 Marulus came out with fifty parables, *Marci Marvli Qvinqvaginta Parabolae*, reprinted in Cologne by Ioannes Gymnicus, in 1529. Some years later he wrote the now lost book on "Psychology"; the term appears to have been coined by him for the book *Psichiologia* [sic] *de ratione animae humanae* ("Psychology, on the Nature of the Human Soul"). He is the author of the *Evangelistarium*, which was printed in seven books in Venice by Jacob Iecus, in 1516.[38] In 1518 he wrote *De Hvmilitate et Gloria Christi* ("On the Humility and Glory of Christ," with March 21, 1518 as the date of dedication) on Christ the Savior,[39] edited by the same publisher, Bernardinus de Vitalibus Venetus (that is, in Venice), who had already printed his *Institvtio*. In the same year Marulus's *Evangelistarium* was re-edited by the German humanist and Franciscan friar Sebastian Münster as his own first publication (Basel 1519).[40] In 1520/21 he wrote the "sermon" *De ultimo Christi iudicio*

---

33. See Usmiani 1957, 22.

34. Knjizevni Krug 1984–.

35. A glimpse of his monastic lifestyle is provided by his contemporaneous biographer Franciscus Natalis, as given by Usmiani 1957, 36.

36. See Usmiani 1957, 48.

37. See Cronia 1953, 11.

38. This work was reprinted in Cologne in 1529; subsequently it was frequently reprinted elsewhere. It was used by Thomas More and King Henry VIII. There is a modern edition in Croatian and Latin by Branimir Glavicic (1985).

39. See Cronia 1953, 11ff.

40. See Raupp 1993.

("The Last Judgment of Christ"). For his *Judit*[41] ("The History of the Holy Widow Judith") of 1521, the first secular work of Croatian literature, printed and reprinted in Venice, he earned the honorific title "Father of Croatian Literature." In 1524 he published a book on the praise of Hercules, *Liber de laudis Herculis*,[42] in which he let the followers of Hercules, the titan of the pagans, compete with the titan of the Christians, that is, Jesus Christ, who, of course, is ultimately the victor. This book is known also as the *Dialogus de Heracule a Christicoles superato* ("Dialogue about Hercules, Who Was Surpassed by Those Who Worship Christ").

While Marulus aimed at the humanist ideal of *uomo universale* ("universal man") of the Renaissance, being interested in painting, local and national history, languages and poetry, his overall goal remained the renewal of Christianity (*renovatio Christiana*).[43] This layman was very critical of the immorality of the clergy, which he attacked in violent terms throughout his works.[44] In a way he wanted to be the Christian Valerius Maximus, whom he studied in his manuscript *Valerii Maximi Compendium*, written "by Marcus Marulus" (*per Marcum Marulum*).[45]

THE "VERITABLE DE LUXE EDITION"[46] BY URBANUS IN ERFURT, 1514

Henricus Urbanus's edition of Marulus's *Carmen* has the following full title: *M. Maruli Carme[n] de doctrina domini nostri Jesu Christi pende[n]tis in Cruce p[er] modu[m] dialogissmi Christi & Christiani* ("M. Marulus's Poem about the Teaching of Our Lord Jesus Christ as He Is Hanging on the Cross by Way of a Dialog between Christ and a Christian"). It is a "very beautiful booklet"[47] of only seven pages (see fig. 2.2). This edition is the only one

---

41. *Istoria svete udovice Judit*, which tells the biblical story of Judith and the slaying of Holofernes, was published in five editions between 1521 and 1627. The story of Judith proved extremely popular with a wide cross-section of the population in the Croatian version. The ethical message of Judith appears to be a call for Christian faith and unity in the struggle against the Turks, who are clearly paralleled with Holofernes. English edition by Cooper 1991.

42. See Cronia 1953, 12. This publication is esteemed highly, as its dedicatory epistle to Thomas Niger expressed admiration for Erasmus of Rotterdam.

43. Cronia 1953, 20.

44. See Usmiani 1957, 31.

45. See Usmiani 1957, 1 and 38. Valerius Maximus was a Roman author (died c. AD 50) known for his *Nine Books of Memorable Doings and Sayings*.

46. Béné 1994, 93.

47. Béné 1994, 99.

known as a separate edition, which thus makes Germany the only country to publish the *Carmen* as a booklet of its own. Germany is also the country that produced the largest number of Latin editions of the *Institvtio*, to which the *Carmen* was normally attached. However, no German version of the poem is known, whereas a sixteenth-century English translation is available (see below).[48] Remarkably, the Jesuit Saint Francis Xavier took the Cologne edition of the *Institvtio* (which includes the *Carmen* in its final pages) with him on his mission trips to Asia.

The first page shows the full title in large print. The second page displays the woodcut by an anonymous craftsman, which makes the Erfurt edition the first that includes a full-page illustration[49] (see illustration at the end of this chapter). Christ dominates the center of the picture on the title page as he is hanging on the T-shaped cross, shown with the crown of thorns and a small loincloth. The Crucified is flanked by the two criminals on their crosses. The soul (in the form of a little person) of the good thief on Christ's right side is received by an angel of heaven, while the soul of the criminal on the left is grabbed by the hair by a devil. Soldiers on foot and one on horseback mock and torture. The five pages that follow in Urbanus's edition present the poem in big, beautifully formed lettering.

The *Carmen* is divided into two parts. The first twenty-eight lines represent a dialogue between a Christian who asks questions and Christ, who provides brief answers. The Erfurt edition[50] clearly indicates the question/answer structure of this first part by the layout of the pages, which shows the alternation between *Christia[nus]* and *Christus*.

Marulus may have modeled his collection of examples in his *Institvtio* after the *Liber de modo bene vivendi* of Pseudo-Bernard,[51] which he translated into Croatian,[52] while the *Carmen* itself may be inspired by Pseudo-Bernard's *Oratio rhytmica* (see above on Saliceti), which Marulus also translated: *Molitva sv. Bernarda* ("Saint Bernard's Prayer"). Pseudo-Bernard's full Latin title, *Oratio rhytmica ad unum quodlibet membrorum Christi patientis et a cruce pendentis*, closely resembles Marulus's *Carmen* with its wording about Christ *pendentis in cruce*. Other possible influences

---

48. See Béné 1994, 133. A Japanese adaptation of the *Institvtio* came out in Nagasaki in 1595. "There may exist a Chinese or Japanese translation which is waiting to be unearthed if it has survived" (Béné 95).

49. Béné 1994, 99.

50. See the facsimile in Béné 1994, I.1.3.1–7.

51. See *Patrologia latina* 184:1199–1306. Its author may or may not be Thomas of Froidmont. Béné 92.

52. See Cronia 1953, 18.

on his *Carmen* may have been Petrarch (died 1374),[53] Lactantius (died c. 320), to whom the *Carmen de passione Domini* is attributed and which Marulus must have read as the first text in the anthology *Poetae Christiani veteres*[54] (see above), and Saint Bonaventure (died 1274) with his poems *Laudismus de sancta cruce* and *Meditatio de passione Jesu Christi*, which were also translated by Marulus.[55]

In the dialogue between the Christian and Christ, the Christian asks seven questions, each consisting of two lines, and Christ gives his answers in the same two-line verse form (given here in English summary):

1. Why did you come to earth? So that man may find his way to heaven.

2. Why do you want to endure suffering and death? So that the loving-kindness [*pietas*] may cleanse man's blood, which then is to be carried into heaven.

3. Why do you spread out your arms and have your feet so closely joined? Because I invite all nations to the covenant of faith.

4. Why do you bend your head and gaze down? Because I want to remind mortals not to be arrogant but rather to bend the neck meekly under the yoke of piety.

5. Why are you naked and why do your bones dry out? I want this so that you feel disgust over worldly luxury.

6. Why does a small cloth cover your loins? From this learn that chaste bodies are dear to me and that I hate it when forbidden love bares someone's shame.

7. Why the blows, the spit, the thorns, and everything else? Because he (here the poem switches to the third person singular) bears to the end every injury; he does not bring on any others. He wants to enjoy peace.

The second part of the poem encompasses fifty lines, in which Christ teaches a lesson about the moral life of a Christian in the light of Judgment Day, which will be terrifying. This lesson appears to be an extension of Christ's answer to the final question, because there is no punctuation between answer 7 and the subsequent verses. The second part of the poem continues seamlessly with these words: "Life is short, labor is limited, payment is most welcome, the benefit is always immense and perpetual."

---

53. Marulus translated Petrarch's Italian *Vergine bella, che di sol vestita*; Cronia 1953, 13; Usmiani 1957, 36.

54. See Béné 1994, 92.

55. See Cronia 1953, 18; Béné 1994, 91–93.

However, if all this does not move a person, one should at least be afraid of the exile of the eternal prison (*carcer*) with its inextinguishable fire and darkness, the ever-gnawing worm, and the ever-bitter plague (*lues*). All these things await those who lust and follow other vices. They do not listen to Christ and do not follow him; they do not fear the judgment on the day of wrath (*dies irae*), when there will be great turbulence that will shake the spheres (*globos*). The moon will turn bloody red; the sun will be gone. The earth (*orbis*) will crash. One will see that the choirs of angels do not make sense anymore. The world will go up in flames. Then "I [Christ] will arrive" (*adueniam*), sitting on a cloud accompanied by the multitude of saints. The terrifying trumpet will sound from above. Without delay, hell and inferno will come to the accused (*tartara & ima reis*). The slave-dealer (*mango*) will then catch those who survived thus far. Nothing will be left hidden or concealed (*nihil occultumve latensve*), including unspoken thoughts.

Christ will give eternal life as reward for one's merits. Those whom malicious error implicated shall have their chained feet untied. Be wide awake on that dark day at the end time (*extremi temporis atra dies*) when things will happen so fast. At this point the verse favored by the pope appears: "Happy is the one who always puts his life to good use" (*Felix, qui semper vitae bene computat usum*) and who always thinks of the end, be he away or at home (*iam fore, iamque suum*). With those words Christ concludes his lesson.

Marulus's *Carmen* was translated into English in the second half of the sixteenth century by Philip Howard, Earl of Arundel (1557–1595), while he was imprisoned in the Tower of London. His translation is known under the title *A Dialogue Betwixt a Christian, and Christ Hanging on the Crosse. Written into Latine by Marcus Marulus, & Translated into English*.[56] This English version, incidentally, served as the introductory poem to the complete translation of *A Letter from Jesus Christ to the Soul That Really Loves Him* (*An Epistle in the Person of Christ to the Faithful Soule*), which was made from the original Latin text of the German Carthusian Prior Johannes Lanspergius (John of Landsberg, 1489–1539), titled *Liber alloquiorum Jesu Christi ad quamvis animam*. Marulus's poem served as the opening to the 1595 Antwerp edition of Howard's translation of Lanspergius's *An Epistle*.[57]

Howard's translation of verse 77 of the *Carmen*, quoted by the pope, goes like this:

---

56. See Béné 1994, II.3.1.

57. See Béné 1994, 106. The contemporary English edition of John of Landsberg's *A Letter from Jesus Christ* is found in the series Spiritual Classics (Landsberg 1981).

Happie is he who still his life, doth well and Godly spend.[58]

Fig 2.2. Title page of Marulus's *Carmen*, edited by Henricus Urbanus (Erfurt 1514). Reprinted from Béné 1994, 1:1.3.2.

---

58. Béné 1994, II.3.6.

Chapter 3

The Empires

The Mouse, the Frog, and the Unidentified Flying Object: Metaphors for "Empires" in the Latin Works of the Croatian Humanist Marcus Marulus and of the German Humanist Ulrich von Hutten[1]

THE DOMINANT POWER IN the Middle Ages was the "Holy Roman Empire of the German Nation," by its official Latin name: *Sacrum Romanum Imperium Nationis Germanicae*, a designation which was established firmly by 1512. There are various aspects to this Roman notion.[2] In Marulus's vocabulary it has no significance, if he used it at all. By its nature, poetic language prefers metaphors. Fables handed down from antiquity became a great source for poets of all times.

The most famous collection of fables is that of the Greek author Aesop, whose short stories of talking and interacting animals were handed down in Latin prose or verse. The first printing with illustrations of *Aesop's Fables* was provided by Giovanni and Alberto Alvise in Verona in 1479,[3] with

---

1. Paper originally written and intended for the meeting of the American Association for the Advancement of Slavic Studies, November 15–18, 2007, in New Orleans, Louisiana.

2. See Awerbuch 1981.

3. See De Simone 2004, 103.

woodcuts designed by one of the city's leading painters, Liberale da Verona (c. 1445–1526).⁴ An edition by Lorenzo Valla (1407–1457) was also available as of 1499.⁵

Fig. 3.1. From *Nuremberg Chronicle* of Hartmann Schedel (Nuremberg, 1493 German edition).

4. It would be worthwhile to examine these incunabula for their depiction or lack of the fable of the Mouse and the Frog. But this is not our purpose here. On Liberale, see *Catholic Encyclopedia*, entry "Verona" (https://www.catholic.org/encyclopedia/view.php?id=11990). As early as 1475/1480, Bonus Accursius printed the collection of these fables, made by Planudes, which, within five years afterwards, William Caxton translated into English, and printed at his press in Westminster Abbey (1484/1485). Numerous other illustrated editions of the late fifteenth century are known: Johannes Zainer's Latin and German editions of Aesop's *Vita et fabulae* (Ulm, 1476–1477), which influenced many subsequent printings of Aesop's fables all across Europe (see De Simone 2004, 51). The Croatian printer Dobrić Dobričević (Boninus de Boninis) printed *Aesopus moralisatus* (Brescia, c. 1487). With the same title, an edition from a southwestern German city is known by Michael Greif (Reutlingen 1489) and from Venice by Manfredus de Bonellis (1491 and 1493); from Florence by Francesco Bonaccorsi (1496). From Basel an edition of 1501 is known by the physician and humanist Heinrich Steinhöwel (of Ulm, d. 1478) together with the writer Sebastian Brant (of Strasbourg, d. 1521), see fig. 3.2; from Sevilla: *Libro del sabio y clarissimo fabulador Ysopo historiado y annotado* (Sevilla: Jacob Cromberger, 1521).

5. *Fabulae ex graeco in latinam per Laurentium Vallum uirum clarissimum uersae Aesopus* (Venice: De Cereto, 1499).

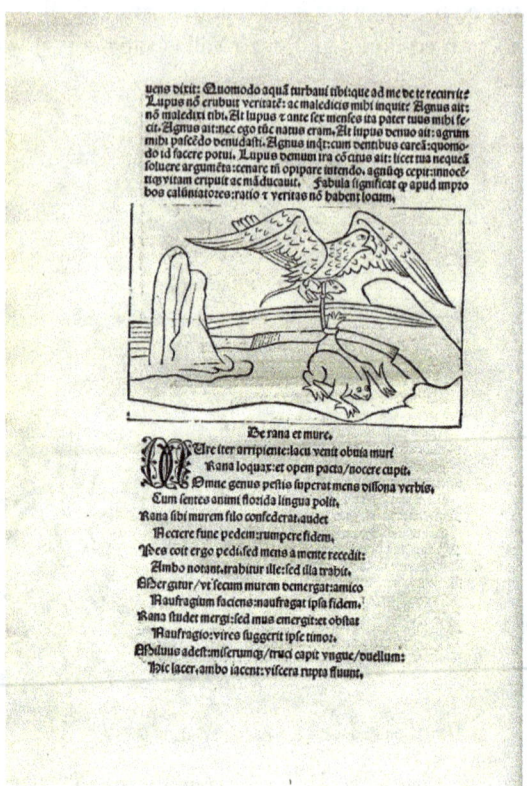

Fig. 3.2. The Frog and the Mouse. Illustration on page 48 by an anonymous woodcutter. From: Heinrich Steinhöwel (and Sebastian Brant), *Esopi appologi sive mythologi: Cum quibusdam carminum et fabularum additionibus Sebastiani Brant* (Basel: Jacobus [Wolff] de Pforzheim).

A "portrait" of Aesop (Esopus, fig. 3.1) is included in the *Nuremberg Chronicle* of Hartmann Schedel (1440–1514), also known as the *Chronicle of the World*, a medieval account of the history of the world.[6] Aesop is the first listed among the Greek writers. Only one of Aesop's fables is of interest here: the fable of the Mouse, the Frog, and a preliminarily unidentified Flying Object. The Englishman Caxton called the fable under consideration here "Of the rat and of the frogge." In the Latin edition of Heinrich Steinhöwel and Sebastian Brant of 1501 the focus also is on the Frog and the Mouse as the caption of the illustration shows (*De rana et mure*).

This fable lent itself particularly well to describe certain religious-political "empires" of the Renaissance period. A look at the famous German

---

6. See Schedel and Füssel 2001.

nationalist, Ulrich von Hutten (1488-1523),[7] an early sympathizer of the Reformer, Martin Luther (1483-1546), shall function here simply as one element or aspect of the European literary context in which the Croatian humanist and lay theologian Marcus Marulus[8] of Split is to be situated; thus the introductory chapter on Hutten serves as an illustration of the wider context of Marulus's literary work. The main purpose is to investigate the use of the fable by Marulus in his Latin texts, his interpretation of the unidentified Flying Object (3.1), his characterization of this bird (3.2), and in this connection, his use of the notion of the "Turkish Emperor" (3.3), his concern for Christian unity between the Frog and the Mouse (3.4), and his specific view of the "wrath of God" (3.5).

Only in recent times does Marulus emerge as a literary and theological figure of European significance, as a "European Humanist" whose opus is an "organic part of the European literary heritage" and "a common treasure, which needs to be discovered together."[9] Neither Marulus nor Hutten were mentioned in a recent study on the development of creating the concept of East and West among Renaissance humanists and their view of the Ottoman Empire.[10] However, the older, monumental work *Turcica* (on European prints concerning the issue of the Turkish menace) lists both, Hutten with his speech that he had planned to deliver to the German princes in 1518, and Marulus with his open letter of 1522 to Pope Adrian VI.[11]

AESOP'S FABLE OF THE MOUSE, THE FROG, AND THE UNIDENTIFIED FLYING OBJECT

A mouse asked a frog to help her get across the river. The frog tied the mouse's front leg to her own back leg using a piece of string and they swam out to the middle of the stream. The frog then turned traitor and plunged down into the water, dragging the mouse along with her. The mouse's dead body floated up to the surface and was drifting along when a kite (bird of

---

7. See Wheelis 1977; Junghans 2001.

8. I use his humanist Latin name as I am dealing here with his Latin texts.

9. Bratislav Lučin, "Introduction," in MR, 30-31.

10. See Bisaha 2004. The "Protestant" Hutten is not mentioned in Fischer-Galati 1959. Hutten, but not Marulus, is mentioned in Guthmüller and Kühlmann 2000, 211. Croatia is not taken into consideration, but Poland (437-443), France (373-394), and England (395-408) are.

11. See Göllner 1961-1978; Hutten, *Ad Principes Germaniae*, vol. 1:70 (no. 100) and 84 (no. 125); Marulus, Letter to Adrian VI, vol. 1:95 (nos. 153 and 154). Göllner also includes the oration by Tranquillus Andronicus (Fran[jo] Trankvil Andreis [1490-1571]), vol. 1:322 (no. 678).

prey) flew by and noticed something he could snatch. When he grabbed the mouse he also carried off the frog. Thus the treacherous frog who had betrayed the mouse's life was likewise killed and eaten.[12]

The Latin versions usually speak of the bird of prey as "a flying kite" (*milvus [volans]*). One of the meanings of the English word "kite" is a soaring bird of prey, especially of the genus *milvus* with long wings and normally a forked tail. The fact that the exact name of the Unidentified Flying Object is not given in this fable allows for various interpretations, in ways as needed by an author, be it a hawk, a falcon, an eagle, even an egret,[13] or as in the case of the medieval author Odo of Cheriton (died 1247), the devil.[14]

ULRICH VON HUTTEN'S USE OF THE FABLE

In the summer of 1516 Hutten had experienced life in Rome under the papacy. The disillusioned young man returned to Germany and enthusiastically joined Martin Luther and his circles, in the hope that he could combine his own "Away-from-Rome" campaign[15] with Luther's rising popularity and interests. Hutten had become an early supporter of Martin Luther primarily because of the Reformer's criticism of the Roman papacy.[16] And Luther became a supporter of Hutten, whose name is connected to the famous *Letters of Obscure Men* (1514/1517). However, the principal author was Crotus Rubeanus (c. 1480–1545).[17] Hutten was an outspoken representative of German national humanism, who nevertheless used Latin as the preferred language for his poetry and pamphlets, and who promoted polyglot studies (Greek and Hebrew) for the better understanding of the Sacred Scriptures. In 1517 he was crowned poet laureate by Emperor Maximilian I (reigned 1493–1519).

12. Gibbs 2002, online: http://mythfolklore.net/aesopica/oxford/index.htm.

13. Martin Luther started his own German edition of Aesop's Fables for pedagogical purposes; see WA 50:432–60 (1530). The fable of the Mouse and the Frog is found on p. 449. Luther identified the bird of prey with a *weyhe* (p. 449, line 29), likely the equivalent of an egret or stork, in Early New High German. According to *Duden Etymologie*, *der Weih[e]*, it may be a bird of prey.

14. Odo's application: *Hoc est quando parochia data est alicui stulto et insufficienti; uenit Diabolus et asportat utrumque capellanum et paroch[i]am*; see University of Mannheim website. Odo is an example of how fables were used by medieval preachers against stupid pastors (*contra stultos rectores*) who are given parishes; then the devil comes and takes away both the chaplain and the parish.

15. Or, "Anti-Rome Campaign" (*Huttens Anti-Rom Kampagne*), Bernstein 2004, 176–79.

16. See Posset 2003c, 14–16 (on Hutten).

17. See Rummel 2002, 23.

Certain verses of Hutten that were dedicated to Emperor Maximilian were accompanied by a pictorial representation of Aesop's fable of the Mouse and the Frog. The picture is a woodcut by Hans Weiditz (c. 1495–c. 1536),[18] an artist better known for his portrait of Emperor Maximilian and for his *Emperor Maximilian at Mass*.[19] Within Hutten's work *Ad Caesarem Maximilianum Epigrammatum Liber Unus*, it is epigram 21, about the emperor and the Venetians, *De Caesare et Venetis*, that was accompanied by Weiditz's woodcut. The book was printed by Johann Miller in Augsburg in 1519, the same printer who published a call for help by the Croatian nobleman Tranquillus Andronicus (1490–1571), summoning the Germans to help against the Turks.[20]

Hutten's focus is on the Flying Object rather than on the relationship of the Mouse and the Frog. He calls Aesop's bird of prey (*milvus*) an *ales* in Latin, which simply means "winged," but is usually used for a large bird of prey like an eagle or a hawk:

> Recently, the shameless Frog stepped out of the swamps of Venice
> and dared to say as he touched the ground: "The land is mine."
> When Jupiter's Bird (*Iovis ales*) saw it from his lookout on high he
> destroyed it with his claw and threw it back into the dirty waters.[21]

In Hutten's text, only the Bird and the Frog are mentioned, not the Mouse. This is the case also with Weiditz's woodcut, which appears to have been created specifically for Hutten's text. To Hutten and Weiditz the identification of the Flying Object as "the Eagle" came quite naturally as they were, of course, familiar with the eagle as the heraldic symbol of the Habsburg Empire. Weiditz depicts the Eagle with the imperial crown of the Holy Roman Empire. The Eagle with its wings dominates the upper center and right field of the picture, representing the northeast in terms of geography. In the background across the entire upper part of the woodcut, we see a mountain range, the Alps. The imperial Eagle has landed on the Alps and is descending upon the Frog that is leaping from the water, the Mediterranean Sea. Hutten and Weiditz focus exclusively on the conflict between the Frog and the Eagle.

---

18. See Böcking 1862, 3:205–68, here 216–17 (with Weiditz's woodcut).

19. See Turrentine 2001.

20. *Oratio contra Thurcas ad Germanos habita* (Augsburg: Johann Miller, 1518). This printing is not included in Bohnstedt's study of 1968, although Hutten is a German pamphleteer, but not writing in the vernacular and likely because of that left aside.

21. *Rana procax nuper Venetas egressa paludes*
Ausa est, quam tetigit, dicere, "terra mea est." Quam procul ut vidit specula Iovis ales
ab alta, onvulsam ad luteas ungue retrusit aquas.
Böcking 1862, 3:216–17.

The Frog, representing the Republic of Venice, has its head raised high with a scepter in the right hand. The scepter is one of the regalia and thus an attribute of a monarch. When shown in the hand of the Frog as the Republic of Venice one must interpret the Frog as having usurped the royal scepter (illegally). In the waters behind the Frog we see a complex of buildings sitting on an island and large boats in the waters, representing the powerful Venetian fleet.

Fig. 3.3. The Eagle and the Frog: The Habsburg Empire (Eagle) quarreling with the Republic of Venice (Frog). Woodcut by Hans Weiditz, from Hutten's Epigram and Exhortatorium to Emperor Maximilian (1519) (British Museum). The woodcut is reprinted in A. G. Dickens 1966, 25; also depicted in Egg and Pfaundler 1969, 44.

Fig. 3.4. *The Four Apocalyptic Horsemen* (1498) by Albrecht Dürer (1471–1528). Illustration of the text Apocalypse 6:1–8. The First Rider is a mounted archer and wears an Ottoman-like cap with a crown, which is a hint at the Turkish emperor.

According to Hutten, "the shameless Frog stepped out of the swamps of Venice." This means that Venice reached far onto the dry land, from the foot of the Alps in Lombardy and the land around Bergamo in the west to the foothills of Tyrolia in the northeast, and all the way along the eastern Adriatic coast down to Dubrovnik and beyond. The Frog in Hutten's words claimed: "The land is mine."

Hutten's epigram describes and Weiditz's woodcut depicts the power struggle between the Empire and the Republic of Venice under the doges Leonardo Loredan, who reigned from 1501 to 1521, and Antonio Grimani, who reigned from 1521 to 1523. Emperor Maximilian I had proclaimed himself as Roman emperor not too far from Venice, namely in the cathedral of Trent, on February 4, 1508. For the purpose of breaking the power of Venice, Pope Julius II (1503–1513), the warrior pope, had formed the League of Cambrai with Emperor Maximilian I, Louis XII (1498–1515), and Ferdinand (of Aragon, 1479–1516) in December 1508; an alliance on paper, supposedly against the Turks.[22] During the "Venetian War," which started in 1508 and lasted for nine years, the emperor took possession of parts of the Venetian Republic's territory. However, by January 1515 the new French king, Francis I (1515–1547), formed a new alliance with Venice against the emperor and the new pope, Leo X (and other allies). The Italian War of 1521 to 1526, sometimes known as the Four Years' War, pitted Francis I of France and the Republic of Venice against Emperor Charles V (1519–1556), Henry VIII of England (1509–1547), and the Papal States. The conflict arose from animosity over the election of Charles as emperor in 1519.

These historical struggles are depicted in the woodcut of the Eagle and the Frog, representing in an abbreviated and simplified form the great battle between the Holy Roman Empire of the German Nation and the Republic of Venice over the hegemony of Northern Italy, one of the major conflicts of European history of the sixteenth century.[23]

Hutten may have been inspired by Tranquillus Andronicus to be concerned, too, with the Turkish menace, and not only with the emperor's cause against the Frog. Andronicus published his anti-Turcica text in 1515: *Ad Deum contra Thurcas Oratio carmine heroico. Eiusdem epistola ad clarissimum ac nobilem virum Hieronymum de Croaria* (*sic*; Nuremberg: Johannes Stuchs, about 1515),[24] and in 1518 he published his *Oratio contra Thurcas ad Germanos habita* (= *Oratio de bello suscipiendo contra Turcos*; Augsburg: Johannes Miller 1518).[25]

One must not forget that men like Hutten were not only concerned with the German empire that was fighting against the Republic of Venice, but that he also feared the Ottoman Empire that advanced from the southeast. We find Hutten's worries expressed in his speech at the Diet of Augsburg in 1518, when he called upon the princes of Germany to wage war against the Turks. The speech, written in Latin, was also printed in Augsburg in 1518, but by another printing press, that of Sigismund Grim[m] and Marcus Vuyrsung.[26]

22. See Wiesflecker 1986, 5:426–27.

23. See Rabe 1989, 20–21.

24. Edited in Böcking 1862, 5:205–28, with a woodcut on 205.

25. See Franolić 1998; see the website "Latin as a Literary Language among the Croats," http://www.croatia.org/crown/articles/6609/1/E-Latin-as-a-literary-language-among-the-Croats.html.

26. *Vlrichi de Hutten equitis Germani ad Principes Germaniae vt bellum Turcis inuehant. Exhortatoria* in Böcking 1962, vol. 1 (no. 19).

Anti-papal feelings in Germany clearly expressed themselves officially at the imperial Diet of Augsburg in 1518 when the estates of the empire identified themselves with the complaints of the German nation (*gravamina nationis Germanicae*). They let the papal delegate, Cardinal Cajetan (1469–1534), know that they rejected any taxation in support of the pope's call to a crusade against the Turkish threat.[27] Hutten, as the German spokesman for the movement of a "church without Rome," called upon the political forces within the Holy Roman Empire of the German Nation against the Turks, but without papal leadership. The Germans must no longer provide financial support for the Roman papacy, but instead they should give their money to the emperor and the empire's war against the Turks.[28] Hutten apparently had persuaded the German estates that their emperor should lead them against the Turks without the pope.[29] German Lutherans began to work with a concept of "empire" that no longer needed the pope. Nevertheless, they remained very concerned about the Turkish menace.

The famous artist Albrecht Dürer had created a woodcut in 1498 that vividly depicts the Turkish menace, which is represented in one of the four apocalyptic horsemen (fig. 3.4). His depiction may very well stand for the German fear of the approaching Turks at the end of the fifteenth and at the beginning of the sixteenth century.

MARULUS ON THE BIRD OF PREY, THE MOUSE AND THE FROG

The Republic of Venice included within its borders the area of the eastern coastline of the Adriatic Sea, known as Croatia. It thus provided additional space for the international "literary republic"[30] of Latinists to whom Marcus Marulus of Split belonged. In the history of this coastline, the role of the Latin language was more important than in most other European territories, and by virtue of the Latin language our Croatian Latinist was united to the international Latin-speaking world. Around 1500 Split was home to a flourishing humanism. The circle of humanists at Split did not produce, however, any other great authors besides Marulus, who equaled the most distinguished Latin writers of that time in Europe. He was part of the universal phenomenon of Latin literates which transcended all barriers. He

27. See Junghans 2001, 80.
28. See Wheelis 1997, 122.
29. See Junghans 2001, 81.
30. Gortan and Vratović 1971, 47; Budiša 1991; see Franolić, website at http://www.hic.hr/books/latinists/01latin.htm.

also shared the Latinists' reliance on literary models of antiquity.[31] He made ample use of the classical tradition, including Aesop.

Identifying the Bird of Prey

In his *Repertorium* Marulus made a note of the three animal characters of Aesop's fable, the Frog, the Mouse, and, simply, the Bird (*auis*). What may be significant is the fact that Marulus entered them under the term "Menace" or "Danger,"[32] which may be the key to the understanding of Marulus's use of the fable later on, namely understood as the "Turkish menace." To him the fable was a story about great, deadly dangers descending on the homeland. We know that Marulus had an edition of *Aesop's Fables* at hand, which is listed in his will as *Apologi quedam de Jsopo Greco*[33] (i.e., "Some Fables of the Greek Aesop"). Whichever edition he may have had at hand, he utilized this particular fable from a point of view that differed from Hutten's in Germany. Hutten features the relationship of Frog and Bird. Marulus employs the story from the perspective of an endangered city, namely his hometown Split. Yet, both Marulus and Hutten are somewhat fixated on the Flying Object. Hutten sides with the Bird as the Eagle, while Marulus sees in the Flying Object the threatening Bird of Prey.

Marulus used the fable twice. In one of the various poems that Marulus directed against the animosities among the Christian nations, *In discordiam principum Christianorum* ("Against Discord among the Christian Rulers"), the fable is used to express concerns about the religious-political situation he lived in. He used it again in 1522 (see below). Marulus—in contrast to Hutten—included not only the Frog and the Bird, but also the Mouse. For Marulus, too, the Frog represents the mighty Republic of Venice. The Mouse, in Marulus's view, stands for the Western adversaries of Venice, as he deplores the fact that the Frog and the Mouse ceaselessly struggle in the same pond. What does he mean by the Unidentified Flying Object, *praedae auidus miluus* ("the flying kite of prey")? For an answer, let us look at how he addresses the political constellation (NB: the translator identified the bird of prey as the "Falcon"):

> While a frog and a mouse ceaselessly struggled in the pond,
> Each a bitter foe preparing the other's death

---

31. See Gortan and Vratović 1971, 38–47.

32. *Scytharum dona: rana, mus, auis et sagittf; quo perimendos sagittis hostes significabant, nisi aquas subiissent ut ranf, aut terram ut mures, aut aera ut uolucres, Repertorium*, entry "Periculum," taken from his readings of Marcus Sabellicus, *Ab orbe condito*. *Repertorium* (Sabellicus 2000, 3:140).

33. See CM 14 (2005) 46.

Falcon, the beast of prey, noticed the fight from the high
Descended and grabbed them both with its crooked beak.
Trust me that such destiny awaits all our rulers
Who continue their wild war against each other.
When they all get exhausted of their mutual slaughter,
Then the barbarian foe will have a free way.
I wish I only were a bad prophet, and the wind
Would take my words high up, scatter them into thin air.
But if they are not united by common foe,
Essential truth this will be, a word from Phoebean tripod.[34]

Marulus's Latin version of the fable does not match any version of the traditional wording, for instance, by Walter of England, Romulus, or others.[35] It is Marulus's own wording which he fit into the poem on the discord among the rulers. In his version, the Mouse and the Frog are not friends, but foes. The Bird of Prey noticed from on high the fight between them and "descended and grabbed them both with its crooked beak." Obviously, the little Mouse would mean the mighty Holy Roman Empire. Did Marulus want to belittle the imperial power as a little mouse? One should not overinterpret here by an awkward allegorization of all the details of the fable which Marulus in all likelihood did not intend. He more likely looked at the broader political picture and used the fable as a story about the great menace (*periculum*, see *Repertorium*) threatening his homeland.

Characterization of the Bird of Prey

For Marulus, the Bird of Prey is "the barbarian foe" that "will have a free way" in order to advance to wherever he wants to fly. Who, then, would the

---

34. Lučin and Novaković 2005, 164 (no. 96); trans. by Kovačiće in MR, 144–47.

> Mus et rana lacu medio dum prflia miscent,
> Alter in alterius damna suprema furens,
> Praedae auidus miluus luctantes cernit ab alto:
> Deuolat et rostro prendit utrumque suo.
> Talia fata manent nostros (mihi credite) reges
> Inter se Martis dum fera bella cient.
> Exhausti alternis fuerint cum caedibus dibus omnes,
> Irruet in uacuam barbarus hostis humum.
> O utinam falsus uates sim uerbaque uentus
> Nostra ferens auras dissipet in tenues!
> Sed nisi discordes iungat commune periclum,
> Phoebea fient uera magis tripode!

35. The Latin text of Romulus is found in Hervieux 1970, 654–712. For other Latin versions, see the University of Mannheim website.

barbarian be? Like other humanists of his time, Marulus resurrected the old label of "barbarian," and like Erasmus of Rotterdam, for example, he applied it to the Turks. Erasmus wrote of them in 1530 as a "barbarous people" (*gens barbara*).[36] With the attribute of the dangerous "barbarian" Marulus can only refer to the Turkish menace. The mighty Bird of Prey of the fable is the barbarian enemy, the "common foe" who, in Marulus's use of the metaphor, is the Ottoman Empire that threatens the lands of Christianity, which is represented by the Frog and the Mouse, who both will be eaten up by the big Bird.

To Marulus this is the truth as if it were spoken from the Oracle of Delphi where the priestess sat on a tripod ("Essential truth this will be, a word from Phoebean tripod"). With this image Marulus hints at the classical Greek antiquity. With his reference to the "barbarians" he evokes the memory of the invasion of the barbarians of late antiquity. Their attack on Rome in the fifth century must have appeared to him as barbaric as the conquest of the Second Rome, Constantinople, by the Ottomans, the "new Barbarians" in 1453.[37]

The Bird of Prey is the contemporary sultan of the Ottoman Empire, Selim I (1512–1520), whose threatening advances alarmed the West. Against this predator the pope,[38] the emperor, and the kings of France and England tried to band together, at least for a short time. In 1513 Marulus had high hopes pinned on Pope Leo X as successor of Julius II.[39] Marulus saw in Leo X the "good shepherd" (*pastor pius*), the "famed son of the house of Medici," the "father doctor" who may heal the wounds inflicted on the "Italic world."[40] In Marulus's perspective from Split, the Frog is Venice, the republic to which his hometown belongs. The Mouse represents the enemies of Venice and they might be as big as the Roman Empire of the German Nation; and the Bird of Prey is the Turkish emperor.

Marulus was, of course, not the only one calling upon the pope for help to unite the Christians against the Turks. We know, for instance, that the pope's confessor, the Franciscan friar Petrus Galatinus (1460–1540), preached to the pope and to the cardinals about this issue on the Feast of the Circumcision of the Lord in 1515. In his sermon he declared that the animosities among the Christian princes were the cause that the Turks capture

---

36. Erasmus, *Consultatio de bello Turcis inferendo*, as referred to by Bisaha 2004, 43–93, 175.

37. On this issue, see Schwoebel 1967, 147–75 (chapter 6, "The New Barbarians"). There is no mention of Marulus in Schwoebel's book.

38. Leo X, a Medici, reigned from March 11, 1513 to December 1, 1521; see Schwaiger 2001, 88–89.

39. On this pope, see Shaw 1993.

40. *In Medicem Leonem X. Pontificem Maximum*; Lučin and Novaković 2005, 160 (no. 92); "To Pope Leo X," trans. by Graham McMaster in MR, 144–45.

all the countries by storm.[41] Finally, in 1518 Leo X called for a crusade against the Ottoman Empire, but in vain,[42] since the Germans did not cooperate.

Marulus's Use of the Title "Turkish Emperor" in the Context of European Pamphleteers

Probably on the occasion of the death of the Turkish ruler Selim I, who died unexpectedly on September 20, 1520, Marulus wrote the *Epitaph to Ottoman, the Turkish Emperor* which celebrates the loss of his temporal power through his death.[43] Marulus gave the Turkish ruler the same Latin title, *imperator* (*Epitaphium Ottomani, Turcarum imperatoris*), "Emperor of the Turks," that the rulers of the Holy Roman Empire claimed. From his perspective, the two dominant powers of the then known world were two "empires," one of the Turks and the other of the Christians. With this wording Marulus fits squarely into the European mosaic because the designation "Turkish Emperor" is common verbiage in the early sixteenth century.

In a pamphlet in German (printed in Augsburg in 1523) we also find the notion *Türkisch Kayser* ("Turkish Emperor"; contemporary German spelling *Kaiser*). The text deals with the Black and/or Red Jews (*swartz auch rodt Juden*) who came out of Africa and gather their forces against the Turkish emperor. According to the report of a Jew, these African Jews send twelve emissaries to the Turkish emperor to admonish him to let them return to their ancestral homeland:

> Should the Turk not believe they were real Jews, they were to prove their identity with great portents.... And this Jew reports that they are all black and red Jews, and have come out of the uttermost deserts or dunes of Africa, who until now have been entirely hidden.[44]

A reminiscence (or is it wishful thinking?) of this legendary Black Jewish army out of Africa that is gathering forces against the Turkish emperor (*Kayser*) may be found in another vernacular pamphlet (of 1530) in

41. See Galatinus, *Oratio de circumcisione dominica*; as quoted in Kleinhans 1926, here 172–73.

42. See Schwaiger 2001, 88.

43. *Epitaphium Ottomani, Turcarum imperatoris*; Lučin and Novaković 2005, 214 (no. 152); trans. by Miljenko Kovačićek in MR, 146–47.

44. The pamphlet is edited with an English translation in Appendix A, no. 19, Gow 1995, 266–72, here 267–68. Does the expression *swartz auch rodt Juden* (line 28) mean that there are two groups of Jews, black and red, as the English translation may imply, or does it mean that the Black Jews are known also (*auch*) as Red Jews?

which the idea is expressed that "the Jews ... would lend their support" to fight the Turks.⁴⁵ The author is a Catholic, pro-Habsburg, by the name of Johann Haselberg, who wrote about the "Military Campaigns of the Turkish Emperor," i.e., Suleiman. The long title of his booklet against the Turks (*Türkenbüchlein*; fig. 3.5) summarizes its content about the actions of the Turkish *Kayser*, who "came from Constantinople with his entire armory, by horse and on foot, on water and land and moved toward (Greek) Weyssenburg, and drawing near to the royal cities Ofen in Hungary and Vienna in Austria." The subtitle reads as follows: "With an appendix on the cruel tyranny of the Turk against the Christian nation."⁴⁶ The woodcut on this title page depicts the two opposing armies; on the left, under the leadership of *Karolus*, "the Roman Emperor who is the Archduke of Austria and the Protector of Christendom; on the right, under the *Suldan Soleyma*[n], the Turkish Emperor, an archenemy [*ain erbfeind*] of the Christian faith." He hoped that a divine miracle would end all religious and even political strife so that Emperor Charles V as the head would sweep the Turks away and bring about a new golden age with the help of the Jews (who are not specifically identified as Black Jews or Red Jews) and all the other "sects":

> Even if the Turkish emperor were three times as powerful as he is, he would still have to flee his homeland before the Christian emperor. . . . The Jews and all the other sects in Christendom would lend their support to the Christian campaign.⁴⁷

Haselberg, like many others, at that time only had the Christian emperor as the universal protector in mind under whom all Christians and Jews should unite (thus, not under the papacy). Evidently, by 1530 Haselberg, the pro-Habsburg pamphleteer, no longer brought the papacy into the political play against the Turks, but only wrote of the unification of all the existing religious factions ("sects"), including the Jews, under the Christian emperor. While Haselberg worked with the concept of Jews and Christians united under the emperor against the Turks, Marulus, in contrast, would have been happy with a united Christian front under papal leadership against the Ottomans.

45. Bohnstedt 1968, 37.

46. *Des Türckische[n] Kaysers Heerzug / wie er von Constantinopel Mit aller rüstung / zu Roß und F,ß / z, wasser vnd Land etc. gen kriechische[n] Weyssenburg kummen / vnd fürter/ Für die königlichen stat Ofen yn Vngern, vnnd Wien in Osterreich gezoge[n] /die belegert vn[d] gestuermet etc. [-] mit angehenckter ermanung / der grausamen tyranney des Turcken / wyder Christliche Nation etc. Karolus Römischer Kayser Ertzhertzog vonn Osterreich etc. Beswchyrmer d[er] Christenhait. Suldan Soleym[n] Türckischer Kayser ain erbfeind des Christschliche[n] [sic] glaubens etc.* Nuremberg: C. Zell, 1530, Austrian National Library; Bohnstedt 1968, reproduction on the title page.

47. Bohnstedt 1968, 37.

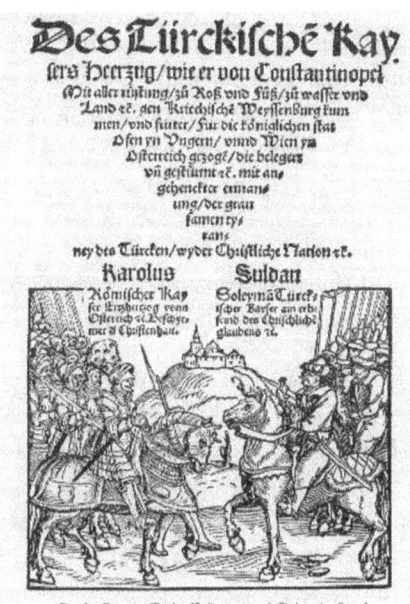

Fig. 3.5. Title page, *Des Türckische[n] Kaysers Heerzug* ("The Military Campaign of the Turkish Emperor"; Nuremberg: C. Zell, 1530; Austrian National Library). For the full title, see note 46.

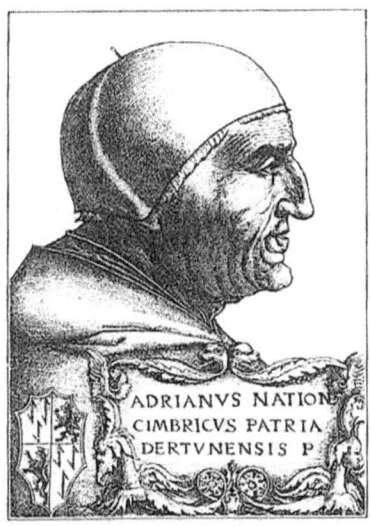

Fig. 3.6. Pope Adrian VI (1459-1523). Copper Etching by Daniel Hopfer. Caption in Latin says: "Adrian of the Cimbrian Nation [Netherlands] whose hometown is Utrecht."

At about the same time, also Luther's vocabulary contained the expression "Turkish Emperor," which actually became in his mind a synonym for a deceiving murderer and robber who is possessed by the devil. Luther used the same title for the contemporary German revolutionary Thomas Müntzer (c. 1489–1525), who was executed a few years earlier: Müntzer is a new Turkish *Kaiser*, as found in one of Luther's pamphlet of 1529.[48]

Marulus's Main Concern Seen in the Greater European Context: Frog and Mouse Must Unite against the Bird

Sultan Sulayman I (Suleiman), the Magnificent (1494–1566), succeeded Selim I and reigned for forty-six years. His accession to the throne of the Ottoman Empire brought about a reorientation of Turkish foreign policy as he led ten military campaigns in Europe and three in Asia. In 1519 Hungary had concluded a three-year truce with Selim I, but Sulayman renewed the war in June 1521 and on August 28, 1521 captured the citadel of Belgrade, the key fortress on the Danube, which opened the road to Hungary. Pope Leo X was greatly alarmed, and although he was then involved in a war with France he sent about thirty thousand ducats to the Hungarians. On December 1, 1521 Pope Leo died. A year later, the main Christian stronghold in the eastern Mediterranean, Rhodos, fell to the Turks, on Christmas Day in 1522. The new pope, Adrian VI (a Dutchmen, who reigned only from January 9, 1522 to September 14, 1523),[49] was alarmed, too.

In the following spring, on April 3, 1522, Marulus in Split decided to call upon the new pontiff. Marulus thought it fitting to use Aesop's fable once more when he asked the new pope for help in providing homeland security against the Turks. Marulus's plea is known as *The Epistle of Lord Marcus Marulus of Split to Pope Adrian VI. About Present Misfortunes and an Exhortation to Union and Peace of all Christians*, and it includes *The Prayer of Marcus Marulus to Christ for Pope Adrian VI*. Plea and prayer were printed in 1522 in Rome by B[ernardus de] V[italibus].[50] Marulus's letter

---

48. *Und was suchte Muntzer itzt zu unsern zeiten, denn das er ein newer Turckisscher Kayser wolt werden?*; in *Vom Kriege wider die Türken* (*On War Against the Turks*), WA 30-II:107–48, here 125.

49. See Schwaiger 2001, 54.

50. *Epistola domini Marci Marvli Spalatensis ad Adrianvm. VI. pont[ificem] max[imvm] de calamitatibvs occvrentibvs et exhortatio ad commvnem omnivm Christianorvm vnionem et pacem* (Rome: Bernardinus. de Vitalibus, 1522). The prayer *Pro Adriano VI. Pontifice Maximo ad Christum oratio* is edited in Lučin and Novaković 2005, 162 (no. 94). Dedication, epistle, and prayer are now available in MR, 90–109, trans. Vera Andrassy.

had been requested by the Dominican Friar Dominik Buća of Kotor (Dominicus Buchia; c. 1480–c. 1560), biblical scholar and preacher, who had asked Marulus to appeal to the pope as the head of the church, not to allow kings and princes to fight each other, but to lead them to unity and prepare a war against the infidels. Marulus mentioned this in his cover letter, in which he asked the friar to forward his text to Rome.[51] Marulus told the pope that the Turkish infidels had not yet besieged the towns of Dalmatia, but all the rest was open to plunder. They intended to attack the towns, too, and declare war on the Venetians, "our masters." The Turks are called the "infidel wolves" (*infideles lupos*),[52] "the Mohammedan beast" (*Maumetana bellua*),[53] and the "most godless of all Antichrists" (*Antichristorum impiissima natio*).[54] Churches have been turned into stables; iconoclasm is rampant. Belgrade had fallen the previous summer (August 29, 1521). Marulus reminded the pope of this fact. The roads would soon be open to Illyria, Germany, Italy, and the rest of the Christian world (*christianorum orbem*).[55] The Turks pillaged monasteries, raped the maidens, circumcised the boys "according to the custom of the Mohammedan faithlessness" (*Maumethana perfidia*)[56] or the "barbarian faithlessness" (*barbarica perfidia*),[57] and turned them into infidels. Marulus uses the Latin notion *perfidia*, not *haeresis* or *secta*. The English translation of *Maumethana perfidia* as "Mohammedan heresy" may be wanting from a theological point of view that would define "heresy" primarily as an inner-ecclesiastical issue (unless one would view Islam altogether as a Christian sect).[58] Marulus wanted to stress the stark contrast between the Christians and the followers of Mohammed. Likely, he did not consider Islam as a Christian sect.

Marulus's plea to the pope is situated in the acerbated religious and geopolitical constellation in which he made use of Aesop's fable of the Frog, the Mouse, and the Bird of Prey (translated as the "Hawk"). Here, the Frog and the Mouse represent the entire "Christian world" (*orbs christianorum*)

---

51. See MR, 90–91.
52. MR, 106–7.
53. MR, 102–3.
54. MR, 94–95.
55. MR, 96.
56. MR, 94–95 and 100–101.
57. MR, 96–97. In Marulus's *Evangelistarium* one finds the notion *impietas* applied to Moslems and Jews: *Iudaica uel Machumetana uel aliqua alia impietate* . . .; book 2 on hope, chapter 1, on Luke 23.
58. On the definition of heresy in the earlier middle ages, Lourdeau and Verhelst 1976.

which Marulus also calls "Christian republic," "Christian kingdoms," or "Christian commonwealth":

> Believe me, the Christian commonwealth [*Res publica Christiana*] will be lost, unless they all, with the same intention, the same faith and in unity, join forces and, having combined their armies and called on the name of Christ to go forth to war and choose death rather than serve the barbaric perfidy [*barbaricae perfidiae*] . . .
>
> It is here [in Marulus's homeland], then, that the enemy should be opposed, that he should be repelled with all our might and effort, so that the flood, which is such a horrendous threat, may not spread and engulf the countries that remain. The common menace [*commune periculum*] should be repelled in a combined campaign! Let no-one think to be safe because a great expanse of territory separates him from the frontiers of the infidels [*ab impiorum finibus*] . . .
>
> Therefore, Holy Father, lest the Christian kingdoms are crushed one after another by the onslaught of the infidel tyrant while they are fighting against each other, it is for you because of your wisdom and the dignity of your office, to see to it that those who are quarrelling are speedily reconciled, that they refrain from [further] injustices, prefer peace over war, and with a united front defend themselves and their property against the attacks of the most rapacious wolf of wolves . . .
>
> Do not stop, Most Holy Father, to help those who are within your boundaries with weapons, money, and necessary supplies [*armis, pecunia, rebus necessariis*] . . .[59]

At the center of his letter, Marulus refers to the fable of the Mouse and the Frog (*apologus muris et ranae*), but without mentioning the Bird of Prey in referring to the title of the fable. Clearly his focus is on the Frog and the Mouse. Yet, in the text itself Marulus includes the third animal character, the *miluus* (kite, bird of prey), which another translator rendered with "hawk." Marulus does not use—from the Latin vocabulary available to him—the other option for the Flying Object, such as the harmless *ales* (which Hutten chose), but qualified by Hutten as "Jupiter's bird," i.e., Eagle (see above). Marulus opts for *miluus*, the flying kite of prey.

> Believe me, now is not the time to remember domestic injustices, and seek retribution, lest we experience the same fate as is described in the fable of the Mouse and the Frog. A frog was dragging a mouse across a pond in order to drown it in

59. My own translation, based on MR, 92–108.

deep water and the mouse was struggling to free itself. A hawk (*miluus*), flying above them and seeing them wrestling on the surface of the water, suddenly plunged down, seized them with his claws and tore them to pieces with his beak. This, it seems to me, will be the fate of those who are now quarrelling among themselves, if they do not stop. For while they are plotting each other's downfall, while they are fighting each other, the barbarian will profit from their division and weakness, attack them as soon as an opportunity arises and conquer them effortlessly.[60]

For Marulus at this point it was rather irrelevant whether the Bird is a hawk, a falcon, or an eagle, as long as it is a bird of prey that is to be feared. In support of his plea, Marulus beseeched the pontiff to follow the example of the biblical king David, and postpone any deserved, just punishment of present-day offenders against the church:

> The biblical story [*sacra historia*] shows that King David proceeded in this way. He did not wish to punish Joab and Shimei, the son of Gera, when they erred [2 Samuel 16:5 and 19:16; 1 Kings 2:5–9]. . . . When he had overcome the enemy, he ordered his son Solomon to punish them when he succeeded him to the throne. Follow his example, Most Holy Father [*Sanctissime pater*], and postpone the penalty which those who have sinned against the Church deserve.[61]

One may assume that here Marulus hints at the pope's troubles with the Lutheran reformers in Germany as those who have offended the church (*qui ecclesiam offenderunt*). Marulus warns the pope with the words of Matt 12:25:

> "Every kingdom divided against itself will be ruined, and every city or household divided against itself will not stand." Those who believe in Christ have one kingdom and one church. If they continue in their discord, their kingdom will crumble. . . . Those who do not believe the Gospel and doubt that this will happen should at least listen to the pagan writer [*gentilem*; Sallust] who says "Concord makes small things grow, discord destroys even the greatest."[62]

---

60. MR, 102–3. However, I changed the word sequence in accordance with the Latin: *apologo detur locus muris et ranae*.

61. MR, 102–3 (my translation, slightly altered here).

62. *Concordia paruae res crescunt, discordia maximae dilabuntur* (my own translation); see MR, 104–7 with n. 13; with reference to Sallust, *Iug*. 10,5.

Marulus Differs on Who Should Be Mindful of the Wrath of God

Marulus's great concern was the ecumenical unity of the Christian nations, which are represented by the Mouse and the Frog and which appear thus so small if compared to the mighty Bird of Prey, the Turks. The contemporary German pamphlets on the Turks (*Türkenbüchlein*) tend to interpret the Turkish menace directly and exclusively as a scourge inflicted by God's wrath and then concern themselves often with the personal sins of the Christians as remedy.[63] In marked contrast, to Marulus it is (primarily?) the animosity among the Christian nations that provokes God's wrath (*ira Dei*). The Catholic Croatian, unlike the German Lutherans,[64] does not simply identify the coming of the Turks as punishment for provoking the wrath of God. According to his open letter to the pope, the discord among Christian nations causes God's anger: "Hating each other, they provoke God's wrath."[65] One may thus question or at least refine the all-too-generalizing statement in a study of the Croatian literature of the sixteenth century that the Turks as such are the punishment of God, a concept which supposedly is found in the works of the Dalmatian and Ragusan authors.[66] It would presume, mistakenly, an identical view of these authors and of Luther, who saw in the Turks the wrath and punishment of God.[67]

In contrast, Marulus sees God's wrath directed toward the disunity among the Christians. However, reformers and humanists alike all worked with the contrast of "faithful" Christians versus "infidel" Turks or Mohammedans and with the concept of the "Turkish menace." The religious differences between Christianity and Islam are clearly spelled out by Marulus as his poem "About the War Between the French and the Spaniards" (undated) shows: "The bitter foe of all Christianity, Mohammed, wants to spread his power upon the entire world." He is the "common enemy."[68]

---

63. See Bohnstedt 1968, 3.

64. Primarily, Martin Luther, Andreas Osiander, Justus Jonas, or Veit Dietrich.

65. ... *odiis flagrantes Dei aduersum se iram prouocant*; MR, 98. Noteworthy and in need of further study is the difference between the German view of the Turkish menace as God's wrath and Marulus's view.

66. See Albrecht 1965, 152–61: "Die Vorstellung der Türken als Gottesstrafe finden wir sogar in den Werken der dalmatischen und ragusanischen Schriftsteller." This author mistakenly refers to Marulus as a "Ragusan poet" (*Ragusaner Dichter*, 83). Ragusa is the Latin designation for Dubrovnik. Albrecht's view is accepted by Göllner 1961–78, 3:83 and 178.

67. On Luther's view, see Brecht 2000; Miller 2002; Miller 2004.

68. MR, 144–45, trans. by Miljenko Kovačićek.

In terms of a historical footnote, Marulus's desire for unity among the Christian nations was fulfilled in part when in August 1523 Pope Adrian VI formed a new alliance with the Frog and the Mouse, i.e., the Republic of Venice, Holy Roman Empire, and the Kingdom of England—but primarily not against the Turkish emperor, but against France. For the time being, the Mouse and the Frog appeared united partly and no longer in a fatal way as the fable has it. Yet, shortly afterwards the pope died and in the course of the sixteenth century the religious disunity of Europe was cemented for centuries to come.

At about the same time, Marulus found an emulator of sorts in the German Lutheran knight Hartmut von Kronberg, who also wrote an open letter to Pope Adrian, *Eyn sendbrieff an Babst Adrianum*,[69] printed at Wittenberg in 1523. However, Kronberg did not use the fable. He sounded more like Hutten, as he demanded that the papacy dissolve its wealth in order to provide funds against the Turks,[70] and also dissolve itself as an institution and abolish its own preachers, who should be replaced by (Lutheran) preachers of the Gospel. Then, after all of Europe has accepted the Lutheran Gospel, the gigantic military action against the Turks may begin and would liberate the many Christian brethren who had been living under the Turkish yoke.[71]

Evidently, Catholics and Lutherans in Germany were drifting apart on their view of the role of the papacy in the defense against the Turkish emperor. Yet, an anonymous Catholic author of 1522, probably from southern Germany or Switzerland (judging by the spelling of his book title, *Türcken biechlin*), was equally very critical of the papacy for its worldly concerns and for draining Christendom of its cash resources that were needed to fight the Turks. He advocated the separation of church and state.[72]

While all these ideas were floating around in the intellectual milieu of his time, Marulus stuck to his adherence to the popes, and he decided to write another poem, sometime in November–December 1523, in order to express congratulations to the newly elected pope, Clement VII (a Medici, who reigned from November 19, 1523 to September 25, 1534). Marulus

---

69. *Daryn mit Christlichem warhaftigen grund angetzeigt wurd eyn sicherer heylsamer weg zu ausreuttung aller ketzereyen: vnd zu heylsamer rettung gantzer Christenheyt von des Turcken tyranney* (Wittenberg: no printer name given, 1523); edited in Kück 1899, 117–20; Bohnstedt 1968, 11 and 53. The pamphlet is posted on a Hungarian website with a different spelling of the title, which may indicate a printing that is different from the one edited in 1899: http://vmek.oszk.hu/html/vgi/vkereses/vborito2.phtml?id=3624.

70. See Bohnstedt 1968, 11.

71. Bohnstedt 1968, 36–37.

72. *Türcken biechlin* (no printer name given, 1522); Bohnstedt 1968, 30.

again called for the political unity of the Christian rulers against the Turkish advances. It was Marulus's last piece of the "*antiturcica* genre."[73] However, he no longer made use of Aesop's fable.

CONCLUSION

In the religious-political context in which Marulus lived, he assigned the Bird of Prey to the Turkish Empire. In doing so, Marulus had a broad, global view. With his great concerns regarding the Turkish menace, the Croatian humanist and lay theologian in one way fits squarely into the cultural context of European humanists with their same concerns about the Turkish menace, though perceived in various degrees of urgency. Marulus and Hutten, just like Erasmus (whom Marulus admired),[74] and others called for a defense against the Turkish attacks. Both Marulus and other humanists were convinced that the lack of solidarity among Christians would help the advances of the Ottoman Empire towards the heart of Europe.[75] In another way, Marulus does not fit as snuggly into this mosaic. As a Catholic Croatian he allowed for or demanded a greater leadership role for the papacy. The Catholic Marulus appealed to the pope for help, in contrast to the Lutherans like Hutten, who relied on the emperor. Hutten and German Lutherans wanted to exclude the pope from the coalition against the Turks, while Marulus expected the pope to take a role of leadership.

In terms of metaphors from Aesop's fable, the Bird of Prey was not employed for the Ottoman Empire by any other poets and authors except by Marulus in his unique situation in the far southeastern part of the Republic of Venice. To the Germans the mighty Bird always was the imperial Eagle as shown on the coat of arms of their emperor. In this connection, Germans like Hutten appear occasionally rather provincial or narrowly nationalistic and self-centered in their own empire as they wanted their emperor to fight the Frog of Venice. Marulus had the wider vision and saw the Christian emperor, although awkwardly compared to the little Mouse, tied to the Republican Frog of the Western world, while from the southeast of Europe the now clearly defined Flying Object has already landed, the ferocious Bird of Prey, the Turkish emperor.

---

73. See MR, 19.

74. See *Marcus Marulus Thomae Nigro, Scardonensi Episcopo, Salutem Plurimam Dicit*; in OO, 11:21–22; see Lučin 2004, especially 100–101.

75. See Maria Cytowska 1974; Housley 1998, 277; Šanjek 1999, 134–35.

Chapter 4

The Pope

Open Letter of a Croatian Lay Theologian to a "German" Pope[1]

THE DOCUMENT UNDER CONSIDERATION here is the rather lengthy, but fascinating *Epistle of Lord Marko Marulić of Split to Adrian VI, the Supreme Pontiff, Regarding the Current Misfortunes and an Exhortation to General Unity and Peace of All Christians*.[2] It is a unique document because it is the only *epistola* that Marulić addressed to a pope,[3] and it appears to be the very first letter to Pope Adrian concerning the misfortunes in Marulić's homeland and the proper role of the papacy for achieving unity and peace among all Christian nations. The *Epistola* is also the last text Marulić published

---

1. I am grateful to Vladimir Bubrin (Canada) for his reading and critiquing of the draft of the paper which was delivered on April 21 during the *Marulićevi dani* 2008 in Split. I am equally grateful to Bratislav Lučin and Neven Jovanović for their comments and suggestions for the publication of the revised and enlarged version of that presentation.

2. *Epistola Domini Marci Marvli Spalatensis ad Adrianvm VI. Pontificem Maximvm de calamitatibvs occvrrentibvs, et exhortatio ad commvnem omnivm Christianorvm vnionem et pacem*. The Latin version with an English translation by Vera Andrassy on facing pages is provided in MR, 90–108. However, I use my own English translation in close consultation with the English version provided on the facing pages.

3. The poem of 1523 addressed to Clement VII was probably not meant to be an *epistola*.

during his lifetime,[4] if one disregards the reprints of his *Judit* that became available a month later in Venice, and the third edition published on January 29, 1523.

There are numerous aspects that may be considered concerning the *Epistola*. Some of them are already covered from a literary-historical point of view,[5] or they are related to documents that emerged after Marulić's *Epistola*.[6] There are still other questions that arise when one investigates the *Epistola* from a historical-theological/church-historical point of view. Some of these issues are to be addressed here (in part 1):

1. The use and non-use of the pope's name in the *Epistola* and its cover letter, which leads to the question whether the text or a draft of it came into existence at an earlier time than immediately after Adrian's election; and it leads to the further issue whether the document is really fully understood if it is considered only and exclusively in terms of "*antiturcica* genre."[7]

2. The problem of the timing and printing of the *Epistola* in spring 1522 (when the new pope had not even arrived yet in Rome, coming from Spain), which promotes the idea that the *Epistola* is more of a timeless and theological document that is not to be considered outdated because of its partially anti-Turkish content.

3. The *Epistola* as an open letter in the context of other sixteenth-century open letters.

In part 2, we will see Marulić as one of several other lay theologians who are loyal to the church of the Renaissance papacy on the eve of the Lutheran Reformation and its early stage.

Before we enter into these topics, we need to make a note on the notion of "nations" in the early sixteenth century, as our topic includes the designations "Croatian lay theologian" and "German pope." We should remind ourselves that "nation" in the modern sense did not yet exist at the time of Marko Marulić, which is a time of pre-nationalist identities. "Croatia" and "Dalmatia" are at times interchangeable.[8] For example, Marulić wrote

---

4. See Tomasović 1994, 30.

5. See Cattaneo 2008.

6. See Marijanović 2003. Stjepan Brodarić (Brodericus, 1480–1539) appeared before Pope Adrian VI as a royal envoy in September 1522, i.e., shortly after the pope was enthroned.

7. As MR, 19, has it. Cattaneo, too, focuses much of his study on this aspect, admittedly not an insignificant one.

8. See Nicholas 1999, 223; Fine 2006.

to the pope on behalf of "our Dalmatia."[9] And, according to the imperial *Edict of the Diet of Worms* of May 1521, Emperor Charles V was "by God's grace Roman emperor elect, . . . king of Germany, Spain, the two Sicilies, Jerusalem, Hungary, Dalmatia, Croatia."[10] The two entities "Dalmatia" and "Croatia" are listed separately. This imperial claim leads to the question: If the emperor was the ruler of Dalmatia and of Croatia and thus their protector, why then did Marulić not write directly to Emperor Charles V for help? We know that the young emperor felt obligated and was more than ready to provide military support against the Turks.[11] Yet, the Croatian nobleman wrote not to the emperor, but to the pope. The issue is not to be pursued here. Always seeing himself as a man of the church (*ecclesiasticus*), Marulić had greater confidence in the papacy than in the empire.

As to the designation "German": Was Marulić aware of the ethnic background of the new pope at the time of the election (January 9, 1522) and at the time when he finalized and dated his *Epistola* (April 3, 1522)? Was Marulić familiar with the notion "Cimbrian Nation,"[12] a contemporaneous expression which signaled the ethnic background of the new pope? "Cimbrian Nation" is a reference to an ancient German tribe, the Kimbers, usually mentioned together with the Teutons. Was Marulić aware that he wrote to a "German" pope?[13] Did Marulić have any inkling that the new pope was living in Spain and elected *in absentia*?[14] It seems not, as one may derive from the simple observation that not even the thirty-nine cardinals who entered the conclave on December 28, 1521 and eventually elected Adrian Florensz Boeyens really knew who this man was: "He was quite unknown in Rome, therefore he had at least no enemies."[15]

---

9. *Dalmatiae nostrae*, MR, 94.

10. Robinson 1904; see website: uk.encarta.msn.com/sidebar_761594139/ edict_ of_the_diet_of_worms.html. On the Turkish conquest of southeastern Europe, see for example, Waley and Denley 2001, 251–62. The "Kingdom of the Two Sicilies" was a territory that included the island of Sicily and all southern Italy almost as far a Rome, almost bordering on the papal state.

11. Especially after Charles V had learned of the attacks against the Island of Rhodos; see the letter of Charles V to Charles de Poupet, Lord of Lachaulx of August 25, 1522, in Kohler 1990, 100–103 (no. 24).

12. See copper etching by Daniel Hopfer (1470-1536) with the Latin caption *Cimbricus*; depicted in Posset 2008b; see fig. 3.6 in above chapter 3.

13. German historiographers/biographers prefer to speak of him as the German pope; see Hocks 1939; Posner 1962.

14. See Pirie 1935, 55–61.

15. Pirie 1935, 58.

SOME ISSUES THAT ARISE FROM THE *EPISTOLA*

The Use and Non-Use of the Pope's Name

It seems that Marulić was writing the *Epistola* not so much to a specific pope, be he Italian, German, Spanish, or whatever, but that he composed a sermon-like pamphlet, at least in parts on the religious role of the papacy. Marulić in writing the text had in mind primarily the moral authority of the institution of the papacy, or he hoped and expected it to become a positive moral force again, despite the series of "Bad Popes" (as later historiographers would view them).[16] This means that the *Epistola* can be read in large parts as a theological source that tells us something about the author's concept of the papacy and the church. Thus, the document can be taken as a source text for Marulić's ecclesiology, as it does not reveal anything specific about Marulić's knowledge about the person of the newly elected pope. The reason for this lack of information in the *Epistola* may be that Marulić's focus was the scandal of disunity among the Christian "nations" in the "West" in facing the military threat of the Ottoman Turks. Both issues, the threat from the Turks and the wars among the Christian nations, are of course closely connected.

Marulić's primary purpose for writing the text appears to have been to motivate the leaders of Christianity in the West to put an end to their wars against each other, including the pope, but not the pope alone. This *Epistola* could have been meant for any pope of that time. This view is supported by the further observations that in his letter Marulić employs the spiritual titles of the popes without mention of the new pope's personal name, which is used only in the very last paragraph as a last-minute "insert." And at that point, the original Latin text does not read "Adrian VI" but only *Adrianus*,[17] i.e., his baptismal name.

It is equally conspicuous that in the text of his cover letter of April 3, 1522 Marulić employs only the papal title *Pontifex Maximus*, not the newly elected pope's full name.[18] At the time of writing the letter, Marulić most likely could not have known the biographical details of this "German" pope and that he breached "papal etiquette"[19] by retaining his baptismal name (Adrian) and not opting for a symbolic change of name as a new

---

16. Chamberlin 1969 includes Alexander VI, Leo X, and Clement VII.

17. MR, 106; the English version on face page 107 has "Adrian VI."

18. MR, 90. One may assume that the wording of the title of the *Epistola* in the printed version as we have it today is probably the work of the printer or of Friar Dominik Buća, who gave the text to the printer.

19. Pirie 1935, 58.

pope. When the humanist Enea Silvio Piccolomini (1405–1464, Pope Pius II [1458–1464]) was elected he chose "Pius" for his papal name, which is a literary allusion to Virgil's *pius Aeneas*.[20] Cardinal Rodrigo Borgia (c. 1431–1503) upon his elevation to the papal throne in 1492 demonstratively took the symbolic name "Alexander," the name that belongs to the greatest pagan conqueror of pre-Christian antiquity.[21] In sharp contrast, Adrian decided to keep his baptismal name.

When we take the concept of the papacy as contained in the *Epistola* into consideration, we get a glimpse of the author's ecclesiology and we must conclude that the *Epistola* is more than simply or exclusively a work of the "*antiturcica* genre."[22] It is also and perhaps more so a document promoting Christian unity, written in the tradition of the earlier calls to unity against the Turks by Enea Silvio Piccolomini in 1453 and the congress of princes at Mantua in 1459.[23] The idea of a European crusade against the Turks runs like "a missionary leitmotif"[24] through the years of the papacy of Pius II. It is conceivable that Marulić wanted to compose a letter similar to the intentions of Piccolomini, a letter which would not have to be addressed to one specific pope such as Adrian VI, to whom eventually the *Epistola* was directed. The text may concern any pope at that time.

That Marulić's text is not exclusively an anti-Turkish document may be argued still from another perspective, namely that the author is scolding all the Christian rulers for their wars against each other. However, Pope Adrian does not fit this mold at all as he was not even in office yet and had no opportunity yet to wage any war. Only with the other addressees in mind (the previous popes and contemporary princes that attack each other by military force) does it make sense that Marulić inveighs against them with offensive and sarcastic-sounding passages like the ones to be quoted below. Evidently, Marulić had in mind primarily the scandal of Christian disunity. Here are some of the most provocative and poetic lines from his *Epistola* directed against the Western rulers, rearranged in a way that the poetic and dramatic quality may become apparent:

> [*Resipiscite*] Come to your senses at long last, [*Resipiscite*] Come to your senses, you lunatics!

---

20. See Helmrath 2001, 118.
21. See Chamberlin 1969, 171.
22. As MR, 19, has it.
23. See Cattaneo 2008, 121–23; Helmrath 2001, 119. The congress of Mantua did not act against the Turks.
24. See Helmrath 2001, 19.

> [*Quousque*] How long will you [*uos*] persist in your madness?
> [*Quousque*] How long will you ignore your [*uestram*] ruin?
> [*Non*] You are not fighting for yourselves [*uobis*],
> [*Non*] You are not winning victories for yourselves [*uobis*],
> but you only are giving to him who is preparing to devour all of you [*uos*]
> the chance of a future victory over you [*uobis*].[25]

With these words and in using the plural forms (*vos, vestra, vobis*) he must have aimed most of all at the obnoxious behavior of the rulers of Europe, although this is found here in the letter to the pope.

As to the expression *resipiscite* ("come to your senses") which Marulić uses here, it is noteworthy that Erasmus in his Greek-Latin edition of the New Testament (*Novum Instrumentum*, 1516) proposed that the central biblical Greek notion *metanoia* should be rendered with *resipiscentia*.[26] It is of course difficult to demonstrate whether or not Marulić had any knowledge of this.

The quoted lines may sound more like a Roman pasquinade, which the new pope would not deserve yet, as he had done nothing, or had failed to do anything which would merit him any ridicule or satirical treatment. Could it be that this dramatic text passage once upon a time had an independent existence and was meant for and inserted into a draft of a text perhaps to a previous pope?[27] Was perhaps Pope Leo X on Marulić's mind when he wrote this part of the *Epistola*? Were some of the major parts of the *Epistola* already written at the time of the fall of Belgrade in 1521 during Leo's reign, or even before the fall of Belgrade? The fall of Belgrade is explicitly mentioned in the *Epistola* (see below).[28]

Pasquinades usually sprung up at the time of a papal interregnum[29] when "socially Rome was a dead city,"[30] and gambling was at an all-time high in the city's gambling dens, where the odds on the candidates to the papal office could run very high. Some gamblers would not shy away from

---

25. MR, 100–101; Cattaneo 2008, 97–98, arranged the lines in a different way to illustrate his point:

> Resipiscite tandem, resipiscite insipientes!
> Quousque ratio uos fugiet, quousque perniciem uestram ignorabitis?
> Non uobis pugnatis, non uobis uincitis . . .

26. See Oberman 1981, 53 n. 23.

27. The question of the literary unity of the *Epistola* is beyond the scope of the present investigation.

28. See MR, 96.

29. See Ludwig 1898–,9:8–10 (Lampoons and Pasquinades).

30. Pirie 1935, 14.

trying to ruin the chances of the opponents. Bad-mouthing and ridicule were also useful: "Scurrilous pamphlets, lampoons and pasquinades flooded the town, always anonymous of course, as backing the wrong horse openly might result in one's losing a good deal more than one's money."[31] This was the milieu in Rome outside the location where the electors stayed. They usually were well informed about what was going on, as much of this "edifying literature was smuggled into the conclave with the object of influencing the cardinals' votes, and no doubt afforded their Eminences and their conclavists [service personnel] a few moments of hilarity at one another's expense."[32]

The passage against the "lunatics" (who fight each other) would correspond with Marulić's specific view of the "wrath of God."[33] He saw it directed against the Christian disunity vis-à-vis the Turkish menace.[34] Once one shifts from the exclusive fixation on the *antiturcica* aspect of the *Epistola*, a whole new range of ideas opens up and the *Epistola* can be understood as a document for the promotion of Christian unity and peace among the Christian "nations" with the pope as their spiritual leader. Thus the document can be used as a source of information of Marulić's concept of the papacy and the Roman Catholic Church.

All this is suggested, first, by the initial impression that Marulić most likely did not have the specific personal or political qualities of Adrian in mind when he composed the *Epistola*, and secondly, by the observation that the new pope's name "pops up" only at the very end of the *Epistola*. Thirdly, Marulić's use of Aesop's fable of the Frog and the Mouse, of Sallust's insight that "unity makes small things grow," of Plutarch's story of Scilurus's "united bundle," and the numerous biblical references to peace, unity, and fraternity[35] point to the possibility that his *Epistola* may not only be classified as an *antiturcica* text, but also as a document of a loyal lay theologian's concept of political ecclesiology.

The Problem of the Timing and the Printing of the Epistola

We do not really know whether Marulić's *Epistola* was conceived originally as a private letter that was to be delivered to the papal court in Rome assuming that the newly elected pope was in residence there already, or as an open

---

31. Pirie 1935, 14.
32. Pirie 1935, 14.
33. MR, 98.
34. On this aspect, see Posset 2008b, 143–44.
35. See MR, 102–6.

letter. And the question still remains: how could Marulić have known that the new pope was not present at the conclave, but was elected *in absentia* and had never set foot on Italian soil before? All we know is that Marulić instructed Friar Dominik Buća to "dispatch it [*Epistola*] to Rome at once."[36]

Dominik Buća (also known as Dominicus Buchia Catharensis, or Buchius, 1480–1560) of Kotor was a Dominican friar and an (occasional?) preacher in Split. Franciscus Martiniacus (Frane Martinčić, c. 1480–1527?) dedicated a poem to Fr. Dominik, who apparently was giving an exegetical lecture series on the Penitential Psalms in Split,[37] but we do not have any dates about his preaching. Marulić refers to Fr. Dominik's "sermons to the people" in his cover letter of April 3, 1522, in which he also indicates that Fr. Dominik was a professor of theology.[38] However, we do not know where he was teaching; evidently not in Rome, as he was instructed to send the manuscript of the *Epistola* to Rome. There are two possibilities:

(a) To the printing shop of Bernardinus de Vitalibus in Rome (Bernardinus had a print shop not only in Venice, but also in Rome). At the shop in Rome, Bernardinus previously had printed Ptolemy's *Geography* in 1507/1508). However, his workshop does not seem to have been open for business in Rome in the spring of 1522 because there appears to be no other print from his Roman press that is dated around that time (1522), except for Marulić's letter. Rome as the location of the printing of the *Epistola* remains itself somewhat of a puzzle.

(b) Directly to the papal court. However, we do not know why there would have been such urgency of forwarding the *Epistola* to the pope in Rome "at once" or "immediately" (Latin: *continuo*). It seems that if the letter was meant to be delivered to Pope Adrian in person, the letter writer or the letter carrier was not aware of the fact that the newly elected pope was not even on Italian soil yet and that therefore there was no urgency at all for the personal and direct delivery of this mail. To whom could or would the letter have been delivered in April 1522, at the time of an interregnum? The vacancy of the Holy See in the fifteenth and sixteenth centuries was usually a

---

36. ... *continuo Romam mittendum*; MR, 90.

37. *Ad reuerendum in Christo patrem fratrem Dominicum Buchium Catharensem ordinis praedicatorum, sacrae theologiae professorem integerrimum, dum in ciuitate Spalatensi contionando poenitentiales psalmos exponeret*; Jovanović 2006, 189.

38. *Reuerendo patri Dominico Buchiae Catharensi ordinis praedicatorum, theologiae professori, M. Marulus in Domino salutem. Cum tuis ad populum sermonibus, Dominice pater, frequenter interfuissem (delectabant enim me plurimum)* . . . ; MR, 90. Buća published a book on the original meaning of the Seven Penitential Psalms: *Etymon elegantissimum satisque perutile in septem psalmos penitentiales* (Venice: Aurelius Pintius, 1531). In the same year, the same printer published Johann Eck's anti-Lutheran book, *Enchiridion locorum communium adversus Lutteranos* (Venice: Aurelius Pintius, 1531).

time of lawlessness and license in Rome. Would any messenger know where to deliver the letter in times of confusion and interregnum chaos? Here is a description of the situation:

> The criminals, who had been liberated at the late Pope's death, when it was customary to proclaim a general amnesty, roamed the streets in gangs, breaking into unprotected houses, plundering, raping and murdering as they went. Unchecked by fear of punishment, the princely houses renewed their feuds, drew chains across the streets to defend their palaces, armed all available retainers and hastened to pay off old scores. The mob attacked the cardinals' palaces, but all precautions had usually been taken by those prelates, their most valuable possessions removed to a place of safety and armed guards stationed within their mansions. It was the traditional privilege of the populace to loot the new pope's residence, being the reason which prompted them always to clamour for a Roman Pope.[39]

It is very unlikely that the letter writer knew that it would take the new pope almost eight months after his election to travel from Spain to Rome, to be crowned on August 31, 1522, immediately upon his arrival in the Vatican.[40]

The urgency to which Marulić refers arguably may have been caused by the immediate threat of the advancing Turks. However, the Turkish menace had closely hit home in Split already in the summer of 1521 with the fall of Belgrade on August 29, 1521, when Leo X was still in office. The fall of Belgrade is mentioned, as said, in Marulić's *Epistola*.[41] If by the said "urgency" the military defense was meant, then one could argue that the idea of appealing to the pope must have or should have come to Marulić's mind already at the time of the fall of Belgrade. This line of argumentation would support the assumption that Marulić's *Epistola* was originally intended already for Pope Leo X and the other Christian rulers at the time, who deserved the mentioned invective more than Pope Adrian (although one should not forget that Leo X called for a crusade against the Turks, but this had come to nothing).

If parts of the *Epistola* were written before or after the fall of Belgrade, then one could further argue that the *Epistola* was not composed for one specific pope, but that it represents more of a timeless document about the role of the papacy, as the text would not necessarily have to be considered as having been directed to one specific pope, but was already conceived,

---

39. Pirie 1935, 114.
40. Pirie 1935, 58.
41. See MR, 96.

perhaps in its basic outline, during the reign of Leo X at the time of the fall of Belgrade and of the various wars that were waged all over Italy. However, since Leo X died on December 1, 1521, Marulić could no longer send his *Epistola* to him; he needed to redirect it to his successor, whose name Marulić may have inserted, as argued above, at the last moment before dispatching it. This chain of arguments would make it more plausible (1) that the mention of the name "Adrian" appears marginal and seems to have been added at the end at the last minute; (2) that a substantial part of the *Epistola* is dealing with the theological concept of the papacy regardless of who the recipient on the papal throne would be; and (3) that the document at times speaks to all the princes of Western Christianity, with the pope's leadership role being stressed in the efforts of securing unity and peace within Christendom. This view of a largely general open letter to a pope about the papacy and its role would explain (4) that the letter as we have it now (as addressed to Pope Adrian) would not have had to come into existence only after Leo's death, or so very shortly after the election of Adrian in January.

By dropping the idea that the text was conceived exclusively for Pope Adrian, we no longer need to look for an answer to the question why there is nothing in it that refers directly to Adrian as regent of Spain and as one of the most significant imperial politicians with considerable, if not decisive, influence upon the young emperor Charles V, whose tutor he once was. If Marulić really would have known these political circumstances and the biographical details of the new "German" pope, one would have expected him to make ample use of them in his *Epistola*. The document is conspicuously unspecific as to the new pope's former role as an imperial politician. All this does not enter into the train of thought of the *Epistola*.

Therefore, it is more likely that the *Epistola*, originally composed as an *exhortation about unity and peace*, was redirected at the last minute "to Adrian." Thus, the challenging idea suggests itself that the *Epistola* was drafted originally as a general text to fit any pontiff, being written as a reminder of what the proper papal duties are. And, in all likelihood the document was meant originally for Leo X and other Christian rulers rather than exclusively for Pope Adrian VI. Or, the *Epistola* was simply meant to influence the new pope whoever he may be.

As to the timing of the letter, some observations as to the length, depth, and style of the *Epistola* also come into play. There are fluctuations in style as one notices the alternating from the second-person singular to the plural form,[42] which is reason to suggest not that it is written impulsively

---

42. Use of the second-person singular in the opening sentence: *Sanctissime pater*; use of second-person plural in the paragraph with the words *Resipiscite*; use of second-person singular: *Pater sancte, . . . caput es*; MR, 92 and 100, etc.

in a quick moment of anxiety, but pieced together from various drafts and that it had a long gestation period.[43] This time period may have stretched at least from the time when Marulić learned of the threat to or the actual fall of Belgrade at the end of August 1521 to the day when he became aware of the death of Leo X on December 1, 1521 and of the election of a new pope early in January 1522.

All in all, it is also not unlikely that the *Epistola* was designed from the beginning as an open letter and intended to be printed immediately, i.e., at a time period which happened to coincide with the celebration of the Feast of Pasquino on April 25, which is St. Mark's Day, when poets and writers were prepared to vent anger and frustration concerning higher authorities. In all likelihood Marulić the literate was familiar with the Roman custom of producing pasquinades. It is conceivable that this awareness was part of his reasoning that the manuscript should be delivered to Rome for publication at about that time, i.e., the high time of literary activities of the year. The aggressive parts of the *Epistola* may have been meant to mimic the popular pasquinades. Other parts of the *Epistola* better fit the other suggestion: that Marulić adhered to the custom of writing open letters out of frustration caused by the lack of unity among the Christians vis-à-vis the Turkish conquest. His text certainly matches contemporary documents that dealt with this issue, one of which was known to Marulić, i.e., the first one to be reviewed here:

The Epistola as an Open Letter to the Pope in the Context of Other Documents Pertaining to the Issue

In May 1512, in the presence of Pope Julius II, Archbishop Bernard Zane (c. 1450–1527) of Split delivered a speech on behalf of Viceroy Petar Berislavić (*ban* from 1513–1520) at the Fifth Lateran Council, which is extant in a print of November of that year.[44] This speech was known to Marulić, who had received it from the editor, Thomas Niger (1450/1460–1531), a higher

---

43. The suggestion that Marulić's shifts from the second-person singular to the plural form and back may be a clever rhetorical device for the purpose of achieving variety is a possibility, but perhaps too far-fetched for an open letter.

44. *Oratio Reverendissimi D. Archiepiscopi Spalatensis habita in Prima Sessione Lateranen. Concilii* (Rome: Iacobus Mazocchius, 1512); Gligo 1983. This printer also published the speech of Balthasar del Rio.

prelate and a diplomat.⁴⁵ He let his cry of alarm be heard all over Europe, especially before Leo X.⁴⁶

On April 27, 1513, Bishop Simon Begnius (Šimun Kožičić Benja, 1460-1536) of Modruš (*Modrusiensis*, located in the mountains of Croatia)⁴⁷ delivered his speech on the issue in the presence of Pope Leo X.⁴⁸ At the seventh session of the Fifth Lateran Council, on June 17, 1513, Baldassare del Rio, chamber servant of the pope (*cubicularius*, no dates known), gave a speech in favor of the war against the Turks, in the presence of Pope Leo X.⁴⁹ Bishop Simon Begnius again turned to Pope Leo with his speech *On the Desolation of Croatia* in 1516.⁵⁰ In 1518 Bishop Erasmus Vitellius (Erazm Ciolek, 1460-1522) as the speaker for King Sigismund of Poland (1506-1548) delivered a speech against the Turks to Pope Leo X.⁵¹ Thomas Niger spoke before the same pope twice, in 1519 and 1521.⁵²

Marulić could have joined this chorus that made itself heard since 1512. One may assume that Marulić, being aware of at least one of these speeches addressed to the pope, did not feel the immediate urge to chime in with that chorus of these official cries of alarm. What could he as a layman have added anyways? Others kept reminding the pope of the grave situation, such as Prince Stjepan Posedarski, who approached Leo X in 1519.⁵³ The urgency to finish a draft of an *epistola* and to have it printed presented itself soon and much more forcefully after he had learned of the fall of

45. See Preface by Thomas Niger in Gligo 1983, 419-22; on Niger see Škunca 2001.
46. See Jurišić 1994,18.
47. Modruš is a village in the mountainous part of Croatia. This now small village is historically known as the see of a medieval Catholic bishopric.
48. *Simonis Begnii Episcopi Modrusiensis Oratio in Sexta Lateranensis Concilii Sessione* (May 1513); Gligo 1983, 589-602.
49. *Baltasaris del Rio Pallatini archidiacono Cesenat. sanctissimi d. nostri Leonis papae decimi cubicularii oratio ad eundem dominum nostrum papam & Sacrosanctum Lateranem Concilium de expeditione contra Turchos ineunda habita Romae in Basilica S. Io. Lateranen in septima sessione celebrata dic XVII Iunii MDXiii* (Rome: Jacobus Mazochius, 1513); from the Hungarian website: mek.oszk.hu/03500/03560.
50. *Simonis Begnii Episcopi Modrusiensis de Corvatiae Desolatione*; Gligo 1983, 605-10.
51. *Orationes reverendi patris domini Erasmi Vitellii episcopi Plocensis. Inuictissimi & uictoriosissimi Regis Poloniae Sigismundi ad sanctam sedem Apostolica[m] & sacram Imperiale[m] maestate[m] oratoris. Habitae per eum in facto generalis expeditionis contra turchos. Vna romae coram Leone Papa. X. altera Augustae coram Maximiliano cesare. Anno Domini. M. D. XViii.*; as posted on the website of Biblioteca Universitaria de Santiago de Compostella. The speech to the emperor is found separately on the Hungarian website cited in note 49.
52. See Novaković 1994, 47.
53. See Novaković 1994, 47.

Belgrade at the end of August 1521. Yet, he still may have been too humble as a layman and, after all, he was not an official speaker of any political authority like the others mentioned here. He also may have felt that plenty of cries of alarm had been uttered already. In any case, the pope was already well informed from various sides. Noteworthy (in terms of a historical footnote) is the fact that after the end of the imperial diet of Augsburg in 1518, Pope Leo X received from the imperial court the negative *Responsio* formulated as an answer to various speeches that had been delivered there in favor of a war against the Turks and the taxation that came with it.[54] These hints at the imperial diet and the pope demonstrate that there was no general indifference in the West concerning the fate of Croatia. The West did not turn "a deaf ear to appeals for help,"[55] but the West did not bring decisive help either to those under attack.

All these considerations on the *Epistola* and on the issues that surround it lead one to postulate that Marulić's *Epistola* is an open letter (into which he may have incorporated a Pasquinade-like passage) with which he as a private person grasped the opportunity to make his outcry heard, which is the reason that he had printed it promptly and made it available to the general public as early as April 30, 1522 in Rome.[56] Marulić may have started to write it as a letter to Leo X, but ended up redirecting it as an *Epistola ad Adrianum VI*. It was probably never meant to be private correspondence, but more likely an impressive instrument of mass communication in order to shape public opinion regardless whether the old pope was dead or the new pope was in Rome or not. By looking at it as an open letter, this document can be read not only as an appeal to an individual pope, but also and more so as an exhortation to all the princes of Western Christianity, including the pope, who were all insulted (rightly so, except for Pope Adrian, who was not enthroned yet at the time) as "lunatics." Their mutual hate is actually a primary, if not the major, concern of the letter writer.

Marulić's *Epistola* perfectly fits the category of the open letter in the sixteenth century. It also may be called a "circular letter" for it was meant for circulation to a wider readership for the purpose of influencing public

---

54. *Responsio principvm Germaniae, data reuere[n]dissimis dominis, Legatis sanctissimi domini nostri Leonis X. & caeteris Oratoribus in Augusta Vindelicorum, Anno M. D. XVIII. Per eruditissimum uirum dominum Richardum Bartholinum Perusinum, Capellanu[m] Reuerendiss[imi] Cardinalis Gurcensis in literas relata* (Basel: Froben, 1518); website: Országos Széchényi Könyvtár—National Széchényi Library; see Kühlmann 2000, 211. On the Turk Tax, see Liepold 1998; Benecke 2006, 288–93.

55. As Tomasović stated "then and now" in Tomasović 1994, 31.

56. See colophon (facsimile edition): *Impressa Romae Per B. V. Anno D. M. D. XXII. pridie kalendas maii feliciter explicit.*

opinion. Most often, the open letter of the time around 1500 was addressed to a powerful person who could not be reached easily in any other way—which was the case with Pope Adrian VI still in Spain; and the open letter may provoke a specific reaction only by being published. At times one encounters the designation *Sendbrief* in German, as it is the case with Martin Luther's open letter in the summer of 1520 to the newly elected Emperor Charles V and to the German nobility, under the title *To the Christian Nobility of the German Nation Concerning the Reform of the Christian Estate*, of which four thousand copies were sold within the first eighteen days.[57] If a text of this sort reaches such proportions in terms of circulation, it becomes an instrument of "mass media" or agitation.[58]

Open letters may be classified as *Flugschriften* in German,[59] which is an eighteenth-century term with the meaning of "leaflets" or "pamphlets." If a document is addressed to a specific person in a high office, but is never meant to be delivered to that person, and even if the text calls itself a *Sendbrief* or *epistola*, it probably is an open letter in the sense of a *Flugschrift*.

We do not know how many copies were printed of Marulić's *Epistola* or who would have purchased one. We also do not know whether a print actually reached the pope, unless we assume that the diplomat Thomas Niger had one and would have delivered it in person to the newly elected pope in Spain. However, this would require, first of all, proof that Niger was in Rome when the *Epistola* came off the printing press at the end of April 1522, and, secondly, that soon afterwards he would have departed for Spain with the printed *Epistola* in his travel bags. There is room for further research on this. Be this as it may, the fact remains that the *Epistola* was printed before the new pope arrived later in summer of 1522. This means that the printing made it a *Flugschrift* for a wider readership. Only at a later date could the print have reached the newly elected pope. The issues that rose here from one document in Marulić's epistolary corpus hopefully help us to polish a few more of the *tesserae* of the "mosaic of Marulić,"[60] the lay theologian. And the entire "mosaic of Marulić" (which admittedly is not yet finished) needs to be shown together with other sketches of contemporary Catholic lay theologians, to whom we turn our attention now, in part 2.

---

57. See Boehmer 1957, 321. Luther's Latin *Epistola ad Leonem decimum* is translated into German as *Sendbrief*.

58. On this, see Köhler 1981.

59. See entry "Flugschriften," Ganzer and Steimer 2002, 244–46.

60. Jozić 2008, 156.

MARULIĆ IN THE CONTEXT OF
EUROPEAN LAY THEOLOGIANS

Before we place the nobleman of Split into the context of other lordly lay theologians of the Renaissance, we need to be reminded that "lay theologians" were usually not part of the picture of the Renaissance scene. Our image of Renaissance men is most likely dominated by the types presented by Eugenio Garin in *Renaissance Characters*, such as the prince, the military captain (condottiere), the cardinal, the courtier, the merchant, the banker, the artist, the voyager, and the philosopher and magus,[61] but not the lay theologian.

One encounters lay theologians throughout the two thousand years of church history. Tertullian of Carthage (c. 160–c. 220) and Origen of Alexandria (c. 185–c. 254) were the two most known in the early church. Great and original theological thinkers, such as the Irishman John Scotus Eriugena (c. 800–c. 850)[62] or the Spaniard Raimundus Lullus (Ramon Lull, 1232–1316)[63] were laymen. The latter had grown up in close proximity to Islamic dominated regions; he was married and had two children.[64]

Lay theologians generally have not found due recognition or have not been studied thoroughly, especially not in terms to their "lay theology." Should the history of the contributions of lay theologians be written, it would have to include the one from Split, Marko Marulić. In the following, several highly sophisticated laymen (philosophers/theologians) who lived during Marulić's lifetime (1450–1524) will be sketched briefly. However, we will disregard the pamphleteers in southern Germany during the early period of the Reformation who may also be called "lay theologians."[65] They are men and women who occasionally vented their opinions in short pamphlets with religious and theological content. They include "housewives" and "journeymen" who were more or less inspired by the rising reform movements of Luther and Zwingli.

Giannozzo Manetti

One of the earliest lay theologians of the Renaissance was Giannozzo Manetti[66] (1396–1459), who became known as a gifted speaker. His great speeches

---

61. Garin 1991.
62. *Ein Laie*, Köpf 2002, 13; on Eriugena, see for example D'Onofrio 2008, 82–98.
63. See Biemer 1989, 145–48; D'Onofrio 2008, 423–29.
64. D'Onofrio 2008, 423.
65. See Russell 1986.
66. On Manetti, see Botley 2004.

as envoy before Pope Nicholas V (reigned 1447–1455) and before the Doge and Council of Venice were events to be remembered.[67] On the occasion of the death of his young son, he wrote the autobiographical *Dialogus consolatorius* in 1438. Manetti was a classical trilingual man with a good knowledge of Greek and Hebrew, besides Latin. He translated anew the Hebrew psalms into Latin, which he defended in an anti-Jewish text known under the title *Apologeticus adversus suae novae Psalterii traductionis obtrectatores*. Manetti is best known for his work of 1451/1452 on the dignity of man: *De dignitate et excellentia hominis*, written at about the time of Marulić's birth. Manetti's life and work were recently recognized as belonging to "The Mature Stage of Humanist Theology in Italy."[68] Marulić the theologian is still waiting for such recognition.

Wessel Gansfort

In the Netherlands of the fifteenth century (the place and time of the Modern Devotion) there was Wessel Gansfort (Basilius Gansfort, or Frisius, 1419–1489)[69] (see fig. 4.1), who "was neither a priest nor a monk, and had no intention of becoming one."[70] He learned Greek, Hebrew, and Arabic, and is an example for the combination of several theological and spiritual traits as he intertwined in his life and work elements of humanism, scholasticism, and mysticism under the impact of the Modern Devotion, not unlike Marulić.[71]

Johann Reuchlin

In late fifteenth-century Swabia (southwestern Germany) there emerged one of the greatest humanist lay theologians of all time, who was about the same age as Marulić, and who became the father of Catholic Hebrew and Greek scholarship. It was Johann Reuchlin (1455–1522), a lawyer by profession, but a polyglot scholar by inclination and interests. The emperor made him a nobleman.[72] Like Marulić he was a versatile humanist. However,

---

67. See Burckhardt 1995, 152.
68. See Vasoli 1998b, 204–6.
69. See Miller 1917, 76, 90–92, 153; Akkerman et al. 1993.
70. Miller 1917, 1:80; Vanderjagt 2005.
71. See Šanjek 1999, 133–36.
72. Ludwig Geiger's nineteenth-century biography of Reuchlin, in German, is still so much in demand that a reprint of the 1871 edition is being offered in 2008: *Johann Reuchlin: Sein Leben und seine Werke* (Boston: Adamant, 2008). Note that fig. 2 does not depict

while Reuchlin was the trilingual man (*vir tri-linguus*) in the classical meaning of the three sacred languages, Hebrew, Greek, and Latin, the "sacred philology,"[73] Marulić was a trilingual author in a different sense. He wrote in Latin, Croatian, and Italian.

Marulić was never married. Reuchlin, the lay theologian, was married twice, and his only child died in infancy. An entire episode of the early sixteenth century is called after him: "The Reuchlin Affair," which designates his battle for the preservation of Hebrew books, including the Talmud.[74] He was the orator of his territorial lord, Elector Philip (1448–1508) of Palatinate and Duke of Bavaria, and "chief disciplinarian," i.e., educator, of his seven sons.[75] As ambassador Reuchlin delivered an oration on behalf of the elector before Pope Alexander VI, on August 7, 1498.

Fig. 4.1. Wessel Gansfort of Groningen, "Light of the World" (M. WESSELVS GANSFORTIVS GRONINGENSIS LVX MVNDI VULGO DICTVS).

Fig. 4.2. "Patrons of Liberty," Detail of a woodcut (attributed to Hans Weiditz), found on the title page of the "Story of the Four Heretics of the Order of Preachers," printed in 1521 in Strasbourg. Reuchlin, at the far left, is a member of the group of "Patrons of Liberty" along with Ulrich von Hutten and Martin Luther.

Orators were knowledgeable in philosophy, theology, and foreign languages, and as humanists like Reuchlin they were indispensable to princes and popes because they were in charge of the official correspondence and

---

a real portrait of the famous humanist from Pforzheim, Germany; it is the only contemporary one that is known. Similarly, there is no contemporary portrait of Marulić either.

73. Kristeller 1961, 79.

74. See Rummel 2002.

75. On Reuchlin as educator and speech writer, see Friedrich 1998.

of making speeches on public and solemn occasions.[76] Orators of that time appear to have required a well-rounded education. This was the case also of our lay theologian *Marcus Marulus Spalatensis*.

Both Reuchlin and Marulić remained loyal to the Church of Rome. Under the given circumstances in the German-speaking lands of the time, this may be a bit surprising as far a Reuchlin is concerned, especially because Reuchlin's nephew, Philip Melanchthon, turned out to become a formidable Lutheran. Only Marulić seems to have been frustrated by the Christian discord in facing the Turkish menace, something that may not be detected in Reuchlin's opus.

Paulus Ricius

Still another lay theologian was the physician and family man Paulus Ricius (Paul Ritz, Paolo Ricci, c. 1480–c. 1541) from Tyrol, Austria.[77] Born into a Jewish family in Grub, Tyrol, he converted to Christianity as a young man in 1505. He taught philosophy and medicine at the University of Pavia (then in the duchy of Milan) before he became the personal physician of the prince-bishop of Brixen in Tyrol, later of Cardinal Matthew Lang (1468–1540) of Salzburg. Since 1514 he was the physician of Emperor Maximilian I (reigned 1493–1519), and later also of King Ferdinand I (1503–1564). He sided with Johann Reuchlin in the great controversy over Jewish books.[78] In 1529/1530 Ricius was elevated to the rank of a baron, now known as "Paul Ritz von Sprinzenstein" (in Upper Austria), a title he passed on to his sons after his death in 1541. This physician and lay theologian published numerous theological works in Latin, including on the holy name of God (*Tetragrammaton*) and Christian-Jewish Cabala.[79] At the time when Marulić's "Song about the Teaching of our Lord Jesus Christ Hanging on the Cross" was

---

76. See Burckhardt 1195, 146. On the development of embassies since about 1450, see Nicholas 1999, 218–20.

77. See Keil and Halbleib 1989, 233–36; Siebert 1994, 255–56; Roling 2003. His castle, *Schloss Sprinzenstein*, is located in western Mühlviertel in Upper Austria. *Sprinz* means "hawk" in the local dialect; see website "Sprinzenstein." Ricius is not an Italian, as is assumed occasionally, as in Dall'Asta and Dörner 2000–11, 3:xlv.

78. See the letter of August 20, 1516 by Hieronymus Ricius, son of *Paulus Ricius Israelita*, to Reuchlin, in Dall'Asta and Dörner 2000–11, 3:298–303 (no. 288).

79. *In cabalistarum seu allegorizantium eruditionem isagogae* (Pavia: Jacob de Burgfrancho, 1510; Augsburg: Johannes Miller [?], 1515); *Lepida et literae undique concinna in psalmum Beatus vir meditatio: concisa et archana de modo orandi in nomine tetragrammaton responsio* (Augsburg: Grimm and Wirsung, 1519); *De anima coeli compendium. Responsio ad interrogationes de nomine Tetragrammaton* (Augsburg: Grimm, 1519).

published in Erfurt, Germany, in 1514, Ricius' book on the Apostles' Creed was printed at Augsburg.[80]

Both Marulić and Ricius were concerned about the Turkish menace. Ricius in his speech/sermon for the Diet of Speyer in 1529 called for the mobilization against the Turks. He placed his oration under the biblical theme of Ezekiel 33:6 ("But if the watchman sees the sword coming and fails to blow the warning trumpet, so that the sword comes and takes anyone, I will hold the watchman responsible for that person's death, even though that person is taken because of his own sin"). It was printed in Augsburg in 1530.[81]

Gasparo Contarini

Another layman who like Marulić lived in the Republic of Venice was the patrician Gasparo Contarini (1483–1542) (see fig. 4.3), thirty-three years younger than Marulić. He contributed to the debate on the mortality of the human soul.[82]

He was a significant representative of the religious renewal in Italy, known as *evangelismo italiano*.[83] When this lay theologian was serving as a Venetian diplomat at the papal court in 1535, as a layman at the age of forty-two he was made a cardinal by Pope Paul III (reigned 1534–1549). The challenges of the Reformation in Germany absorbed much of his energies.

---

80. *In apostolorvm symbolvm Avgvstini* [sic] *Ricii orathoris* [sic], *philosophi et theologi ocvlatissimi a priori demonstrativvs dialogvs* (Augsburg: Johannes Miller, 1514); see website: "Austrian Literature Online." It is not clear why the title has Augustinus Ricius and not Paulus Ricius. There is the similar title under Ricius' name: *In apostolorum simbolum (juxta peripateticorum dogma, dialogus per plane ac summo ingenii ac[u]mine lumini gratiae lumen concilians nature* (same location, date).

81. *AD PRINCIPES, MAGISTRATVS, populosque Germanif, in Spirensi co[n]ventu PAVLI RICII Oratio* (Augsburg: Alexander Weyssenhorn, 1530); see website: "Austrian Literature Online." *Statera Prudentum. Ipse est pax nostra . . . Christo Nazareno regni celoru[m] Duci / Tribunis, Antesignanis, et Cohortibus Crucis Co[m]pendiariu[m], et o[mn]i attentione dignum hoc Pavlj Rjcjj Opus desudat* (Augsburg: Philipp Ulhart, 1532); a copy is extant in Bayerische Staatsbibliothek, Munich. Among Ricius' other works are *De sexcentum et tredecim Mosaicae sanctionis edictis* (Pavia: Jacob de Burgfrancho, 1510; Augsburg: Johannes Miller, 1515); *Apologetica ad Eckiana responsa narratio* (Augsburg: Grimm, 1519). On the order of Emperor Maximilian I, he translated four tracts of the Talmud into Latin in his *Talmudica nouissime in latinum versa periocunda commentariola* (Augsburg: Grimm and Wirsung, 1519); against Johann Eck: *Naturalia et prophetica de anima coeli omni attentione digna aduersus Eckium examina. . .* (Augsburg: Grimm and Wirsung, 1519/1520); *De coelesti agricultura* (Augsburg: Steyner, 1541).

82. *De immortalitate animae*; see Vasoli 1998a, 382.

83. See Simoncelli 1979.

He was defamed later on as a Lutheran.[84] Like Marulić he deliberated on the role of the papacy, which resulted in his publication *De potestate pontificis* (1529, 1534). However, the issue of the political unity of the West against the Turkish advances did not seem a concern for him as it was for Marulić.

Ioannes Ludovicus Vives

As the final example of lay theologians in the Renaissance we mention the Spaniard Ioannes Ludovicus Vives (Juan Luis Vives, 1492–1540) (see fig. 4.4), forty-two years younger than Marulić. His Jewish family was converted forcibly to Christianity. Due to the threat of the Inquisition, the convert Vives left for Paris in 1509, where he studied arts and humanities. In 1517 he became tutor to the French nobleman Guillaume de Croy (1498–1521), who at nineteen was a cardinal and archbishop of Toledo. In 1524 Vives married a wealthy woman, Marguerite Valdaura. He admired Erasmus of Rotterdam and Thomas More as he developed an interest in philosophy and theology. He lived in Bruges, Belgium, on a pension from King Henry of England. There he continued to write and revise many works until his death in 1540.

When Marulić was working on christological themes around 1520, Vives was writing a commentary on St. Augustine's *City of God*. While Marulić's *Evangelistarium* was printed in Basel in 1519 by Adam Petri, Vives' commentary on Augustine was reprinted by Froben in the same city in 1522.[85] Vives also composed an open letter to Adrian VI on the troubles of Europe and the Turkish menace, but half a year later than Marulić, on October 12, 1522; it was printed in Louvain and titled *Ad Adrianum de Europae statu ac tumultibus*. In it Vives saw in an ecumenical council the "saving medication" (*medicina*) for these tumultuous times,[86] unlike Marulić, who set his hope on the papacy.

---

84. See Gleason 1993; Posset 2008a.

85. Vives, *Commentarii in XXII libros De Civitate Dei Divi Aurelii Augustini* (Louvain, 1521; Basel: Froben, 1522).

86. See Vives 1964, 5:171–72.

Fig. 4.3. Bust of Gasparo Contarini. From: *Embassies and Ambassadors in Rome* (Milan and Rome: Casa Editrice D'Arte Bestetti & Tumminelli, no date), 57.
Fig 4.4. Ioannes Ludovicus Vives.

Vives wrote on many things, including political pamphlets against the Inquisition.[87] In 1527 he fell out of favor with King Henry by opposing the royal divorce from Catherine of Aragon, and was imprisoned for six weeks, after which he left England for the Netherlands to devote himself to writing. He died in 1540 when he was undertaking a literary defense of Christianity, *On the Truth of the Christian Faith* (*De Veritate Fidei Christianae*), published posthumously.

The theology and philosophy of these laymen of the Renaissance (and others not mentioned here)[88] represent, so to speak, all the colors of the rainbow. On the eve of the Reformation and its early years, a time aptly characterized as the years of theological "wild growth" (*Wildwuchs*),[89] they felt at home under the then very wide roof of Catholic theology.

The fact that lay theologians around 1500 are underexposed in historical-theological research may help explain why also Marulić, the Croatian

87. Among his numerous works are: *Christi Iesu Triumphus. Virginis Dei Parentis Ovatio* (Paris, 1514); *Meditationes in septem psalmos, quos vocant poenitentiae* (Louvain, 1518); *De Institutione Feminae Christianae* (Louvain, Oxford, 1523); *De subventione pauperum* (Bruges, 1526); *De Europae dissidiis et bello turcico* (Bruges, 1526); *De conditione vitae Christianorum sub Turca* (Bruges, 1526); *Sacrum diurnum de Sudore Domini nostri Jesu Christi* (Bruges, 1529); *Meditatio de Passione Christi in psalmum XXXVII* (Bruges, 1529); *De Veritate Fidei Christianae*, Bruges, 1540). See Eire 2008.

88. Another fine example of a lay theologian from the Venetian-Croatian region was the much younger Matthias Flacius Illyricus (Matija Vlačić, 1520–1575); on him see Olson 1981; Olsen 2002.

89. Junghans 2001b.

churchman and theologian, is so little known. These men—including Marulić—belong to the elite of European lay theologians. If ever a book were written on the history of loyal lay theologians in the Catholic Church, Marulić undoubtedly would take a place of honor.[90]

CONCLUSION

The *Epistle of Lord Marko Marulić of Split* is an unusual document in that it was written by a Croatian layman to a "German" pope who himself was a rather strange, alien figure on the papal throne during that time. True, Marulić with his *Epistola* was not "the first Croat to ask a Pope for help,"[91] but he was, indeed, the first layman[92] (unless further research proves me wrong) to address the new pope with these concerns, that is, a pope who had been elected *in absentia* and who was not even enthroned at the time of the publication of Marulić's *Epistola* in Rome. In contrast (but according to proper etiquette), Brodarić and also Krsto Frankopan presented their pleas after the pope's enthronement, in September 1522 (Brodarić) and in July 1523 (Frankopan).

As an open letter, Marulić's text presented itself as a sermon-like exhortation, based on the author's understanding of the spiritual and political nature of the papacy. His admonition concerned the general unity and peace among all Christian nations vis-à-vis the Turkish menace. An earlier draft (including a Pasquinade-like passage) could have come into existence already at the time of the fall of Belgrade in 1521 during the reign of Leo X. The insertion of the name "Adrian" only at the very end of the letter would support such a thesis. Evidently Marulić had no similar expectations of the rest of the political leaders of the Christendom of his time, be it the doge of Venice[93] or the emperor of the Holy Roman Empire.

The *Epistola* may serve not only as a peculiar church-historical document written by a layman. Marulić was clearly aware of his non-existent

90. Future research will have to find out whether these lay theologians had contact with each other. Marulić most likely had no contact with them—a whole different social group of laymen were the lay cardinals that existed at his time. They would require a monograph of their own. There were four classes of cardinals: cardinal bishops, cardinal priests, cardinal deacons, and lay cardinals. All but the lay cardinals had the right to vote at a conclave; see Pirie 1935, 2.

91. Novaković 1994, 47.

92. This is contrary to Novaković 1994, 47, who wrote that Marulić was not "the first layman to address his plea to Adrian VI." More correctly one could say that he was not the only layman who addressed the new pope.

93. In the summer of 1521, Ivan Statilić of Trogir (Statilius, 1472–1542) was sent to the doge in Venice as envoy of King Louis II of Croatia and Hungary in order to beg for help; see Novaković 1994, 45–46.

rank in the church hierarchy. When he says that he is aware of his "smallness," he most likely meant his low status in the church as a layman in the pew, as compared to the hierarchy and the papacy. At the beginning of the open letter he states that he has "no authority whatsoever" to speak up and to address the pope. He means to say that he has no mandate from any political or ecclesiastical ruler or from any interest group.

However, this document is also a theological source text for the further investigation of the ecclesiological concepts (the church and the papacy) of the prolific lay theologian of Split. He is best situated within the context of other lay theologians loyal to the papacy during the Renaissance. His open letter reveals a certain self-understanding as a man of the church and a "humble and supplicant" (*humilis et supplex*)[94] sheep of the papal flock. The historical-theological study of his *Epistola* may contribute to the further illumination of his theology for piety and of his life as a Catholic lay theologian of European stature.

---

94. Used in the title of the *Epistola*; MR, 92.

Chapter 5

The Bible

The Illustrated Biblia cum comento *from the Library of the Father of Croatian Literature, with Samples of His Marginalia*

The "Father of Croatian Literature," Marcus Marulus, is convinced that "God is the author" of the Scriptures.[1] To him the Word of God is the "sword of the Spirit," as in his *Dialogue about Hercules* he lets the Theologian say this by quoting Ephesians 6:17.[2] Marulus copied in full length the saying of 2 Peter 1:20 under the keyword "interpreter" (*Interpres*): "There is no prophecy of Scripture that is a matter of personal interpretation, for no prophecy ever came through human will; but rather human beings inspired by the Holy Spirit spoke of the holy God."[3] At the end of his *Dauidias* he proclaims that the Holy Spirit "with divine light did illuminate our mind" with "what is vouched for by the ancient books, the Scriptures of our faith."[4] Marulus feels indirectly inspired by the Holy Spirit, who speaks through the "Scriptures of our faith." We therefore do well in keeping his overall religious and theological conviction about the Bible as inspired Scripture in mind.

1. *Veteris Nouique instrumenti quorum Deus est autor.* Evangelistarium I, *Praefatio.*
2. *Gladium spiritus, quod est verbum Dei;* LMD, 1:123.
3. Repertorium (hereafter quoted as Rep) II, 80.
4. *Sed sacer ... spiritus ... / impleuit nostrum diuino lumine mentem / ... quae nostra fides scriptis testata uetustis / hausit* (Davidias 14, 18–19; 22–23); Lučin 2007, 204.

ENTERING THE WORLD OF MARULUS: THE CULTURAL-HISTORICAL BACKGROUND, LIBRARIES IN THE RENAISSANCE[5]

The Renaissance man Marcus Marulus always remained a man of books and was very much part of the European phenomenon we call *civilisation du livre*[6] or "book culture"[7] of the Renaissance humanists and of the Modern Devout or New Devotionalists of the *Devotio Moderna*.[8] In forming his private library Marulus pursued an activity typical of humanists,[9] who in the fourteenth century started with collecting works of Greek and Roman literature. The passion for the ancient world increased with each new discovery of a lost or forgotten work of classical antiquity. Francesco Petrarca (1304–1374) is the early great representative of this development.

Johannes de Ragusa, OP (of Dubrovnik, Ivan Stojković, c. 1390–1443) collected Greek manuscripts which he bequeathed to the Dominican library in Basel at the end the Council of Basel (1431–1437) that he had attended. A friend of Erasmus of Rotterdam composed the manuscript catalogue of Stojković's collection which is extant.[10] The Greek New Testament manuscripts were later studied by Johann Reuchlin and by Erasmus of Rotterdam.[11]

A more detailed comparison of Marulus's and Erasmus's and others' libraries would be of great interest, but would go beyond the scope of this presentation. Erasmus's own library mirrors a preference for Greek authors, often in Latin translation,[12] but not for Hebrew books. The same inclinations (and neglect) are apparent in Marulus's book list as he, too, shows this preference for Greek books in Latin translations with little or no apparent interest in Hebrew books, something for which their contemporary Johann Reuchlin is famous. This much seems clear: around 1519/1520 Marulus

---

5. Parts of this study were presented at the Marko Marulić Days 2009 in Split, Croatia. I am grateful to Vladimir Bubrin and Bratislav Lučin for helpful hints in finalizing my presentation for publication. The *Marulianum* in Split kindly provided a DVD, produced by Branko Jozić, with the more than two thousand pages of the four volumes of Marulus's desk copy of the *Biblia Latina*, which is extant in the library of the Observant Franciscan friars in Split. The four volumes were on display during the Marko Marulić Days 2009.

6. Heger and Matillon 1986.

7. See Kock 2002.

8. On the Modern Devotion and the Brethren of the Common Life, see Fuller 1995; VanEngen 2008. On Marulus's connections to the movement, see Šanjek 1999, 133–36.

9. See De Smet 2002.

10. See Sicherl 1977, 45–46; Lučin 2004, 97–98.

11. See Rummel 1986, 36–37.

12. See Husner 1936.

read some of Erasmus's writings,[13] but they are not listed in his inventory. It appears that he did not work with the Greek-Latin edition of the New Testament which Erasmus made available from Froben in Basel since 1516.[14] Marulus also did not possess any of Reuchlin's publications.

The works of Cardinal Nicolaus Cusanus (de Cusa, from Kues in Germany, 1401–1464) were available at the Venetian book market.[15] However, Marulus did not possess any of his books nor of the Greek scholar and bishop Bessarion of Nicea (1403–1472), a cardinal since 1440, who promoted the collection and translation of Greek classical and patristic literature. His extensive collection was given to the Republic of Venice for St. Mark's Library (Biblioteca Marciana).[16] Venice received yet another collection of great books from another cardinal, Dominicus Grimanus (Domenico Grimani, 1461–1523). His library became very famous as it contained Greek, Hebrew, Aramaic, Arabic, and Armenian books.[17] Marulus dedicated his *Dauidias* to Cardinal Grimanus (but it was not published).[18] The library was huge. According to estimates, it comprised about fifteen thousand titles.[19] Erasmus visited this cardinal's library when it was still in Rome in 1509.[20] It appears that Marulus did not have the opportunity to visit it, not even after it was relocated to Venice.

These hints at some Renaissance libraries of Marulus's time may suffice for the purpose of illuminating at least in part the cultural, intellectual, and spiritual-theological context of Marulus's own library, which is revealing not only in what it contained, but also in what it did not. And, it was small compared to the libraries of the above mentioned booklovers. Nevertheless, his library allows us to form an understanding of what a Renaissance man and lay theologian in Split was interested in at that time.

---

13. See Lučin 2004, 100.

14. *Novum instrumentum cum annotationibus* (1516); *Novum Testamentum omne, multo quam antehac diligentius ab Erasmo Roterodamo recognitum* (1519); *Novum Testamentum cum annotationibus* (1522).

15. *Opuscula theologica et mathematica. . . .; Opera*, Venice: Johannes and Gregorius de Gregoriis, de Forlivio, 1497–99.

16. See Labowsky 1979.

17. See Freudenberger 1936, 21; Tamani 1975; Diller et al. 2003.

18. See Marcovich 2006, 5–6 (dedication). The *Dauidias* was never published during Marulus's lifetime, perhaps—according to Marković—because of the intervention of the one to whom the work was dedicated. Marcovich in his preface (p. vii) surmises that Grimanus saw in Marulus's opus "heretical typology" at work.

19. According to Marino Sanuto's diaries, as mentioned by Freudenberger 1936, 18.

20. See Freudenberger 1936, 19.

Marulus's Library[21]

The edited version of Marulus's testament (representing the state of his library in 1521–1524) provides ten groups of books which are headed by classifications in capital letters as follows: ECCLESIASTICI (forty-two titles); POETAE (fifteen titles, one of which—with his marginalia—is extant in the library of the theological faculty in Split);[22] HISTORICI (twenty-two titles); GEOGRAPHI (two titles); GRAMATICI (thirteen titles); COMENTO (four titles); EPISTOLAE (six titles); DE RE RUSTICA (four titles); ASTRONOMI (three titles); PHILOSOPHI et oratores (thirty-two titles),[23] including a work of Cicero which is preserved today in the library of the Observant Franciscans in Split.[24]

Marulus's testament is somewhat confusing because under the subheading *Libri zentiliu[m]* (*sic*; i.e., "Books of Gentiles") he seems to have lumped together the other nine groups. The problem with the division of "church books" versus "pagan books" is that we find at the end of the group of the POETAE two books that are definitely not authored by "gentiles."[25] Furthermore, it would be odd to have to assume that Marulus understood the philologist and Scripture scholar Lorenzo Valla as a heathen author when he listed his two titles under the heading of GRAMATICI: *Laure[n]tij Vallensis Elleganti* and *Compe[n]dium Elegantiaru[m] Vallae*. And, one may have doubts also whether the heading *Libri zentilium* was meant to be extended to *Franciscus Barbarus De re vxoria*, i.e., to the book "concerning wives" of the Venetian senator Francesco Barbaro (c. 1398–1454) and to *Pogij Facetiae*, i.e., to the stories of Giovanni Francesco Poggio Bracciolini (1380–1459). Finally, it wouldn't make much sense to consider *Guarinus Veronensis* (1374–1460) a pagan author (he is listed with the note *quedam*

---

21. According to his testament *Nobilis domini Marci Maruli testamentum* (hereafter abbreviated MT). We focus here on Marulus's own inventory list.

22. This extant volume is the one that is listed as *Liber poetarum ecclesiasticorum et Sedulij simul*, which Marulus bequeathed to Dominus Hieronymus de Papalibus; MT, 64. It was discovered by Mladen Parlov. On Marulus's copy, see Parlov 2000.

23. See MT, 40–46; Lučin 1997.

24. *Marci Tulii Ciceronis oratoris clarissimi rhetoricorum ueterum libri duo; Rhetoricae novae ad Herennium libri quatuor* (Venice: Ioannes de Forliuio and Iacobus Britannicus Brixianus, 1483).

25. The *Libellus Jacobi Boni Epidauri De raptu Cerberi* is a reference to the known Iacobus Bonus (Jakov Bunić, 1469–1534), who wrote the first epic in Croatian literature, *De raptu Cerberi* (Rome, 1490–1500). The listing of *Mathei Andronici Trag[uriensis] Epitalami[um]* is a reference to Andronicus, who is the author of *Epitalamium in nuptias Vladislai Pannoniarum ac Bohemiae regis et annae Candaliae reginae* (Venice: Bernardinus Venetus de Vitalibus, 1502).

op[er]a under Marulus's final group of "philosophers and orators"). Perhaps the classification *Libri zentiliu[m]* was meant only for the ancient, non-Christian "poets" (the second of Marulus's groups) and it was only by accident or by mistake that the last two titles slipped into this group. Or, could it be that Marulus understood by "zentiles" everybody who wrote on secular, i.e., nontheological matters?

It remains an unsolved mystery what Marulus meant with the heading of *Libri zentiliu[m]* and what he wished to comprise with it.[26] Be that as it may, Marulus was part of the Italian revival of classical literature that was celebrated by the humanists, and he simultaneously was a collector and reader of books of "church writers," or "church books" (*Ecclesiastici*), which he listed as the first and as the largest of his ten groups. Since Marulus also lived in an age of Christian Hebrew and Greek scholarship, one is led to the following question, which is important for understanding Marulus and his interest in the Sacred Scriptures:

Anything in Greek and Hebrew?

Marulus lived at a time when other humanists undertook a reappraisal of the *Hebraica veritas*.[27] We do not know whether Marulus had the opportunity to learn Hebrew. At his time, a Jewish community and a synagogue existed in Split.[28] One may assume that if Marulus were interested, he could have found a teacher of Hebrew in Split.

Marulus was not studying the linguistic and exegetical side of theological issues and what contemporary "biblical humanists" called the search for the "Hebrew Truth" and the "Greek Truth" of the Scriptures. He was not the classical trilingual scholar whose expertise would have to include Hebrew and Greek. If he were interested in those aspects of learning, he surely would have purchased Erasmus's Greek New Testament (1516 et al.) or a book like Johann Reuchlin's explanation of the Seven Penitential Psalms, *In septem psalmos poenitentiales*,[29] a booklet, printed in 1512 at Tübingen, of one hundred printed pages with an attachment of the seven psalms in Hebrew with a literal, word-for-word Latin translation directly from the

---

26. See MT, 40.
27. See Coudert and Shoulson 2004.
28. See Kečkemet 2000, 6–8. I use the copy of the Karlo Grenc Foundation in Split.
29. Full title: *In septem psalmos poenitentiales hebraicos interpretatio de uerbo ad uerbum, & super eisdem commentarioli sui, ad discendum linguam hebraicam ex rudimentis*. I used the microfiche edition of the Thrivent Reformation Research Program of Luther Seminary Library in Saint Paul, Minnesota.

Hebrew, with the explicit purpose of publishing it for those wanting to learn Hebrew and go back to the Hebrew original of biblical texts.

Marulus apparently was not interested either in the fresh translation of the entire Psalter from Hebrew into Latin, *Psalterium ex Hebreo*,[30] which was available since 1515 from the Venetian book market, and which the Augustinian friar Felix de Prato (Fra Felice, c. 1460-1559) published through the printing press of Peter Liechtenstein in Venice. This was an edition approved by Pope Leo X,[31] reprinted in Marulus's lifetime in Venice in 1519. In it Marulus could have found support for his own way of typological Scripture interpretation since Friar Felix frequently pointed out how David's words signify the mystery of Christ, as they express in particular Christ's passion (as in Ps 22, for example). Marulus evidently also did not consult the *Biblia Hebraica* which Felix de Prato edited in Venice through the Bomberg press in 1517.

We know that Marulus learned a bit of Greek in school, as he went to the humanist school (not clerical or monastic) in Split. A man by the name of Hieronymus Genesius (Ienesius) Picentinus taught Greek and he was active in Split from 1473 to 1477.[32] Marulus, however, did not refine his knowledge of Greek in later years, as is implied by the minimal use of Greek letters in his works. He sporadically wrote words in Greek into the margins of his *Biblia Latina*[33] and his *Repertorium* does contain Greek letters and words,[34] and also Greek terms in transliteration.[35] Greek texts, however, which he had at hand in the bilingual sections of his copy of *Poetae Christiani veteres*, are left untouched, as there are no marginalia found with them, not even for the Latin translations on facing pages.[36]

From the sources available to us one must conclude that books written in Greek or Hebrew were not part of Marulus's library and not of interest

30. Full title: *Psalterium ex Hebreo diligentissime ad verbum fere tralatum: fratre Felice ordinis Heremitarum sancti Augustini interprete per summum pontificem Leonem Decimum approbatum* (Venice: Liechtenstein, 1515).

31. On Felix, see Posset 2001, 237.

32. *Sub Colla Firmiano, Tydeo Acciarino et Hieronymo Ienesio Picentino, a quo etiam Greca elementa accepit, eius aetatis uiris eruditissimis, in Latinis litteris adeo profecit* (. . .); Franciscus Natalis (Božićević), *Vita Marci Maruli Spalatensis per Franciscum Natalem conciuem suum composita*; Božićević 2007, 30–31. For dates of Genesio's activity in Split, see Praga 1933.

33. See below with fig. 5.8.

34. For example, *APOCALIP[SIS]: Ego su[m] et* ; Rep I, 282 (in the section on Paul's Letter to the Romans; [sic] *figural[ite]r*; Rep II, 111 (in the section on Jerome).

35. For example: *Nom[en] te[m]p[er]antif Grfcu[m] sophrosyne* . . . ; Rep III, 306 (in the section on Plato).

36. See folios 148–221.

to him. If one defines "biblical humanists" as scholars concerned with the study of the original biblical languages, one must admit that Marulus was not one of them. Nevertheless, one needs to remember in this connection that Marulus was very much a searcher for the "Gospel Truth" (*Evangelica veritas*), for which his *Euangelistarium* is known. Its editor in Basel, Franciscan friar Sebastian Münster, later a Lutheran, sang its praises.[37] In this search Marulus resembles the early Reformers in Germany, who just like him were concerned with the reform of pastoral care, at least in the early years of the Reformation. Yet, one notices that Marulus did not possess any of their works. In his library nothing can be found of Johann von Staupitz (c. 1465–1524), Martin Luther (1483–1546), or Philip Melanchthon (1497–1560).

Marulus's Books of "Church Writers"

The first category of Marulus's books, the "church writers," may provide a better understanding of what the pious poet and lay theologian of Split was interested in. It comprises two Latin Bibles and titles that are related to the Bible, to pastoral care, spirituality, and Christian poetry. Notably, Marulus's ECCLESIASTICI includes the second volume of *Poetae Christiani veteres* (Venice, 1502).[38] However, surprisingly, his list also shows the title of the first-century Jewish historian Flavius Josephus on the history of the Jews, based upon the Bible and other Jewish writings, *De antiquitatibus Judeorum*[39] ("Antiquities of the Jews"). One would expect it under the classification *Historici*. Marulus understood it apparently as a book of a "church writer," most likely because he used it to excerpt stories for his Christian spiritual and moral pedagogical purposes,[40] not for writing history. One may see the books of that group in terms of the contemporaneous "theology-for-piety," to use a translation of the awkward German expression *Frömmigkeitstheologie*.[41] Somewhat surprising, too, is the fact that Marulus

---

37. See Charles Béné, "Marulić and Europe," Dossier 147.

38. The title of volume 2, *Sedulius, Juue[n]cus Arator poetae* (given in Marulus's book list, MT, 38), is deceiving because this volume contains many more poems and other texts including biographies beyond the three authors mentioned in the title. Samples of this poetry in English translation (for example of Iuvencus, Cyprian, and Sedulius) are available in White 2000.

39. MT, 38.

40. See the chapter 5.19 of *Euanglistarium*, "Avarice is the cause of many evils," in MR, 82–83, with the reference to Josephus.

41. Coined by Berndt Hamm, for his study of the late medieval theology of Johannes von Paltz (died 1511), a contemporary of Marulus; see Hamm 1982. This German term

was the owner of a priest's prayer book, the breviary. Should one assume that the pious man used it daily? Or, did it just collect dust on his bookshelf? Was his breviary identical with the *Brevijar hrvatski* ("Croatian Breviary") that is known to have been printed by a Venetian printer in 1493?[42] Since it is lost, we cannot know the answer to this question.

SAMPLE PAGES FROM THE FOUR VOLUMES OF THE *BIBLIA LATINA*

His two Bibles are listed at the beginning of his *ECCLESIASTICI*. A modern handwritten note at the beginning of the first volume says that it is the *Biblia (cum postill.) [Venetiis, Bonetus Locatellus pro Octaviano Scoto, 1489]*.[43] Marulus bequeathed it to the Observant Franciscan *Conventus Paludis* in Split. He listed it as *Biblia cum Nicolao de Lyra*.[44] The first extant page of this Bible (fig. 5.1) starts with the incomplete sentence from the Song of Songs: . . . *sum sed formosa filie hierusalem sicut tabernacula cedar: sicut* . . . The left margin shows Marulus's marks in brown ink, i.e., his Roman numerals III to VI, which indicates that the previous page(s) must have displayed the numerals I and II. They refer to the biblical hermeneutics of Tyconius (died c. 400)[45] and his book on the "Seven Rules" or "Seven Keys" of Scripture interpretation, which is summarized here by Nicholas of Lyra (c. 1270–1349) in his prologue to the Latin Bible which Marulus was numbering in the margins.

The sacred text is printed in larger print in a central text "box" (or "window"). The first three volumes comprise the Old Testament with a total of more than 1,640 pages. The New Testament is found in the fourth volume, which takes up more than 530 pages. The fourth volume also includes at the end the treatise of Nicholas of Lyra *On the True Messiah*,[46] on less than

---

is not generally accepted.

42. See Franolić 2008, fig. 19 (with a woodcut on the title page showing Saint Jerome with the lion in his study).

43. Locatellus (Lucatellus, Boneto Locatelli) was a priest from Bergamo, active as a printer from c. 1485 to c. 1510. He was one of the most prolific printers in Venice. Early in his career he established a close working relationship with Octavianus Scotus and his output came to be almost entirely for Scotus or his heirs. They also financed the printing of numerous scholarly works of theology, philosophy, and medicine, around 120 editions before 1500 alone.

44. MT, 64. This friary also received Marulus's *Compendium Biblie volumen* and *Homilie Origenis*.

45. See Babcock 1989.

46. On Lyra's booklet, see Klepper 2007, 82–108.

ten pages. There are two pages of index (*Registrum*) with five columns per page. Thus, Marulus's edition of the *Biblia Latina* comprises more than two thousand densely printed pages.

The layout of a typical page of Marulus's Bible looks like this: A "box" at the center, usually at the upper half of a page, contains the biblical text in large print in two columns (figs. 5.2 and 5.3). Together with the biblical text appear the *Prologus* and the *Argumentum* which are treated, in terms of layout, as if they were the sacred texts themselves (since they appear within the "box"). The *Prologues* are specific letters of the church father Jerome.

The comparison of a page from two different copies of the same print (here, of the book of Isaiah, f. 31) demonstrates that Marulus's study edition is perhaps the least expensive print that was available (compare figs. 5.2 and 5.3). Marulus's copy of the *Biblia Latina* has no rubrications (fig. 5.2).[47] A more luxurious copy has the rubrications for capital letters which are properly executed in red and in blue, signaling the beginning of a new chapter (fig. 5.2).[48] Rubricator's handwork was very costly. Early printers often left small square spaces in printed texts for their customer to hire artists to provide decorative initials. This is the case with Locatellus and the print of 1489. Furthermore, a deluxe edition included the illustrations in color.[49]

The biblical text "box" is surrounded by the apparatus of comments in a smaller print, occasionally with an illustration. The scholarly apparatus customarily consists of four parts:

(a) There are *Expositions* which are always those of the Franciscan Friar William Brito (c. 1230–1300) and which concern Saint Jerome's *Prologues*. Brito's identity is revealed only at the end of the Old Testament volumes.[50] His *Expositions* stem from about 1270.[51]

(b) The *Postils* are always those of Nicholas of Lyra, who is a *Hieronymus redivivus* and who, like Brito, is a medieval French Franciscan friar. *Postil* or *Postilla* is a "commentary." Its name is explained either as the abbreviation of the Latin expression *post illa [verba textus]*, i.e., what comes "after

---

47. Except for the appendix in volume 4 of his *Biblia*, i.e., Lyra's treatise (booklet) *On the True Messiah*. Unfortunately, there is no full *Biblia Latina* generally accessible in order to make further comparisons.

48. As shown on the website: http://intellectadesign2.blogspot.com/2008/03/festival-de-livros-religiosos-raros.html (accessed October 2009). It is not a complete *Biblia*.

49. The hand-colored woodcut of fig. 19 (beginning of the book of Genesis with the story of creation and the historiated initial I) is exhibited on Ebay (accessed August 8, 2009).

50. *Explicit postilla fratris Nicolai de lyra super vetus testamentum cum expositionibus Britonis in prologos Hieronymi*; vol. 3, f. 242.

51. See Daly 1966, 4–7.

the words [of the Bible]" in the form of comments, or as the diminutive form of *postea* ("marginal note" in medieval Latin).⁵² These are continuous comments on the Bible that Lyra provided by drawing much of his insights from the medieval Jewish exegete Rashi (Solomon Gallus, 1040-1105).⁵³ One may date his *Postils* between 1320 and 1330, i.e., more than half a century after Brito's *Expositions* and more than two hundred years after Rashi's commentaries. Lyra's contribution to biblical scholarship cannot be exaggerated. He functioned like "a vacuum cleaner that sucked up the wealth of medieval biblical learning."⁵⁴ Lyra is a "goldmine."⁵⁵

He is the "key factor" in the history of Bible interpretation; his return to the theological supremacy of the Scriptures and specifically to the literal sense is the fundamental mark of a theology that is returning to the sources. The literal sense does not allow subjective interpretations of a commentator.⁵⁶ Yet, Lyra's *Postils* did not go unchallenged. About one hundred years later (c. 1430) they triggered criticism from a Spanish bishop:

(c) Critical notes against Lyra's commentaries are expressed in the *Additions* of Bishop Paul of Burgos (c. 1350-1435), who wrote circa 1430.⁵⁷ Those *Additions* vary in number; sometimes there are up to ten on a given chapter. There is clear evidence that Marulus made use of both Lyra's comments and Burgos's additional notes. In his book *On the Humility and Glory of Christ*, concerning the feast of Passover, Marulus agrees with "the opinion of [the bishop of] Burgos" (*Burgensis sententia*) which is expressed in Burgos's *Additions* to the commentaries of Nicholas of Lyra on the Bible.⁵⁸

(d) The scholarly apparatus usually includes the sharp, defensive replies that are called *Responses*. They are always those of the Saxon Franciscan Matthias Döring (c. 1400-1469),⁵⁹ who wanted to defend his French confrere Lyra. The *Responses* are to be dated c. 1440 (i.e., ten years before Marulus's

---

52. See Bihlmeyer and Tüchle 1960, 2:419 (ch. 145).

53. See Hailperin, 1963; Bunte 1994.

54. Hagen 2004.

55. Smith 2008, 62.

56. See D'Onofrio 2008, 522.

57. Originally, the *Additions* were more than one thousand marginal notes which Burgos had entered in a volume of Lyra's *Postils*. The bishop sent them to his son Alfonso. Many of the *Additions* imply that Lyra was not competent in Hebrew and that Lyra also misinterpreted Thomas Aquinas when he quoted him; see Krey 2008b, 1:501.

58. *In Additionibus commentariorum Nicolai Lyrae super Bibliam*; De humilitate, 440-41. This is a very rare locus where Marulus explicitly mentions Lyra and Burgos.

59. Döring held the office of provincial of Saxony in his order. He was an opponent of the Observant Franciscans; he represented the University of Erfurt at the Council of Basel (1431-37); see Krey 2008a, 205.

birth). If there are no *Additions* to be found, there was obviously no need for any *Responses*. Yet, not all of Burgos's *Additions* provoked Döring's *Responses*.[60] In figures 5.9 and 5.10 we can see examples of an *ADDITIO* by Burgos (besides the eucharistic symbol). The printer was kind enough to signal with capital letters not only the beginning of an *Addition* but also the beginning of Friar Döring's defensive reaction, the *REPLICA[TIO]*[61] (fig. 5.10).

Samples of Bible Illustrations

The earliest illustrated print of a Latin Bible (in the history of Bible printing) is probably the one of 1481 by Anton Koberger (1445–1513) in Nuremberg.[62] The 1489 Bible print in Marulus's possession may be the first *Venetian* print that includes pictures by one or several anonymous woodcutters. There are thirteen illustrated pages in volume 1, none in volume 2, sixteen in volume 3, and one in volume 4 (a woodcut diagram, genealogy). This comes to a total of thirty pages that show illustrations of various sizes. The first illustration is found in Jerome's *Prologue* and shows Jerome with the lion in his study (fig. 5.4). This picture is one of two historiated initials, both found in volume 1. What we see here is the initial F in the *prologue* or *letter to Bishop Paulinus*. The initial F marks the beginning of Jerome's text that speaks about *Frater Ambrosius* (Brother Ambrose). It takes some imagination to detect the shape of the letter F in this picture: The arch over Jerome's study represents the horizontal top line. The vertical part in the letter F is represented by the wall in back of Jerome (fig. 5.4). Other contemporary prints may only show an embellished initial (fig. 5.4a).

Most of the illustrated pages of volume 1 are found in First Kings, some pages with up to three pictures per page. In volume 3, two woodcuts illustrate the book of Isaiah, one is in Daniel, and one in Maccabees. The book of the prophet Ezekiel has twelve illustrated pages. One of the most remarkable is found on folio 140v showing the ground plan of the "Wonderful Stream of Water and the Temple" according to Ezek 47 (also showing the library stamp; fig. 5.5). In Ezek 47, the "Wonderful Stream of Water" is described as flowing

60. Döring's *Response* is also called *Tractatus* as in *Incipit tractat[us] mag[ist]ri Mathie*; vol. 1, f. 24, right column, second line from the bottom.

61. The Latin word *replicatio* is usually abbreviated in the *Biblia Latina* with REPLICA; it literally means a "rolling back" or "turn over" of what was said; it should not be confused with "replication" or "replica" in terms of a reproduction of something.

62. Samples of hand-colored woodcuts of the Koberger Bible of 1483 (two volumes, in German translation) can be seen on the website: https://www.smu.edu/Bridwell/SpecialCollectionsandArchives/Exhibitions/Lightboxes/?itm={190D8A76-2C89-4E7C-87F5-A06A0370714B}.

out from beneath the threshold of the temple (*Sanctum sanctorum*). The very detailed map depicts the flow of the water starting in front of the temple (top of picture) toward the east (*Oriens*, at the bottom of the picture). The water flows past the southern side (i.e., toward the left side in the picture) of the *Holocaustum* (in the center of the picture) and exits at the east gate (at the bottom of the picture). This woodcut illustration in his *Biblia* is based upon a much earlier drawing which may be found in manuscripts.[63]

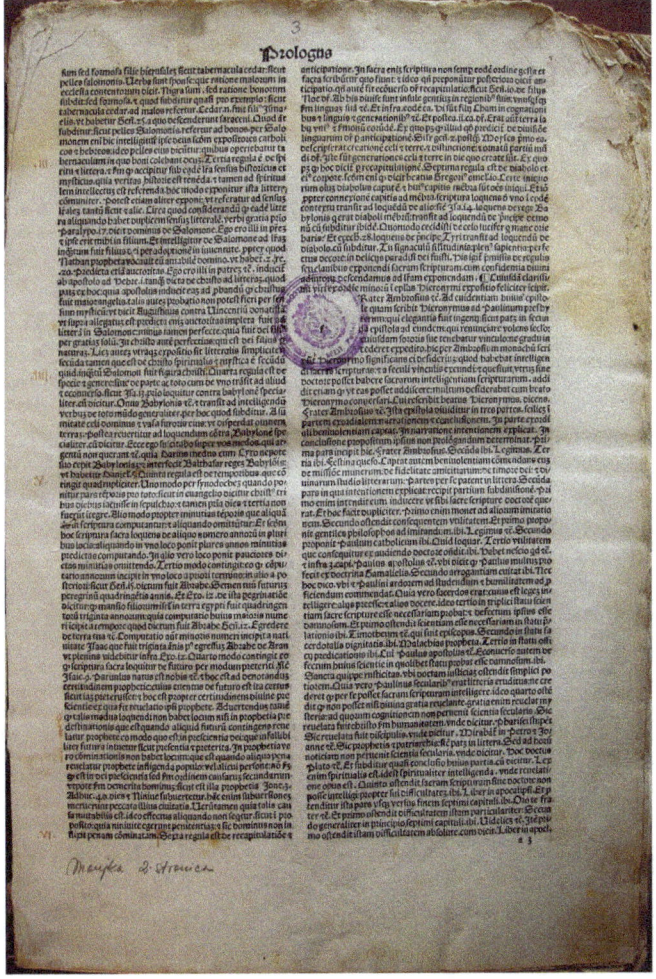

Fig. 5.1. First extant folio (f. 3) of Marulus's *Biblia cum comento*, with library stamp.

---

63. I.e., a codex in the Bodleian Library, Oxford; see Rosenau 1974, fig. 4.

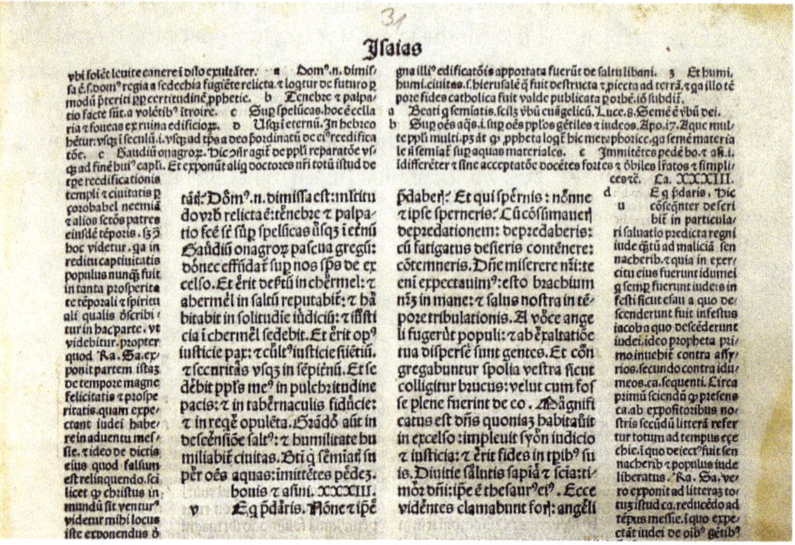

Fig. 5.2. Folio 31 from the book of Isaiah in Marulus's desk copy,
without the finishing touches of a rubricator (inexpensive edition!).

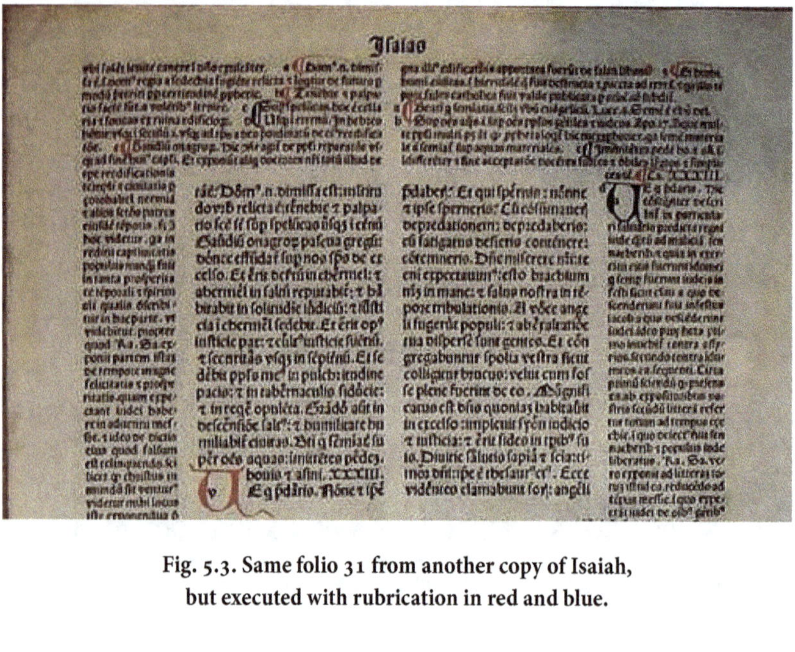

Fig. 5.3. Same folio 31 from another copy of Isaiah,
but executed with rubrication in red and blue.

THE BIBLE   99

Fig. 5.4a. Initial F in *F[rater] ambrosius*, in *Biblia Latina* (Speyer: Peter Drach, 1489); from website "Herzogenburg, Stiftsbibliothek," https://homepage.univie.ac.at/Martina.Pippal/Herzogenburg.htm.

Fig. 5.4b. First woodcut illustration in Marulus's Bible edition, showing Saint Jerome in his study. It is the historiated initial F in *F[rater] ambrosius*.
Detail of f. 3v in *Biblia Latina*, vol. 1.

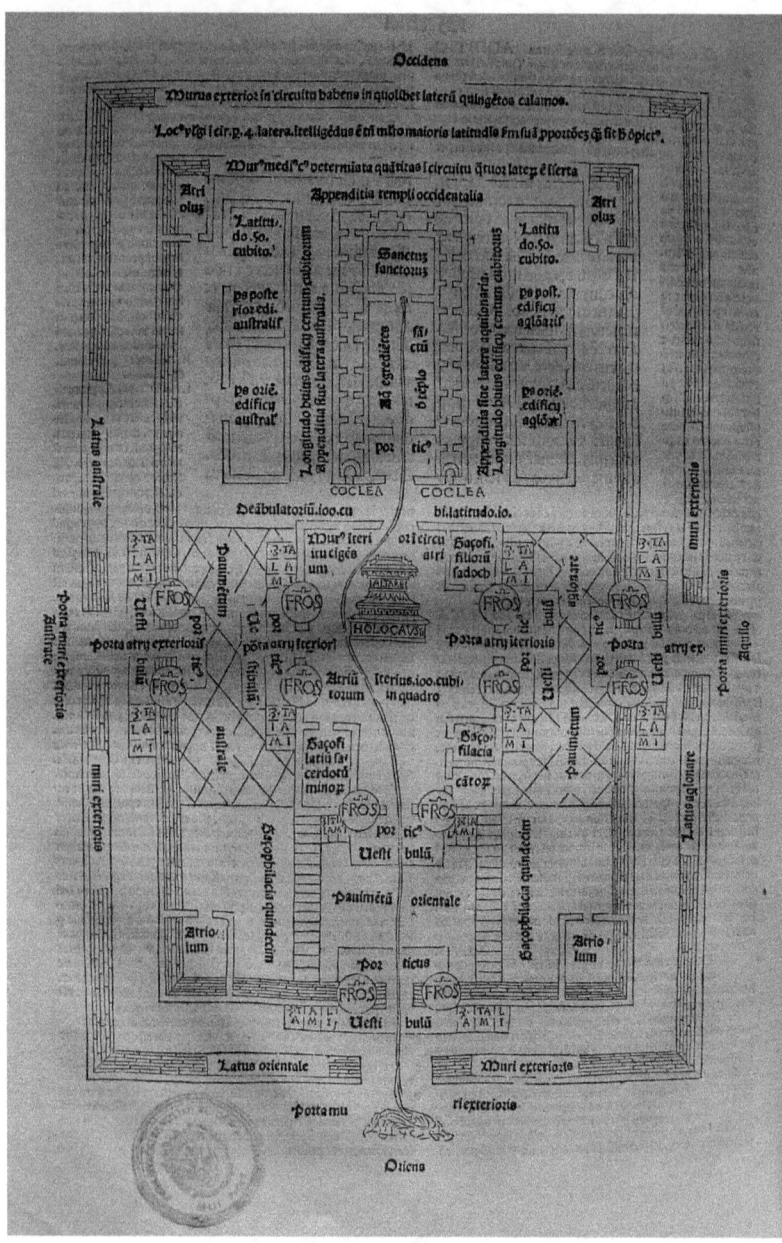

Fig. 5.5. Ground plan of the "Wonderful Stream of Water" and the temple area, according to Ezekiel 47; *Biblia Latina*, vol. 3, f. 140v; with library stamp.

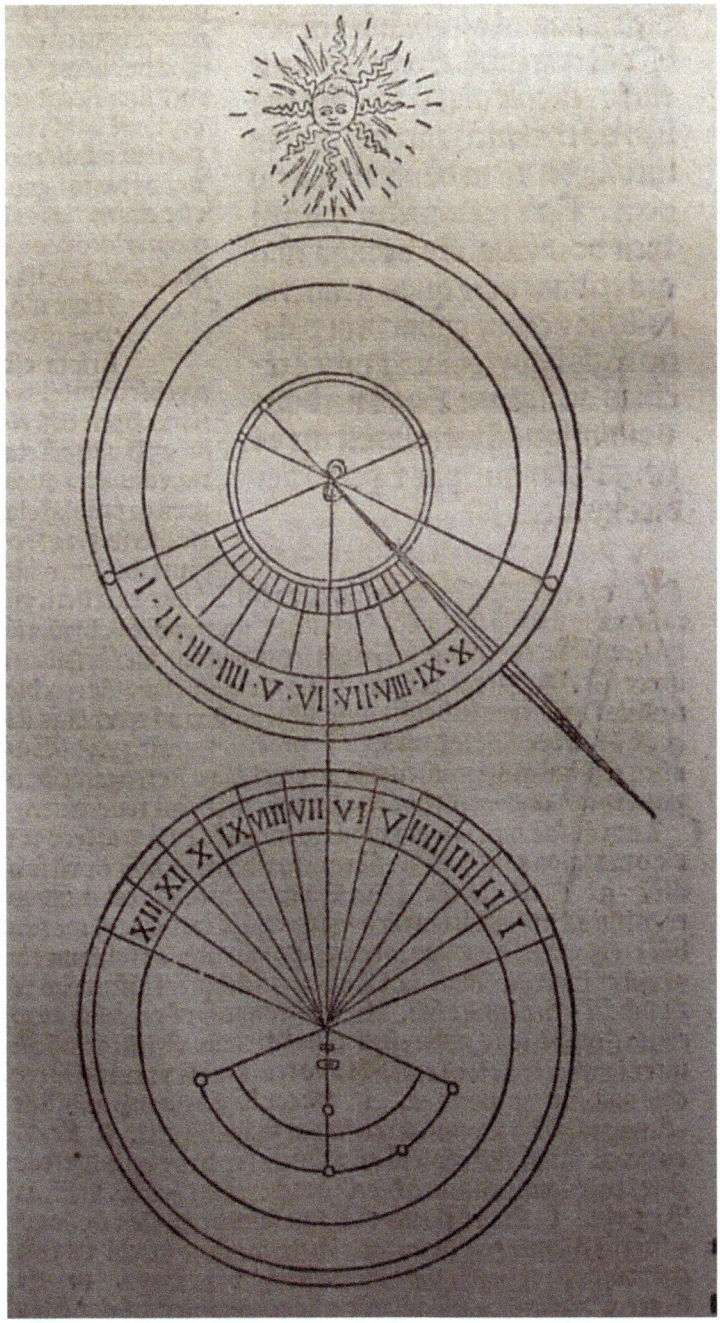

Fig. 5.6. Sun face (top) and sun dial, on Isaiah 38:7–8; *Biblia Latina*, vol. 2, f. 36.

Fig. 5.7. Franz Posset during the Marulić Days 2009 with the display of Marulus's *Biblia Latina* from the Library of the Observant Franciscans in Split, with excised folio 284.

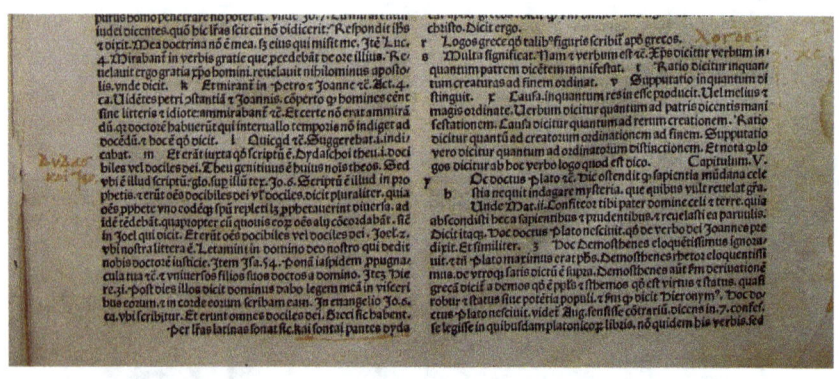

Fig. 5.8. Marulus's entry in Greek/Latin: ΔυΔασκοί *Theu* (lower left margin); his first christogram with a curly vertical line and the word λογοσ [sic] (right margin); *Biblia Latina*, vol. 1, f. 6.

THE BIBLE

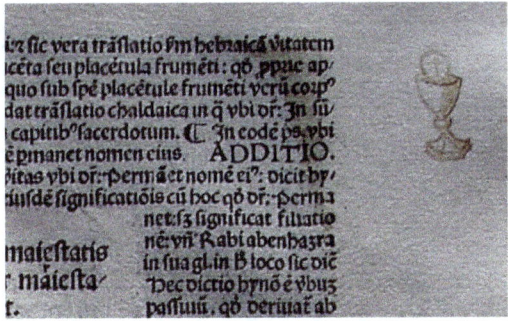

Fig. 5.9. First of the two eucharistic symbols (chalice and host), on Psalm 71:16; next to Burgos's *ADDITIO*; *Biblia Latina*, vol. 2; detail of f. 158.

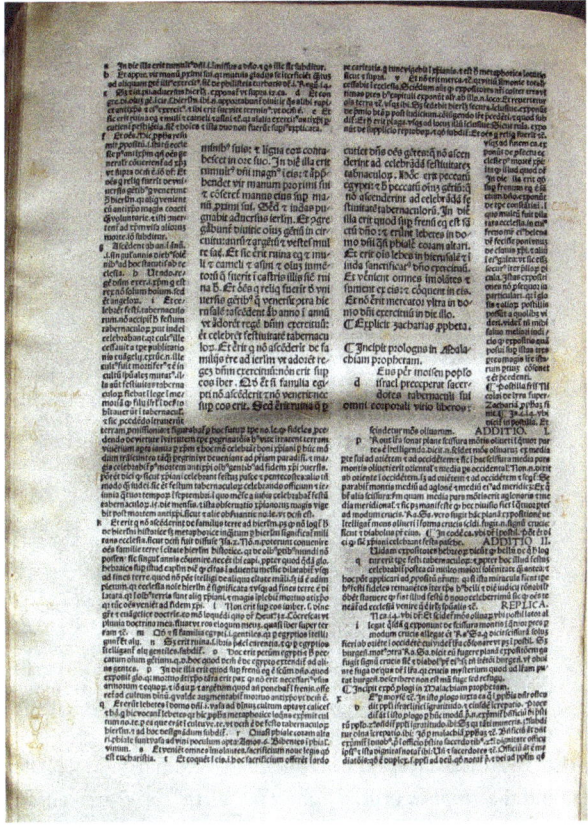

Fig. 5.10. Second eucharistic symbol, in Zechariah; lower left corner of f. 211v, *Biblia Latina*, vol. 3. Also visible is a cross without a socle for *ADDITIO I* in the right margin.

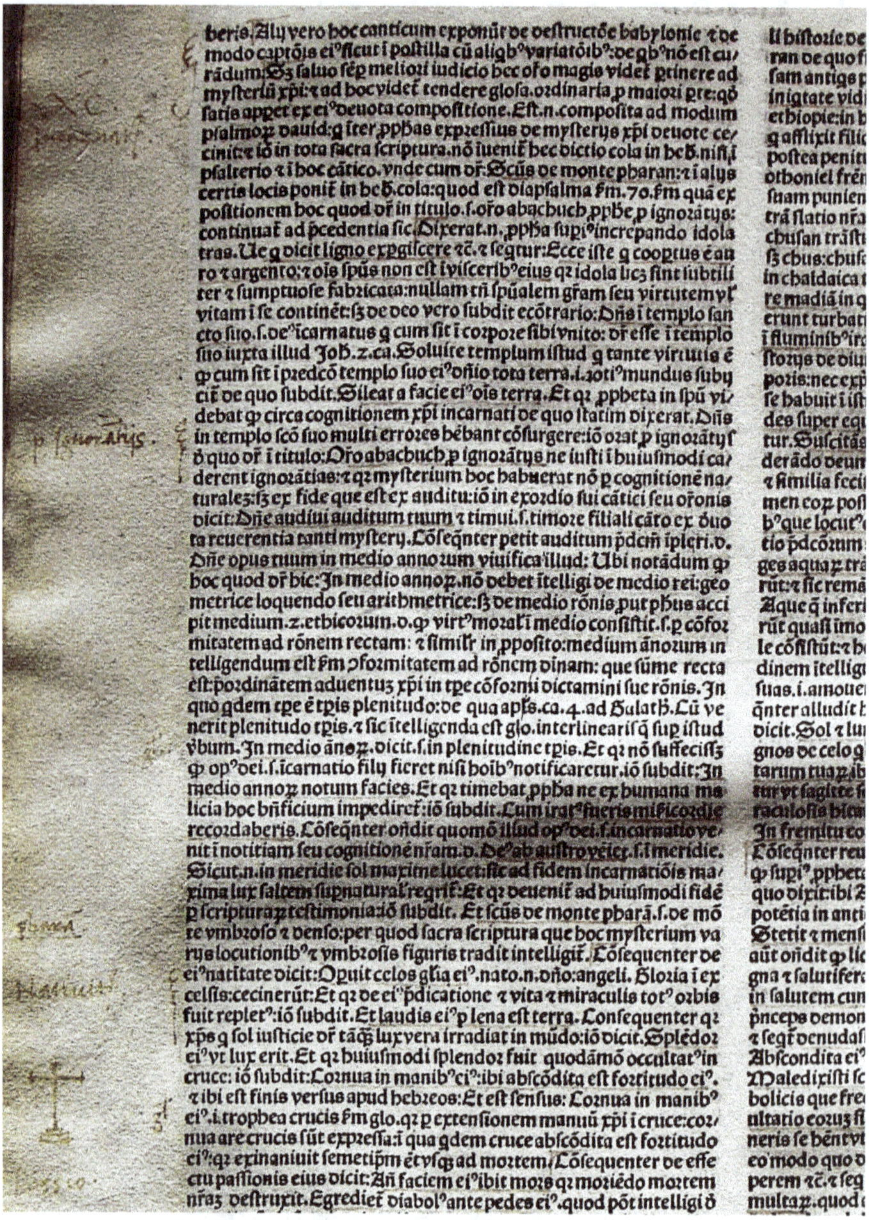

Fig. 5.11. The cross on a socle at the bottom of the left margin, correlated to Lyra's comment about the *Trophea Crucis*. *Nativitas* ("birth") is written above the cross, *Passio* ("suffering") under the socle of the cross. Marulus's entry of his christogram is seen at the top of the page; Habakkuk, *Biblia Latina*, vol. 3, f. 198v.

THE BIBLE 105

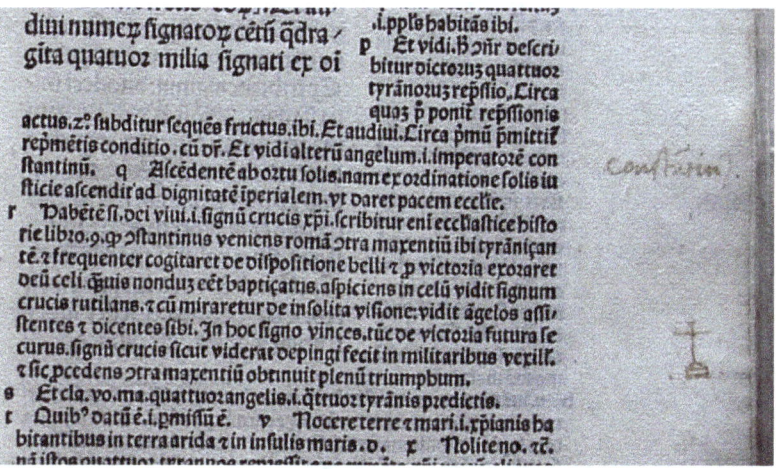

Fig. 5.12. Marulus's note *Consta[n]tin[us]* and his drawing of a cross on a socle for Lyra's *Comments* on Revelation 7; *Biblia Latina*, vol. 4, detail of f. 254 (wrongly numbered as 154).

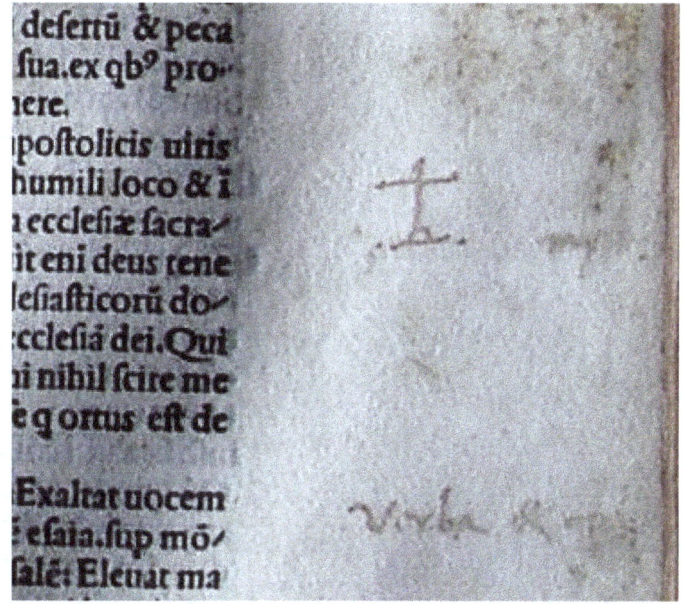

Fig. 5.13. Marulus's cross on a socle and the abbreviation *myst[ica]* in Jerome's *Expositiones in Hebraicas Questiones*, f. 228 (*Super Esaiam*, i.e., on Isaiah).
Photo: K. Grenc.

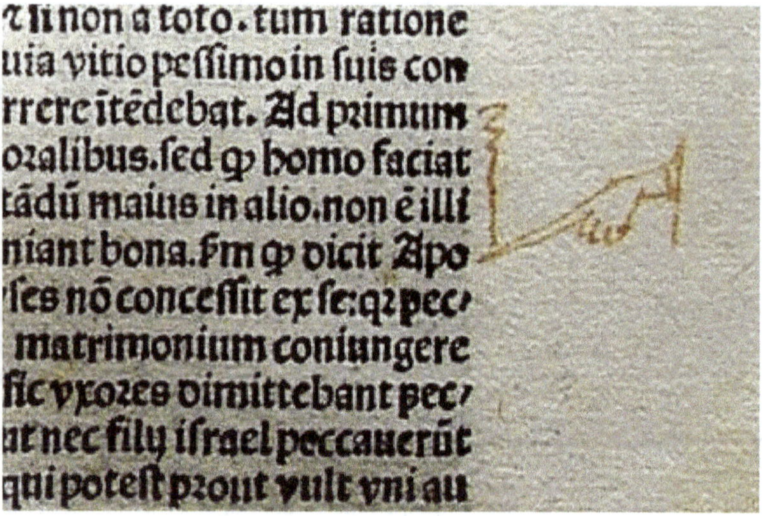

τli non a toto. tum ratione
uia vitio pessimo in suis con
rrere itēdebat. Ad primum
oralibus. sed q homo faciat
tādū maius in alio. non ē illi
niant bona. fm q dicit Apo
ses nō concessit ex se: q2 pec
matrimonium coniungere
sic vxores dimittebant pec
at nec filij israel peccauerūt
qui potest prout vult vni au

Fig. 5.14. The first *manicula* in Marulus's *Biblia Latina*; on Genesis 19, with the elongated finger, and curly vertical line; *Biblica Latina*, vol. 1, f. 45.

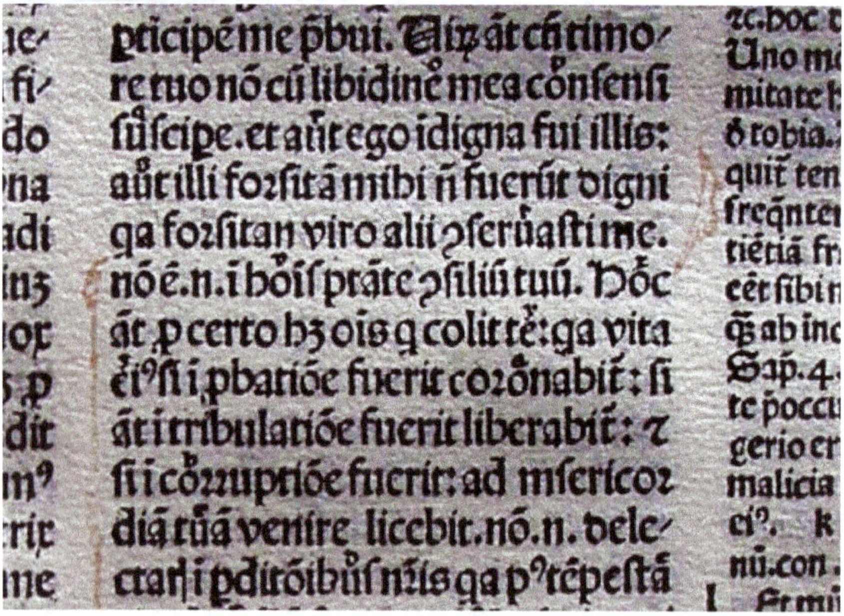

pricipē me pbui. Uirū āt cū timo-
re tuo nō cū libidinē mea cōsensi
suscipe. et aūt ego idigna fui illis:
aūt illi forsitā mihi ñ fuerūt digni
qa forsitan viro alii ɔseruāsti me.
nō ē. n. i hoīs ptāte ɔsiliū tuū. Hoc
āt p certo hz oīs q colit tē: qa vita
ei9 si i pbatiōe fuerit coronabit: si
āt i tribulatiōe fuerit liberabit: τ
si i corruptiōe fuerit: ad misericor
diā tuā venire licebit. nō. n. delectaris i pditōibus nris qa p9 tēpestā

Fig. 5.15. A *manicula* is entered into the right margin of the biblical text "box:" of Tobit; and a curly vertical line on the left of the biblical text "box"; *Biblia Latina*, vol. 2, f. 54.

Such an early drawing may have been the model after which the woodcut in Marulus's *Biblia* was produced as many illustrations and diagrams included in the printed Bibles of that time are based on earlier medieval drawings.[64]

A Missing Illustration

Marulus's Bible was vandalized. In Second Kings (in the Vulgate terminology, and thus in Marulus's copy, it is *Regum IIII*),[65] the major part of the second column of folio 284 was excised (vol. 1 of his *Biblia Latina*; fig. 5.7); it would have shown King Ahaz's sun dial (*Horologium*), which is mentioned in 2 Kings 20:11 (מעלות [*ma'alot*]). The illustration which was excised from folio 284 may have been something like the illustration in the book of Isaiah, folio 36, concerning Isa 38:7–8. It is the second of two illustrations in the book of Isaiah (sun face [at the top] and sun dial; fig. 5.6).

Samples of Marulus's Marginalia

The four volumes of Marulus's *Biblia Latina* show traces of his reading in the form of various marginalia. All are written in brown ink. Some mark of his pen is found on just about every folio. It is not possible to give a number of all his marginal notes and scratches. But this much is clear: They hardly ever appear in the biblical texts themselves. They show up alongside the texts of the commentaries or prologues. For instance, when Marulus reads chapter 4 of Jerome's *Prologue*, he copies two words from the commentary. They are printed in transliteration, but Marulus enters them in a combination of Greek and Latin lettering (fig. 5.8): (1) *Theu* [*sic*] (lower left margin); (2) [*sic*] and also his first christogram with a curly vertical line (right margin) (*Biblia Latina*, vol. 1, f. 6). There is only one other instance where Marulus uses Greek characters in the marginalia of his Bible. It is his abbreviation for "Christ" (Latin/Greek) entry *Resurrectio*, next to his curly vertical line, in Acts of the Apostles (vol. 4, f. 207v).

Marulus employs various ways to mark the printed text. Besides underlining and "hooks" within the text, he often uses curly marginal markings, abbreviations such as *NB* for *Nota bene* ("Please note!") and entries of names and notions.[66]

---

64. See Cahn 1994.

65. In modern Bibles, 1 Samuel and 2 Samuel are identical with what the Vulgate calls 1 and 2 Kings; modern 1 Kings and 2 Kings are 3 Kings and 4 Kings in the Vulgate.

66. His marginalia occur also in the other books that are extant from his library.

It is difficult to establish a hierarchy of his marginalia. However, it seems fairly obvious that a text which Marulus marks with certain drawings of religious symbols is more important than just an underlining or a curly marginal marking. Thus, at the bottom of the hierarchy are his lines, be they underlining or vertical curly markings. Names and notions that are picked from the printed text probably rank higher. Of special interest are his numerous christograms and his drawings in the form of *maniculae* ("little hands," pointing hands), cross on a socle, and eucharistic symbols.

(1) The eucharistic symbols (chalice and host, figs. 5.9 and 5.10) are entered twice in the Old Testament volumes (none in the New Testament): first on Psalm 71 (vol. 2, f. 158) and then on Zechariah (vol. 3, f. 211v). Marulus is particularly fond of Ps 71:16: "May wheat abound in the land, flourish even on the mountain heights. May his fruit increase like Lebanon's, his wheat like the grasses of the land." About this psalm verse Marulus is learning from Lyra's *Postil* that it is to be understood in a spiritual way of the eucharistic bread. Lyra sees the expression *memorabile triticum* ("memorable wheat") fit to be applied to the sacramental body of Christ, the holy Eucharist. Under the species of bread from wheat (*sub specie panis tritici*) the body of Christ is contained. At this point Marulus enters the expression *Euch[aristia]* into the left margin of folio 158. A bit further below, Marulus marks with a vertical curly line Lyra's reference to the "mystery of Christ." Even Paul of Burgos is in rare agreement here with Lyra because he too sees the "Hebrew Truth"[67] being confirmed in all this.

The second of the two eucharistic symbols is drawn into the margin at the comments on the concluding verses of the book of Zechariah (14:20b–21; in vol. 3, f. 211v). Lyra says there that the prophet Zechariah is "speaking metaphorically" (*propheta metaphorice loquens*)[68] when he says: "On that day ... the pots in the house of the Lord shall be as the libation bowls before the altar. And every pot in Jerusalem and in Judah shall be holy to the Lord of hosts; and all who come to sacrifice shall take and cook in them ..." This text is understood in terms of the Eucharist. Lyra explains that all what is said of the divine worship of the Old Testament is said (metaphorically, typologically) of the New Testament.[69]

(2) The drawings of a small cross on a socle are found nine times in his *Biblia*: in vol. 2, f. 246, on Canticle 8; vol. 3, f. 56v, on Isaiah 66; f. 198v,

---

67. *Sic vera tra[n]slatio s[ecundum] hebraica[m] v[er]itatem in hoc loco*; f. 158.

68. Note that he says "metaphorically" (not typologically). The issue of metaphors in Lyra and in Marulus needs to be investigated. For example, Lyra points out that *cerua* in Psalm 21 is said *metaphorice* of the humanity of Christ; vol. 2, f. 123.

69. *[Propheta] exprimit cultum novi testamenti per ea quae erant in cultu veteri testamenti*; f. 211v.

on Habakkuk 3; f. 208v, on Zechariah 9; f. 211v, on Zechariah 14 (fig. 5.10); in vol. 4, f. 95 on John 5; f. 203, on Hebrews 11; f. 254, on Revelation 7 (Constantine's vision of the cross; fig. 5.12) and on the subsequent page, f. 254v. On Habbakuk 3 (fig. 5.11) we see the word *Nativitas* ("birth") written above the drawing of the cross and *Passio* ("suffering") under the socle of the cross.[70] His drawings of a cross on a socle may be found not only in his *Biblia Latina* but also in autographs[71] and in other extant books of Marulus's library[72] (a sample is shown in fig. 5.13).[73] In his copy of the *Poetae Christiani veteres*, the cross on a socle appears four times (and thus it is as rare as in his *Biblia*).[74]

(3) The *maniculae* are found seventeen times: in vol. 1, f. 45, 59, 74v, 98, 144, 168, 175v, 250; in vol. 2, f. 48v, 54 (within the biblical text "box" of Tobit!); in vol. 3, f. 153; and in vol. 4, f. 29v, 135, 155, 161v, 173, 225v. The first pointing hand appears on Genesis 19 (f. 45, fig. 5.14). The elongated finger points to the word *Apostolus*, where the commentator provides a cross reference to the apostle Paul concerning the comments on Genesis 19. The *manicula* in the book of Tobit (fig. 5.15) is notable for its unusual placement on the folio: it is drawn by the right side of the biblical text "box" in the upper center. This seldom occurs, as Marulus's pen very rarely seems to dare to touch the biblical text. Apparently, the biblical text in Tobit, which deals with Sarah's prayer for death, was impressive. Marulus lets his "little hand"

---

70. Small crosses without a socle appear, for instance, in Zechariah; vol. 3, f. 211v (see fig. 10) and in Letter to the Hebrews; vol. 4, f. 203.

71. See *Repertorium*, f. 136; *De Veteris instrumenti uiris illustribus*, f. 42v. Zvonko Pandžić shows twelve examples of the drawing of the cross on a socle (in the books from Marulus's library) in Pandžić 2009, fig. 19.

72. For example, in the large volumes of Jerome's *Letters*, a cross is detected once in vol. 1, f. 11v; and once in vol. 2, f. 127; and two times in the form of a simple cross without a socle in vol. 2, f. 54 and f. 294. In the extant copy of Jerome's *Expositiones Diui Hieronymi in Hebraicas questiones super Genesim necnon super duodecim Prophetas minores et quatuor maiores nouiter Impresse cum Priuilego*, Marulus entered the drawing at least seven times, either as a simple cross or a cross on a socle.

73. See folios 44, 128, 217, 228 (fig. 13), 239, 288, 348. Some of Marulus's drawings of the cross are reproduced in Pandžić 2009.

74. Namely in Sedulius, f. 31; in Iuvencus, f. 53; in Proba, f. 135; and in (Pseudo)-Cyprian's *De ligno crucis*, f. 139. Further research is needed to find out whether these drawings are used in still other places and whether they are used consistently.

point to the Latin word *Hoc* in the Vulgate version of Tobit 3:21.[75] Marulus's drawings of pointing hands appear also in other nonbiblical books.[76]

(4) Christograms appear about 250 times, with 225 of them, by far the lion's share, in the three volumes of the Old Testament. Only twenty of them appear in the New Testament volume. These large numbers are an indication for Marulus's christocentric spirituality. The christogram is employed primarily in order to alert to the christological reading of the Hebrew Scriptures;[77] seventy times in Lyra's comments on David's Psalter alone. In some books of the Old Testament, Marulus enters more than a dozen christograms each, whereas in others he has no opportunity to do so (for example, in the books of Joshua).

In his copy of *Poetae Christiani veteres*, Marulus enters the christogram seven times: four times in Sedulius (f. 14, 15, 23, 31), one time in Juvencus (f. 69), and two times in Arator (f. 117 and 123). In the marginalia on Jerome's *Epistles*, the abbreviation for "Christ" is given with three Greek letters (*Chi Rho Sigma*), being derived from the Greek spelling of the first two and the last letter of the Greek *Christos*. The name *IESUS* is spelled out at least two times in capital letters in each volume. These entries, together with the drawings of the cross, and, most of all, with the numerous christograms, can be of great service in guiding us through Marulus's *Biblia Latina* to his christological reading of the Scriptures.

His *Nota bene* entries and the long "curly vertical lines" were not taken into consideration here as they are far too numerous. There are a few annotations which go beyond names or notions, and may consist of entire sentences. One such instance is especially notable: Marulus's comment on Saint Paul's raincoat in 2 Tim 4:13 (vol. 4, f. 185v). Being the longest (five

---

75. The text in full (without abbreviations) which Marulus marked with his *manicula* and curly vertical line reads as follows: *Hoc autem certo habet omnis qui colit te quia vita eius si in probatione fuerit coronabitur si autem in tribulatione fuerit liberabitur et si in corruptione [correptione] fuerit ad misericordiam tuam venire licebit. Non enim delectaris in perditionibus nostris quia post tempestatem tranquillum facis et post lacrimationem et fletum gaudium et exultationem infundis. Sit nomen tuum Deus Israel benedictum in saecula*; f. 54.

76. In the first volume of Jerome's *Letters*, Marulus enters them at least seventeen times and in the second volume about thirty times. The drawing may be seen also on f. 216 in Jerome's *Expositiones in Hebraicas Questiones* on Isaiah, *Visio Tertia* (Third Vision). In Marulus's copy of *Poetae Christiani veteres*, two *maniculae* are entered shortly after each other, within six lines of Arator's text, f. 118. The same phenomenon of two "little hands" appears also on f. 123, here within four lines, and still for Arator's text. Besides these *maniculae* there are more to be found on f. 94, 98, 99, 116, which makes a total of eight in Arator, six in Juvencus (f. 41, 42, 45, 46, 48, 77), and two in Sulpicius (f. 247, 270).

77. On this issue, see Erdmann 2000.

lines), this note is important not so much for its theological significance, but for its unusual length and triviality, i.e., concerning Paul's *p[a]enula*: "When you come, bring me the cloak I left with Carpus in Troas" (2 Tim 4:13). Lyra took the "cloak" as a symbol of Saint Paul's Roman citizenship.[78] Marulus wants to complement (or perhaps correct?) Lyra's comments, saying that originally the *paenula* was a Roman raincoat about which the Roman Emperor Galba once quipped:

> *Penula apud Romanos uestis erat, qua in pluuia utebantur. Galba penulam roganti respondit: non pluit, non est opus tibi; et si pluit, ipse utar. Abusiue tamen penula pro omni eo quod tegit.*
> Among the Romans the *penula* was a garment that they used when it was raining. To a man who once asked him for his raincoat Galba replied: "It is not raining, you do not need it, and if it rains, I will wear it myself."

However, improperly used, a *penula* may be a cover for just about anything.[79]

CONCLUSION

We have taken a look into the library of a pious Renaissance man at Split, a city then under the rule of the Republic of Venice. Marulus was part of the Latin cultural, spiritual, and theological developments of the West. He apparently was not much interested in Greek and Hebrew Scripture studies or in speculative, Scholastic theology. Neither Thomas Aquinas's *Summa Theologiae* nor works of Bonaventure, Scotus, or any other Scholastic are on his inventory list. He preferred books of pastoral theology for piety, such as the more pastoral *Opuscula* and the biblical commentary *Catena aurea* of Thomas Aquinas, as well as handy collections of Latin "sermons," including those of Bernard of Clairvaux.

We know of two Bibles in his library, but only in Latin. The *Biblia Latina cum comento* is full of his marginalia. As we looked, so to speak, over his shoulder, we saw him taking up his pen in order to enter numerous and varied notes and marks. We were able to get an idea of his biblically shaped, Christ-centered, spiritual thought, and thus we gained a few insights into his pious soul.[80] In reading the commentaries, Marulus's own strong inclination

78. Lyra: *nomen est ciuitatis . . . vestis consularis . . . factus ciuis romanus*; f. 185v.

79. I gratefully acknowledge the help of Zvonko Pandžić and Bratislav Lučin with fully deciphering Marulus's handwriting (from a sharpened reproduction) and with the identifying of the text to which it refers, namely to Quintilian's wit and humor in *Institutio oratoria* VI.3.

80. However, one must realize that Marulus's thought world is also strongly

and apparent tendency to interpret everything in terms of biblical typology was kept under control. Nicolaus of Lyra, whose commentary Marulus used, was a representative of literal-historical exegesis (without denying the spiritual aspects). Without Lyra's rigorous attempt to stick to the literal and historical sense of the Scriptures, Marulus's Bible interpretations may have gone haywire and out of control as the pious Bible scholar was fond of the spiritual, typological, christological reading of the Old Testament. All in all, Marulus was reading the Latin Bible within the tradition of patristic and medieval spiritual exegesis, well grounded (or at least supposed to be grounded) in the literal-historical sense that Lyra primarily pursued. Furthermore, with his Christian spiritual reading of the Bible of the Hebrews, Marulus adhered to the fundamental concept of the essential unity of the two Testaments, moving in the tracks of the medieval Christian tradition.

Marulus appears untouched by the emerging trend among contemporaneous Renaissance scholars of searching for what they called the original meaning of the Bible, the *Hebraica veritas* and the *Graeca veritas*. However, when he read in the commentary part of his *Biblia Latina* about the "Hebrew truth" (*Hebraica veritas*)—for instance, in regard to the christological reading of Gen 22—Marulus underlined the text (in Burgos's *Additio IV*, fol. 48) and marked it with his characteristic curly vertical line and a christogram. But did he do so for the mention of the "Hebrew truth" or for the christological reading of the Old Testament passage?

Marulus was a pious Christian scholar who saw himself inspired by no other than the Holy Spirit.[81] Not the mythology of the pagans was his source, so he says, but the inspiration of the Holy Spirit, who provided what "our faith" (*nostra fides*) in Christ has ladled from the ancient Scriptures:

> It was the Holy Spirit [*sacer Spiritus*] Descending from ethereal
> heights above Who with divine light did illuminate
> Our mind and thus gave us to sing, not strange
> Poetic fictions or the various shapes
> Into which men and gods were once transformed, But what is
> vouched for by the ancient books,
> The Scriptures of our faith.[82]

---

impacted by ancient classical philosophy.

81. *Haec mihi cantati non doctus fauit Apollo, / Non Helicon, turba nouem celebrata sororum, / Sed sacer aeteria delapsus spiritus arce* (. . .); MR, 204.

82. MR, 204–5; I use the English translation of Sanja Matešić with minor modifications.

Chapter 6

The "Rock"

Marcus Marulus's Theological Patrimony Concerning the Interpretation of "You Are Peter and Upon This Rock I Will Build My Church"

DURING THE MARULIĆ DAYS of 2013 we ponder over "The Heritage of Classical Antiquity in Renaissance Texts." For Marcus Marulus the ancient heritage includes not only classical antiquity, but also and always the ecclesiastical patrimony of the early church,[1] which he cherished immensely. In the following, only one word, "rock," will be the focus of our attention, primarily with respect to what the early church and the long Catholic tradition bequeathed to him, the "Father of Croatian Literature," concerning the proper understanding of the "rock" in Matt 16:18, which is one of the most contentious verses in the entire New Testament.

Many people have seen the cupola of Saint Peter's Basilica in Rome on television during the recent reports about the transition from the reign of Pope Benedict XVI to Pope Francis. Viewers may wonder what the full inscription on the inside ring at the base of the dome says. It reads: *TV ES PETRVS ET SVPER HANC PETRAM AEDIFICABO ECCLESIAM MEAM*; it is the Latin version of the biblical verse Matt 16:18. The time when the inscription was finished (c. 1620) was the era of the Catholic Counter-Reformation—about

---

1. Béné 1981.

one hundred years after Marulus's year of death (1524)—a time when his Latin books were still in high demand in certain German-speaking regions.

The present topic is not so much an elaboration of what the verse may or may not have meant in the era of the Counter-Reformation, but what it meant to a Croatian nobleman on the eve of the Reformation, around 1500, when Saint Peter's Basilica as we know it was not even built. This nobleman is one of the first Croatian Scripture scholars to become internationally known, and it is worth finding out what he has to say, especially since he is known as the "Father of Croatian Literature" in the vernacular. His Latin works are the only texts in which the contentious "rock" appears. The riches of these works are still to be excavated in future research on Marulus's *Gedankenwelt*.

When we approach the topic of what Marulus thought of the biblical verse, we need to consider briefly the *Sitz im Leben* of his work by referring to the cultural-historical and church-historical context in which he lived, a context which shows a distinct interest not only in the patrimony of the church fathers and of the Sacred Scriptures but also in classical, pagan antiquity. With his philosophical and theological focus and with his retrieval of biblical and patristic theology, Marulus fits squarely into the wider picture not only of the Renaissance humanism coming from Italy with its return *ad fontes*, but also of the *Devotio Moderna* coming from the Low Countries.[2] Besides that, Marulus is an ideal candidate for what in recent decades has been labeled the "theology-for-piety".[3] Late medieval *Frömmigkeitstheologie* was a pastoral theology and promoted pastoral ministry through biblical preaching and through it the fostering of the spiritual life of the laity and Christian values in everyday living. Marulus, too, is concerned (to some degree) with the ethicizing of theology, which is one of the typical traits of the contemporaneous theology-for-piety.[4] Marulus himself expressed this element of contemporaneous spirituality in one of his most famous poems,

---

2. On the *Devotio Moderna* and the Brethren of the Common Life, see Fuller 1995; Van Engen 2008.

3. The expressions *Frömmigkeitstheologie* and connected to it the *Bernhard Renaissance*, i.e., the popular revival of interest in the works of Saint Bernard of Clairvaux, were coined by Hamm 1982. *Frömmigkeitstheologie* is best translated into English with "theology for piety." In the light of the contemporary *Bernard Renaissance* to which Berndt Hamm (1945–) alerted the scholarly world, the research results by Zvonko Pandžić, presented in his *Nepoznata proza Marka Marulića* (Pandžić 2009), become more acceptable; I rely on the German summary at the end of the book (with respect to Bernard of Clairvaux and Pseudo-Bernard, 152–55). According to Pandžić, Marulus read and translated much of the work of Saint Bernard and Pseudo-Bernard (!) as it became accessible to him in Split.

4. *Ethisierung der Theologie*; Hamm 1990, 139.

which the late Pope John Paul II quoted in 1998 at the occasion of his visit to Croatia:

> *Felix qui semper vitę bene computat usum.*
> Happy is the one who always puts his life to good use.[5]

Marulus was interested in questions of the then "modern" spirituality (*Devotio Moderna*) with its simplified devotions for lay people as disciples of Christ. Marulus concentrated on the reform of Christian spirituality and Christian living. In considering Marulus's *Sitz im Leben*, it was predictable that he should have translated the most significant book of the *Devotio Moderna* and of the theology-for-piety, i.e., the *Imitatio Christi*, into the vernacular. It is a book with many biblical references; it is "the world's most influential devotional manual."[6] No wonder that it was of great interest to the Scripture scholar of Split. He believed, though, that Jean Gerson (1363–1429), a representative of the theology-for-piety,[7] was the author of the *Imitatio Christi*, which he translated into "Dalmatian."[8]

However, the scholarly consensus is that Thomas à Kempis (1380–1471) was the author. Marulus most probably used one of the numerous Venetian editions printed during the 1480s and 1490s.[9]

We have no indication, although Marulus must have esteemed Jean Gerson highly, that the Split humanist and lay theologian knew anything about Gerson's ideas about ecclesiastical politics, such as his criticism of papal authority (conciliarism). The "ecclesiality" (*Kirchlichkeit*) of the representatives of theology-for-piety is striking. They were not interested in criticism of the ecclesiastical establishment. They may actually be considered great advocates of ecclesial conformism with the traditional sacramental life

---

5. Penultimate verse (77) of the *Carmen de doctrina Domini nostri Iesu Christi pendentis in cruce* (*The Song About the Teaching of Our Lord Jesus Christ Hanging on the Cross*), LS, no. 168. The poem was published in Latin and English on facing pages in Posset 2004. For the contemporary English version by Graham McMaster, see MR, 159–63. See also Béné 1994.

6. Becker 2002, 11 and 13.

7. Gross 1994.

8. Note the choice of words for the translation: *De latino sermone in dalmatichum* [sic], as quoted by Fine 2006, 194. The translation, *Od naslidovan'ja Isukarstova*, is one of the few prose works in Croatian generally accepted as that of Marulus (the others are the dedicatory epistle and two short summaries in his *Judith*, as well as commentaries to the verses of the epic, and two letters to Katarina Obirtić). For the linguistic aspects on the translation into Croatian, see Horvat and Gavrančić 2010. Marulus was well aware of the difficulty of the task when he undertook the translation of the *Imitatio Christi*. When he could not find appropriate solutions in the Croatian vocabulary, he would create loan words and introduce neologisms.

9. Cf. Backer 1864.

of the laypeople and the traditional veneration of the saints of the church. They were not interested in academic debates and scholarly disputations. Their preaching, if they were priests, was aimed at edification. Their focus was on the simplicity of a Christian, virtuous lifestyle.[10] Berndt Hamm's characterization of theology-for-piety (although without any reference at all to Marulus) sounds very much as if it were a description of Marulus's intentions found with his spiritual-theological works. With Franjo Šanjek[11] we may solidify the viewpoint about the connection between Marulus and the spiritual movements of humanism and the reform of Christian life through the *Devotio Moderna* and theology-for-piety (although Šanjek does not use the notion *Frömmigkeitstheologie*).

Marulus fits quite well into the just sketched historical context of late medieval spirituality and also into the context of the history of *Seelsorge* (pastoral care and pastoral ministry, which is an all-too-neglected field of scholarly investigation). As a layman Marulus has left a mark on history through his efforts as persuasive propagator of the Catholic faith (*propagator fidei*, to use the title of Mladen Parlov's book, which takes Guilielmus Eysengrein's expression for Marulus).[12]

He exercises indirect pastoral care through his religious literature for the elite, primarily for the humanists.

With Branko Jozić we observe that Marulus less shared the Renaissance optimism of his time (overrated as it may be) than he participated in the trends of the *Devotio Moderna* and perhaps in maintaining the traditional *contemptus mundi* viewpoint, "a reflection of the dualist polarization that the Christian worldview has never entirely managed to escape."[13] Spiritually appealing to Marulus was the religious literature of the *Devotio Moderna* and theology-for-piety because both dealt with the life of the individual layperson. Marulus with his "modern" spirituality shows a similarity to the Dutch contemporary, Wessel Gansfort (Basilius Gansfort, or Frisius, 1419–1489). After all, the Netherlands were, as we recall, the headwaters of the *Devotio Moderna*. However, the spiritual waters of that movement flowed from the Low Countries upwards back through the Upper Rhine Valley and from that region down the Danube Valley and also across the Alps into northern Italy and into Marulus's homeland. He was thus a

10. A brief, good description of this kind of theology is found in Hamm 1990, 139–40.

11. Šanjek 1999. The *Devotio Moderna* as Marulus's spiritual background is featured also in Pandžić 2009.

12. Parlov 2012; cf. Guilielmus Eysengrein, *Catalogus testium Veritatis* (Dilingae: Excudebat Sebaldus Mayer, 1565), 197v.

13. Jozić 2009.

contemporaneous example of a spiritual outlook that was similar to that of Wessel Gansfort, who "was neither a priest nor a monk, and had no intention of becoming one."[14]

Both Marulus and Gansfort are known for the combination of several theological and spiritual traits, as they intertwined in their life and work certain elements of humanism, scholasticism, and mysticism—all under the impact of the *Devotio Moderna*. Erasmus of Rotterdam, too, grew up under the influence of the *Devotio Moderna* and pursued interests similar to those of Marulus. All in all, Marulus was part of the broader cultural and intellectual movement "back to the sources" (*ad fontes*), which was at work in both the *Devotio Moderna* and in Renaissance humanism.[15] In addition, he was part of what has become known as late-medieval theology-for-piety.

With his specific spiritual, fundamentally non-political, *Weltanschauung* Marulus was not concerned with any high-church political issues of his time, important as they may have been to others. Issues of ecclesiastical law (canon law) with regard to the final authority in the church were not the themes that he wrote about, even though they had been smoldering since the fourteenth century. A struggle raged between the conciliarists and the papalists as to whether an ecumenical council or a pope alone would hold the highest authority in matters of faith.[16] But Marulus in Split appears disconnected from the conciliarist movement and untouched by the staunch opposition of the Renaissance popes to any conciliarist programs. He may have also been unaware of the papalist representatives who sought support from contemporaneous canonistic literature about the absolute supremacy of the popes. And yet, the starting point of the papalist camp for all its defenses of papal primacy and power was the verse with the "rock," Matt 16:18.[17] The question then would be: Did Marulus share the papalist interpretation of Matt 16? No, since he did not use Matt 16 in church-political terms or for any political purposes, be it pro or contra, either as to papal supremacy or as to conciliar authority in the church. Rather, he utilized the theological patrimony of the church fathers of the early church in order to clarify his spiritual and theological understanding of the "rock" in Matt 16:18. The controversial metaphor occurs in the following, wider context of

---

14. See the subsection "Marulić in the Context of European Lay Theologians" in Posset 2009, 149–50.

15. "Introduction," in MM, 20–23.

16. Burns and Izbicki 1997.

17. Stinger 1998, 161.

Matt 16:13–18,[18] which, with its christological significance, is always part of Marulus's thinking when he mentions the "rock":

> *venit autem Iesus in partes Caesareae Philippi et interrogabat discipulos suos dicens quem dicunt homines esse Filium hominis / at illi dixerunt alii Iohannem Baptistam alii autem Heliam alii vero Hieremiam aut unum ex prophetis / dicit illis vos autem quem me esse dicitis / respondens Simon Petrus dixit tu es Christus Filius Dei vivi / respondens autem Iesus dixit ei beatus es Simon Bar Iona quia caro et sanguis non revelavit tibi sed Pater meus qui in caelis est / et ego dico tibi quia tu es Petrus et super hanc petram aedificabo ecclesiam meam et portae inferi non praevalebunt adversum eam.*[19]
> When Jesus came to the region of Caesarea Philippi, he asked his disciples, "Who do people say that the Son of Man is?" They replied, "Some say John the Baptist, others Elijah, still others Jeremiah or one of the prophets." He said to them, "But who do you say that I am?" Simon Peter said in reply, "You are the Messiah, the Son of the living God." Jesus said to him in reply, "Blessed are you, Simon son of Jonah. For flesh and blood has not revealed this to you, but my Father who is in heaven. And so I say to you, you are Peter, and upon this rock I will build my church, and the gates of the netherworld shall not prevail against it."[20]

Remarkably, within the same chapter 16, a few verses later, Jesus is upset with Peter, who dared to rebuke him when he began to tell his disciples that he would suffer death in Jerusalem. These verses do not mirror a Peter who is solid as a rock. In fact, Jesus calls him "Satan": "Then Peter took him [Jesus] and began to rebuke him, 'God forbid, Lord! No such thing shall ever happen to you.' He [Jesus] turned and said to Peter, 'get behind me, Satan!'" (v. 23).

Could it be that within one and the same chapter of the Gospel the apostle Peter is called "Satan" and "rock"? The juxtaposition might be a hint that Peter is not meant to be the "rock." We are not pursuing biblical exegesis here, but we want to investigate how Marulus understood the "rock" of Matt 16:18. In the interpretation and hermeneutics of biblical texts he often finds orientation from the deliberations of the church fathers, primarily Jerome, and also Augustine. Both are to him guarantors of the "Evangelical Truth."[21]

---

18. For our purposes here, we focus on Marulus's Latin works in OO. For an introduction in English to the thought-world of Marulus, see MR.

19. Weber 1994, which is deciphered text of Marulus desk copy of the Bible, IV, f. 25v.

20. My translation.

21. *Hoc egit noster Hieronymus, hoc Augustinus, hoc alii ex doctoribus Euangelicę*

RETURNING TO THE FAVORITE CHURCH FATHER, SAINT JEROME

Marulus's return to the ancient sources is a return particularly to the theological insights of the church father Jerome. Jerome remains his favorite patristic author,[22] as is the case with most of the contemporary Renaissance humanists.[23]

To illustrate this importance, one of Marulus's contemporaries north of the Alps, the eminent Catholic Hebraist Johann Reuchlin of Pforzheim, wrote that he venerates Saint Jerome like an angel from God (*angelus* originally meaning "messenger").[24]

In the *Repertorium*, under the Latin headword *Interpres* ("Interpreter"), we find evidence for Marulus's interest in this issue of scriptural interpretation. He collects sayings from Jerome's opus[25] with respect to textual interpretation[26] and he learns that the allegorical meaning moves and delights a person more than any other interpretation.[27] From Jerome he also takes the information that the Greek Septuagint translators of the Hebrew Bible did not want to put forth any mystical meaning. One must read the divine word (*sermo diuinus*) figuratively or *typicos* (which Marulus spells in Greek letters: τυπικωσ [*sic*]), in terms of "types." The reason for the typological or figurative reading of the Scriptures is to bring out the truth of the story.[28] And so Marulus learns from Jerome some hermeneutical insights, i.e., that such interpretation does not disturb the historical truth.[29] Yet, a

---

ueritatis quamplurimi. Dialogus de Hercule a Christicolis superato, LMD I, 124.

22. This insight, then, makes the thesis even more likely that Marulus is the author also of *The Life of Saint Jerome* (Život *svetoga Jerolima*) in Croatian; Pa ndžić 2009 (German summary, 152).

23. Ridderbos 1984; Rice 1985; Hamm 1990, 127–235.

24. *Quamquam enim Hieronymum sanctum veneror ut angelum*, in *De Rudimentis* 549; pereface, in Dall'Asta and Dörner 2000–11, 2:43 (letter no. 138).

25. Rep II, 42–43, 44–45.

26. And also from various other authors: *Emilius Probus* (Rep II, 37); *Apophthegmata Plutarchi* (Rep II, 39); *Tullius De Finibus* (Rep II, 42); *Aulus Gelius* on Homer and Virgil (Rep II, 92); Sabellicus on the Septuagint (Rep II, 103); *Josephus De Historia Iudeorum* (Rep II, 125); *Eusebius De Preparatione Evangelica* (Rep II, 126); Origen (Rep II, 128).

27. *Alegorica significatio plus movet et delectat 290*; Rep II, 45. On Latin *interpres* in the Bible, see Rep II, 54–55, 68, 73, 76, 80.

28. *LXX interpretes mistica prodere noluerunt. 1. Extasis, mentis excessus 1. . . . Non omnia uere facta, sed in figuram fieri iussa 12. Obscuritas tribus rebus constat 16.* τυπικωσ *figuraliter 30. Hanc habet consuetudinem sermo diuinus, ut per tropologiam et metaphoram historię exprimat ueritatem*; Rep II, 111.

29. *Historię ueritatem tropologia non confundit*; Rep II, 111.

story is often metaphorically composed.[30] Any spiritual interpretation must always follow the order of the original story.[31] From Jerome he copied the following rule for biblical interpretation: When a prophecy about the future is told very clearly, one should not weaken what is written through some uncertain allegorization.[32]

HEBRAICA VERITAS

In the process of studying the ancient ecclesiastical heritage, Marulus became familiar with an important hermeneutical principle found in Jerome's works: "The gospels are not to be interpreted in any other way than according to the Hebrew Truth" (*Hebraica veritas*).[33] By this Jerome most likely meant the literal, original meaning of the biblical text, and also that the New Testament needs to be interpreted from the background of the Hebrew Bible.

Since Marulus lacked expertise in the biblical languages (Greek and Hebrew), one cannot count him among the "biblical humanists" in the strict sense.[34] Nevertheless, Marulus shows great interest in Greek and Hebrew words. Whenever he encountered words of these languages in the Latin literature he collected them for his *Repertorium*. However, concerning the Greek meaning of the "rock" of Matt 16:18 and/or the potential Hebrew background of it, there are no independent or autonomous linguistic opinions discernible in Marulus's works. In other words, any consideration on his part of the "rock" was solely based upon the exegetical tradition of the early church.

---

30. *Historia sępe metaphorice texitur*; Rep II, 112.

31. *Spiritalis interpretatio sequi debet ordinem historię*; Rep II, 112.

32. *Regula Scripturarum est: ubi manifestissima prophetia de futuris texitur, per incerta alegorię non extenuare quę scripta sunt*; Rep II, 112.

33. *Euangelistę secuti Hebraicam ueritatem non alicuius interpretationem 376*; Rep I, 112. On Hebraica Veritas, see Hobbs 1990. Jerome's maxim of searching for the "Hebrew Truth" became a hot issue in Marulus's days, but only outside his familiar surroundings, mainly in German-speaking lands, on the eve of and during the Reformation.

34. For a definition of "biblical humanism" see Augustijn 2003. Expertise in Hebrew would be much easier to acquire (at least in German-speaking lands) a few decades after Marulus's death, when a much younger fellow Croatian, Matthias Flacius Illyricus (Matija Vlačić, 1520–1575, or by the family's other name, Franković), of Labin (Albona) in Istria, went to Wittenberg. At the age of twenty-four he became a professor of Hebrew there. Olson 1981, 2.

MARULUS'S CATHOLIC PATRIMONY

Viewing Marulus within the Catholic tradition might sound trivial, but it is not as simple as it sounds, because it is not clear at all what the Catholic tradition is with respect to the interpretation of the "rock" in Matt 16:18. Three options are available from sixteenth-century Catholic Bible studies, indicating that the interpretation is highly controversial: the "rock" is (a) the person of the apostle Peter, (b) the faith of Peter as he expressed and confessed it with respect to Christ as the Son of God, or (c) Jesus Christ himself.[35]

One may wonder which concept Marulus adopted from the theological heritage that had come down to him. This, however, might be an altogether misguided question. Marulus did not make a conscientious effort to sift through any potential options. He operated primarily with the concept that he encountered during his return to the biblical and patristic sources. In order to substantiate this thesis, we shall observe (a) how he handles the commentaries that accompany his edition of the *Biblia Latina*, and (b) what he adopts from the ancient Christian patrimony for his *Repertorium*.

We get a foretaste of Marulus's thinking about Saint Peter when we read his celebration of this apostle in an undated Latin poem. In it Marulus did not process a single trace from Matt 16:18.[36]

WHAT DOES MARULUS READ ABOUT THE "ROCK" IN THE COMMENTARIES WITHIN THE *BIBLIA LATINA* OF 1489?[37]

Marulus read in his *Biblia Latina cum comento* all the *postils* (*postillae*) by the renowned late-medieval Bible interpreter Franciscan friar Nicholas de Lyra. Lyra's comments were criticized more than one hundred years later by the Spanish bishop Paul of Burgos. The bishop's valid points of criticism were always added within the *Biblia Latina* as complementary notes to Lyra's comments. These comments of the Spanish bishop are called *Additiones*. Marulus read them, too.

When Marulus studied the commentaries in his *Biblia Latina* (and he did this thoroughly), he left numerous marginal notes and underlinings.[38]

---

35. Bigane 1981, 214–52; Froehlich 1989. Examples for the options may be found at: http://www.catholic.com/tracts/origins-of-peter-as-pope.

36. LS, no. 172.

37. MM 74, 77, 86, 148, 168, 169, 172, 177, 178, 188, 194, 208.

38. Posset 2010. See above chapter 5.

In Lyra's comments pertaining to the "rock" and to the "church" Marulus marked, quite conspicuously, an Old Testament passage, whereas he left Lyra's New Testament comments on the "rock" in Matt 16:18 largely unmarked. The reason for leaving the comments on this verse untouched was most probably that he did not find the interpretation of Matt 16:18 at all controversial.

Lyra's Second Postil for Ezekiel's Vision of the New Temple, Concerning the "Rock"

Lyra offers (on several pages, f. 143v–144v) his understanding of the spiritual side of Ezekiel's prophecy in what he calls "the other exposition of the commentator" (*Alia expositio postillatoris*; see fig. 6.1). Marulus marks the beginning of Lyra's interpretation of the prophetic text of Ezekiel 40 with an abbreviation in the margin: *Eccl[esi]a* ("Church," barely visible; see fig. 6.2).

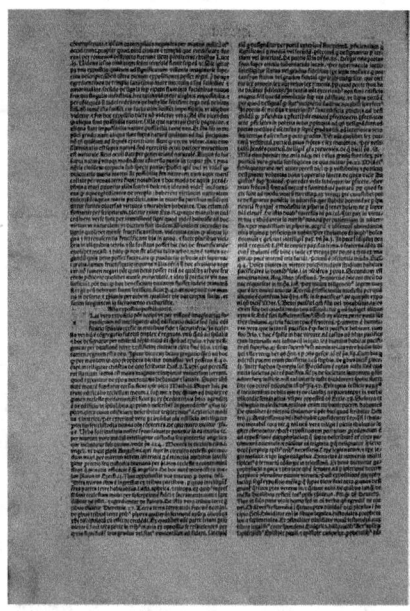

Fig. 6.1. Folio 143v of Marulus's *Biblia*, with paragraph *Alia expositio postillatoris* of Ezek 40, and marginalia on the lower left side (hardly visible).

THE "ROCK"

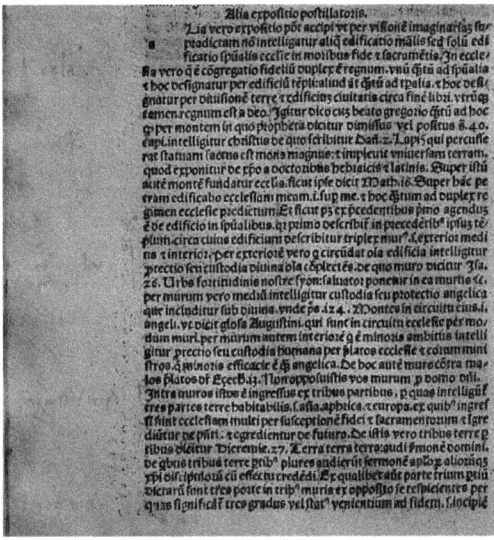

Fig. 6.2. Detail, folio 143v of Marulus's *Biblia*, with the paragraph *Alia expositio* and the marginal note *Eccl[esi]a*.

This marginal note is entered at the line where Lyra states that there is not only the material side of the prophet's vision of the edifice of the temple, but also the spiritual side, which concerns the church and her sacraments (f. 143v). This is so because the mountain on which the church is built is Christ! For his interpretation Lyra refers to the church father Gregory the Great.[39] Christ as the Mountain is interpreted by Lyra by two biblical cross-references: one to the book of Dan 2:34 about the strong stone (*lapis*) striking the statue made of various metals and breaking it; the other to Matt 16:18. Lyra continues (in Latin): *i. [e.] super me* ("that is, upon me"; see detail of f. 143v),[40] which means that Christ says (according to Lyra) that he is building his church upon himself. Marulus now knows from his reading of those biblical comments that Christ is the Rock, which is the christological interpretation of Matt 16:18.

---

39. *Igitur dico cum beato gregorio . . . per montem . . . intelligitur christus* [sic]; f. 143v.

40. *Super istum autem montem fundatur ecclesia sicut ipse dicit Math. 16. Super hanc petram edificabo ecclesiam meam. i. sup. me*; f. 143v; MM, 148.

Lyra's Comments on Matthew's Gospel

Lyra always offers a strictly Christ-centered interpretation, pointing out that the expression "upon this rock" means "upon Christ" (*super Christum*; f. 25v). In his *Additiones* on Lyra's comments for this verse, Bishop Burgos, of Jewish descent, has no criticism of the given interpretation. And, remarkably, the third commentator whose remarks are also always included in the *Biblia Latina cum comento*, i.e., Friar Matthias Döring (c. 1400–1469), has no reason to defend his confrere (which Döring normally does when Bishop Burgos dares to criticize Lyra's comments).[41] Therefore, one may conclude that Lyra's authoritative, Christ-centered interpretation of the "rock" had gone unchallenged through centuries of biblical exegesis. Thus, Marulus has no reason whatsoever to question Lyra's teaching that the "rock" means Christ, and not Peter. Marulus has no underlining or any marginal note here on Peter or *petra*. There was nothing unusual in what he read in the comments in his *Biblia*. By following the accepted medieval exegetical tradition, Marulus remains firmly convinced that the "rock" on which the church is built is Jesus Christ himself. Christ, who is God and man, is the warrant that the church would last until the end of the world.[42]

THE "ROCK" IN THE REPERTORIUM

The autograph of Marulus's *Repertorium historiarum per alphabetum* (as the full title says), with about 1,600 pages in its printed edition (published only recently), is splendid proof of his contribution to the rebirth of the classical and ecclesiastical antiquity in his time.[43] In looking up the books which he listed in his personal testament, we find that he included the *Repertorium* under "historical" texts, *Historici*.[44] This might be misleading: paying attention to certain keywords, one may actually detect Marulus's *theological* thinking and his spiritual priorities. The keywords reveal him as a representative of what around 1500 is labeled "theology-for-piety". For instance, under A, the last three lemmas are "Angel," "Apostles," and "Anti-Christ" (*Angelus, Apostoli, Antichristus*). Under B one finds, for example, "Baptism" and "Benediction."

The three hefty volumes of the *Repertorium* constitute much of Marulus's theological inheritance, in a personalized lexicon put together for his

---

41. MM, 168–69.
42. Parlov 2001 ("Marulić's Conception of the Mystery of Church").
43. Glavičić 1998–2000.
44. As edited in CM 14 (2005), 42.

private use. The notion of the *Repertorium* as a "dictionary" reminds one of a contemporaneous book title which displays both expressions: *Dictionarius seu repertorium morale* by the medieval monk Petrus Berchorius, OSB, but the opus became available in print only much later, i.e., in 1516/1517 (published by Jacob Sacon in Lyon), and one may wonder whether Marulus was inspired by it for the title for his own *Repertorium*, if, indeed, he had knowledge of it.

Where in the three volumes of the *Repertorium* should we start to look? We may narrow it down when we bear in mind Marulus's theological conviction, developed from his Bible studies, that Jesus Christ is the God-man and the Rock, as Marulus found in the commentary part of his *Biblia*. Thus, when we investigate the *Repertorium*, an additional hermeneutical and simultaneously dogmatic principle comes into play, the result of Marulus's study of Lyra's biblical interpretation. When Marulus collects data on Jesus Christ, he does so under the Catholic dogmatic premise of the divinity and humanity of Christ, which is proper Catholic Christology and which he finds displayed in the medieval commentaries within his Latin Bible. Marulus approaches the Scriptures and the church fathers from the position of Catholic theology, and not from historical-critical exegesis in the form of the later historical criticism. If the observations just made (concerning his theological standpoint) would remain unacknowledged, we would likely misunderstand him.

It is useless to search for Marulus's insights into the meaning of the "rock" under the entries of the letter P for Latin *petra* ("rock") or for the name *Petrus*. And, one must remember that with respect to the "rock" of Matt 16:18 Marulus does not rely on typology or tropology, or on any allegorical interpretation, because the literal sense for him is clearly at hand in Matt 16:18, namely that Christ is the Rock.[45] We are led instead to search (perhaps to some people's surprise) under the letter D, for *Deus Christus* ("God-Christ"), and we are most successful with the passages from the books of Origen and of Jerome.[46] Marulus collects excerpts first from Jerome (c. 347–419), then from Origen, although Origen (185–c. 254) is the much older source.[47]

---

45. However, in many other instances, especially in his interpretations of the Old Testament, he loves to employ allegories and typology, including rock and stone; see samples below.

46. For our focus on Christ, we will investigate (not exclusively) the entries under D: *Deus, Deus Christus, dii gentilium*; Rep I, 240–341.

47. Why this is so is not our immediate concern here.

Marulus's notes taken from Saint Jerome on "God" and "God-Christ" comprise several pages in the printed edition of the *Repertorium*.[48] These Trinitarian and christological elaborations are the proper theological context for statements about the "rock." Immediately after the relatively long entries on God (*DEVS*) follows one on "God-Christ" (*D[EV]S CH[RISTV]S*). It is in the context of the sections about the divinity of Christ where one finds excerpts relevant to our topic: "The Rock is Christ" and the [little] "rocks are the apostles."[49] This is one of Marulus's most significant christological and ecclesiological insights drawn from his patristic sources. He repeatedly copies those excerpts which say: "The Rock is Christ. Christ is God."[50] "Christ is the Rock."[51] The same conviction and a similar word play on the one Rock (Christ) and the other rocks (the apostles) emerge, for example, in a medieval source which Marulus did not excerpt—a work of the "last of the church fathers," Saint Bernard of Clairvaux (1090–1153). Bernard wrote of Christ as the Rock and Peter as the marble column. According to Bernard, the Lord said to Peter that he would build his church upon himself (i.e., upon Christ) and not upon Peter.[52] It is unlikely, though, that Marulus knew of Saint Bernard's saying. But the hint in Bernard (in the context of the contemporary Bernard Renaissance around 1500) may support the impression of there being a general patristic and medieval conviction, summarized by Lyra and handed down to Marulus, that the "rock" is Christ.

Marulus's excerpts concerning the meaning of the "rock" continue as follows: The name "Peter" is derived from *petra*.[53] According to John 1:42 (quoted in the Vulgate version) Simon, son of John, is to be called "Cephas" which is rendered "Peter," an insight which Marulus includes in his entry on the "Apostles."[54] However, what Marulus did not know or excerpt was Jerome's other statement, i.e., in his commentary on Gal 2 that "Peter" is the

---

48. Rep I, 321–25; 328–32; 333–34.

49. *Petra Christus. Petrę apostoli 55*; Rep I, 322; see also Rep I, 95 (on *Apostoli*).

50. *Petrus Christus 194. Christus Deus, Gygas 195*; Rep I, 323.

51. *Christus petra . . . 291*; Rep I, 323.

52. '*Tu es Petrus, Tu es*', inquit, '*Petrus*' *dictus a me petra, tu eris columna marmorea*, '*et super hanc petram*', *id es super meipsum*, '*aedificabo ecclesiam*'. *Noluit ille qui petra erat fundari ecclesiam supra Petrum, sed super petram*; *Sententiae* III, 112; alternate text as found in the note of the critical Latin edition of Bernard's works, *Sancti Bernardi Opera*, vol. 6–2:194; see Posset 2003a, 84–86. Bernard's image of *columna* for "apostles" is likely derived from Paul in Gal 2:9: "James and Kephas and John, who were reputed to be pillars . . ."; see also Marulus's excerpt from Jerome, Rep I, 100 (entry *Apostoli*): *Petrus et Ioannes columnę*.

53. *Petra et ab eo Petr(us) petra . . . 355*; Rep I, 324.

54. Rep I, 49 (entry *Apostoli*).

translation of the Hebrew and Syriac "Cephas," which in Latin and Greek is *petra*.⁵⁵ Marulus neglects this linguistic insight, a neglect which may function as further proof that biblical word exegesis was not his primary concern.

In his entry *DEVS CHRISTVS IESVS* Marulus simply repeats from Jerome's opus that Christ is the Rock, found in the context of a reference to "Syon" (Zion), which also means "Christ."⁵⁶ One may assume that the reference to Zion meant Isa 28:16: "See, I am laying a stone in Zion, a stone that has been tested, a precious cornerstone as a sure foundation." It is noteworthy that a Refomer, Martin Luther, should in a sermon of 1522 have incorporated the reference to the stone in Zion of Isa 28:16 in the same way. Luther preached as follows: The "rock" means nothing else but the Christian evangelical truth as is said also in Isa 28 (verse 16).⁵⁷ When Marulus continues with his excerpts from Jerome, he writes (not unlike Luther) that from Christ the Rock "the rivers of the evangelical teaching burst out."⁵⁸ Marulus also notes that Christ is the stone of contradiction and the rock of scandal.⁵⁹ Another large excerpt on the "Church" (*Ecclesia*) is also from Jerome, with this decisive phrase: "The Church of God [is built] upon the Rock Christ."⁶⁰ In this connection it is a bit surprising that our Scripture scholar does not quote for further support the verse of 1 Cor 10:4 (*petra autem erat Christus*, "and the rock was Christ"). Perhaps he felt no need for arguing as he might not have sensed at all that this could be a controversial issue, as it would become in the early Reformation in Germany.

Marulus collects excerpts concerning Christology and ecclesiology and concerning the conviction that Christ is the Rock not only from Jerome but also from Origen. The rock metaphor occurs twice; first in Marulus's entry *DEVS* ("God"), where his excerpts contain this series of christological notes: "Christ is the true light; Christ and the Church are like the sun and the moon . . ."; and "Christ is the Rock."⁶¹ In the second instance we read: "Christ is the Rock, and Christ is the Pastor."⁶² Origen is an important

---

55. *Patrologia latina* 26:341.
56. *Syon Christus 60. Petra 66*; Rep I, 329.
57. "Nun Felß hayßt nicht anders dann die christliche Ewangelisch warhait . . . Das ist auch gesagt durch Esaiam am 28. woelcher Christus allhie glosiert: 'ich will ain steyn legen in Sion . . .'"; WA 10-III:210,17–24.
58. *Christus petra de qua erumpunt flumina euangelicę doctrinę*; Rep I, 332.
59. *Christus lapis offensionis et petra scandali 210*; Rep I, 330.
60. *Ecclesia Dei supra petram Christum*; Rep I, 368.
61. *Christus lux uera . . . Christus petra*; Rep I, 338.
62. *Christus petra. Christus pastor*; Rep I, 339.

source for the understanding of the "rock" in the early church and consequently also for Marulus.

When Marulus mentions Matt 16:18 in his *Repertorium*, he does so under the heading of "faith proper" (*fides recta*) in his section of excerpts from the Gospel of Matthew. In that instance Marulus is concerned with Peter's faithful acknowledgment of Christ being the Son of God; he is concerned with the "gates of hell," which to Marulus mean the vices and the heresies that shall not prevail.[63] This entry in the *Repertorium* is significant for the simple fact that it shows Marulus's categorizations and his listing of Peter's faith in Jesus Christ by utilizing the wording of Matt 16:18. And, most of all, in this very context Marulus does not focus on the person of Peter as the "rock." Peter's proper faith in Jesus Christ is the salient point here. Marulus knows from the patristic patrimony what today the *Catechism of the Catholic Church* states in referring to Peter's faith in Matt 16:18: "'You are the Christ, the Son of the living God.' On the rock of this faith confessed by St. Peter, Christ built his Church" (*Catechism*, no. 424). As a typical representative of late medieval theology-for-piety, Marulus understands the proper faith in Christ as the faith that is accompanied by good works. Marulus notes that the person who listens to the Word of God and acts accordingly resembles the one who builds upon the rock (employing the wording of Matt 16:18).[64]

When Marulus is reading his Bible and annotating the medieval comments found in his Latin Bible edition (as we have seen above) and when he is gathering his excerpts for the *Repertorium*, he does not have the opportunity to tell us anything explicitly about his own convictions concerning the "rock." His *Repertorium* only tells us what he has found during his studies and what he considered worth selecting and keeping. The *Repertorium* by its nature does not lend itself to elaboration on personal theological convictions. What is important, though, is to pay attention to the perspectives under which Marulus gathers his excerpts because these perspectives reveal what was important to him. From those perspectives we can observe that he is being led to conclude that the "rock" is not the apostle Peter, but Christ alone. And, we see that when he cites Matt 16:18 he does so with respect to the correct faith (*fides recta*) which Peter has confessed—and with the addition that it is a faith that is active in good works. Marulus has ethicized theology for practical purposes as a representative of the theology-for-piety.

---

63. Rep I, 394.

64. Under the subheading of "Faith without Works" (*Fides sine operibus*) he has this observation: *Qui audit et facit, assi(mu)labitur ędificanti supra petram*; Rep I, 394. The critical edition has *assi(mi)labitur*, but the word should be deciphered as *assi(mu)labitur*. In Marulus's extant autographs one finds *assimul-* (*Vita Hier.* 38 = LMD II, 86); the spelling *assimil-* is not confirmed.

From the selections presented in his *Repertorium* we obtain a fairly good idea of what Marulus was after. However, as said, excerpts alone do not necessarily express his opinions. For a detailed analysis of Marulus's conviction we would have to turn to the authentic works from his own pen.[65] In conclusion, however, we may use Marulus's words from his late work (1519) *The Humility and Glory of Christ*, paraphrasing Matt 16:18 (Marulus uses "house" as substitute for "church"): *Christus est igitur petra, super qua domus fundata*, an interpretation he has learned from the theological patrimony of the early church: "Christ then is the Rock upon which the house is built which will stay stable even when it suffers from the winds and floods of temptations."[66]

---

65. Cf. Parlov 2001, 178.

66. *Christus est igitur petra, super qua domus fundata, licet uentos et flumina tentationum patiatur, stabilis tamen permanet*; De humilitate 554–55.

Chapter 7

"The Tree of the Cross"

and Other Early Christian Latin Poetry with Marulus's Marginalia

INTRODUCTION

In keeping with his theological interests and in the true spirit of humanism, Marko Marulić—Marulus, acclaimed as the "Father of Croatian Literature"—was keenly interested in Christian poetry, as a brief look into the inventory of his library shows.[1] Following the spirit of his time, Marulus turned to the early sources (*ad fontes*) and studied early Christian Latin poetry. The lay theologian showed the same interest as the contemporary monastic humanists who collected or wrote Christian poetry.[2] The genre of the biblical epic was popular in Late Antiquity.[3] Marulus showed great interest in it and thus entered into the stream of what is called the European tradition of *Sacra Poesis*.[4] According to Carl P. E. Springer, "The biblical epic represents a unique form of cultural

---

1. See MT.
2. See Posset 2005.
3. See Herzog 1975; Kartschoke 1975; Rädle 2003; Springer 2003.
4. Wehrli 1969; Novaković 2000.

expression,"[5] and as such it is more than just a biblical paraphrase. Biblical epics may be defined as "poems written in the dactylic hexameter, which owe their narrative continuity to a biblical sequence of events."[6]

Which early Christian poems stirred Marulus's special interest? We are fortunate to be able to answer this question at least partly thanks to a book from his library entitled *Poetae Christiani veteres*, discovered by Mladen Parlov in 2000.[7] It includes numerous handwritten marginal additions, including curly vertical lines, little drawings made in the margin consisting of *maniculae* ("little hands," usually with an elongated digit), and drawings of a cross on a socle. The latter in particular signal statements or references to the cross of Christ.

The *Poetae Christiani veteres* is our main source; it was printed in 1501 in Venice by Aldus Manutius, whose printer's device is found on folio 9.[8] This title comprises altogether three volumes, which were printed between 1501 and 1504. Marulus's second volume survived and is kept today at the library of the faculty of theology in Split. We know that Marulus referred to this book by the names of the first three and best-known poets represented in the second volume: *[Liber] Sedulij, Juue[n]ci et Aratoris etc* ("The Book of Sedulius, Juvencus and Arator").[9]

He bequeathed the book to Hieronymus de Papalibus, son of Lord Matheus, along with Virgil's *Opera* and another book which is listed but not extant, *Liber poetar[um] ecclesiasticor[um]* ("The Book of Ecclesiastical Poets").[10]

Of particular note is Marulus's apparent lack of interest in the three biographies that are part of the introduction of the edition on his desk: of Iuvencus from Jerome's *Illustrious Men*,[11] of Sulpicius Severus by Gennadius,[12] and of Proba (with entire passages in Greek). Marulus does not underline anything or enter any notes except at the biographical sketch of the Roman poetess Proba (f. 3, see below).

5. Springer 2003, 103.
6. Roberts 1985, 4.
7. See Parlov 2000.
8. I am grateful to the Marulianum Institute for providing the Venetian print of *Poetae Christiani Veteres* with Marulus's marginalia on DVD. The DVD displays two pages together, numbered accordingly, as the book itself has no pagination; I follow the numbering in the DVD.
9. MT, 34.
10. *Opera Virgilij, Liber poetarum ecclesiasticorum et Sedulij simul*; MT, 64.
11. Jerome had written a survey of 135 Christian writers; see Jerome and Gennadius 2000, 117–18 (on Iuvencus).
12. Gennadius and Jerome 1953, 385–402. Gennadius was a late-fifth-century priest and writer.

The extant second volume is comprised of not only works by early Christian poets, but also includes seven works by poets of the Renaissance, contemporaries of Marulus: Gregorius Tiphernus (1414–c. 1462) and "R Z," who can be identified as the poet laureate by the name Raphael Zovenzonius (Raffaele Zovenzoni, 1431–c. 1485). Why these two contemporaries are included in a volume on early Christian poets remains unclear. The second volume runs to a total of about six hundred pages including the introductions and postscripts to the various works. We have to be selective.

Here we will follow Marulus's theological interests, which he signaled by "crosses on a socle" drawn in the margins of his desk copy (see figs. 7.1, 2, 4, 5). There are four poems Marulus decorated in this way. We encounter them only in the first part of the extant volume (f. 1–146): Sedulius's *Easter Song* (*Carmen paschale*, with more than one hundred pages, f. 9–35), Iuvencus's *Poem on the Gospels* (*Evangelica historia*, of almost one hundred pages, f. 37–86), Proba's *Cento* (with about twenty pages, f. 125–36), and Pseudo-Cyprian's *Tree of the Cross* (*De ligno crucis* [*versu heroico*]), with two printed pages, f. 139–40). Whereas the first three are rather lengthy, we concentrate on the latter, by far the shortest.

Not meriting a drawing of a cross from Marulus are the following works of early Christian poets, which are only to be mentioned here: The *Historia apostolica* ("The Apostolic History") by Arator, a subdeacon probably from Liguria; the two poems by (Pseudo-)Lactantius, *De passione Domini* ("The Passion of the Lord") and *De resurrectionis dominicae dei* ("The Day of the Resurrection"); and the two poems by Pope Damasus, *De laudibus Pauli apostoli* ("In Praise of Saint Paul") and *Elegia in Hierusalem* ("Elegy on Jerusalem"). Also undeserving of Marulus's specific attention are the three contemporary Marian poems, that is, the two by Tiphernus (*Deprecatoria ad Virgniem elegia* and *Oratio ad beatissimam Virginem*) and the epigram by Zovenzonius, *Ad beatissimam Virginem*.[13] After having entered a curly vertical line toward the end of the text of "The Tree of the Cross" (f. 140), Marulus skipped the two Marian poems of Tiphernus (f. 140–41) and continued with his marginalia at the beginning of *Precatio Matutina ad omnipotentem Deum* ("Morning Prayer to God," f. 141).

Marulus appreciated Venantius Fortunatus's poetry, and freely paraphrased, in Croatian, a poem on the resurrection of Christ.[14] However, Venantius is not included in the volume of Christian poets under consideration here. It is surprising, though, that Marulus ignored Lactantius's "Passion of

---

13. Marulus's marginalia are completely absent from all of Zovenzonius's texts.

14. *Ad Felicem episcopum de pascha*; *Carm.* III, 9, *Od uskarsa Isusova*; Lučin 1992 (Marulić's paraphrase of Venantius Fortunatus).

the Lord" and Zovenzonius's two poems related to Christ's suffering and death on the cross: *In diem palmarum* ("On Palm Sunday") and *In Passione domini nostri Iesu Christi* ("The Passion of our Lord Jesus Christ"). Marulus's neglect of Lactantius's poems as observed in his Venetian collection may be explained by the fact that Marulus had a separate edition of Lactantius available in his library,[15] perhaps an edition like the Roman edition of 1474, and therefore would not have marked the poem in his Venetian edition.

To those who would like to see in Marulus a political poet, it might be disappointing that he totally disregarded Zovenzonius's poetic prayer to Christ against the Turks (*Ad Christum ut perdat Turcas* [*Carmen Saphicum Raphelis Zouenzonii poetae*]). None of Zovenzonius's poems show any traces whatsoever of Marulus's pen, nor does Damasus's "Elegy on Jerusalem." One may have expected Marulus to mark up both poems, since he himself wrote on the same themes in his *Molitva suprotiva Turkom* ("Prayer against the Turks") and *Tuženje grada Hjerozolima* ("Lament of the City of Jerusalem").[16]

MARULUS AND HIS MARGINALIA IN "THE TREE OF THE CROSS" AND OTHER POEMS

We will first take a brief look at poems or parts thereof that Marulus decorates with his rare but characteristic cross on a socle in the margins, and we shall concentrate in particular on "The Tree of the Cross." They are dealt with in chronological order of writing, not in the sequence found in the Venetian edition.

Iuvencus (First Half of the Fourth Century): "Just as Moses lifted up the serpent in the desert, so must the Son of Man be lifted up" (Evangelica historia, bk. 2, f. 53)

Around 330 AD, Iuvencus, a Spanish nobleman and priest, composed the *Evangelica historia* (or *Evangeliorum libri quattuor*)— "Poem on the Gospels." It represents the earliest effort to render the four Gospels into poetry, styled after the classical epic of Virgil's *Aeneid*. The *Evangelica historia* remains an important and fascinating witness to the reception of the Bible in the Latin West. For his efforts and his faithfulness to the scriptural narrative, Iuvencus stands at the head of the genre as the "Father of Biblical Verse" in the West. The poem was approved by Jerome in his *On Illustrious Men*

---

15. See MT, 38.
16. Both poems are included in Lučin 2007, 236–53.

and the text remained popular throughout Late Antiquity and much of the Middle Ages. In Anglo-Saxon England, it was among curricular texts in the monastic school system. Aldhelm, Bede, and Alcuin, for example, all knew and emulated the style and language of Iuvencus. Surprisingly, the *Evangelica historia* has never been translated into English.

Iuvencus coined the new christological title *Dominus lucis* ("Lord of Light") in the final verse of his opus.[17]

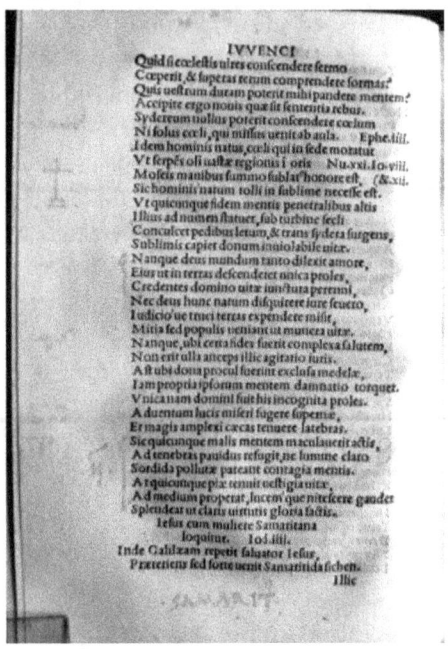

Fig. 7.1. Iuvencus, f. 53, with a cross on a socle in the left margin.

However, this exceptional title (in line 812) goes unnoticed by Marulus, who with his curly vertical line marks only three other verses[18] in the conclusion of the opus, and enters the name *Co[n]stant[inus]* into the right margin (these concluding verses, 806–12, deal with Emperor Constantine. Elsewhere, for instance, during his Scripture studies, Marulus shows a great interest in Emperor Constantine). Marulus enters the marginal note

17. See Jacques Fontaine 1984, 131–41.

18. His curly vertical line refers to the lines in italic below:

Haec mihi pax Christi tribuit, pax haec mihi secli, Quam fouet indulgens terrae regnator apertae Constantinus, adest cui gratia digna merenti Qui solus regum sacri sibi nominis horret *Imponi pondus, quo iustis dignior actis.*

Constantin[us] and draws a little cross on a socle in the margin of folio 254 of his *Biblia Latina* (vol. 4, New Testament).[19]

It concerns the comment on Rev 7 by the medieval Franciscan exegete Nicholas of Lyra, who identified one of the "angels" of Rev 7 as the Emperor Constantine. On his march on Rome, Constantine had a vision of the cross of Christ and heard the promise that he would be victorious "in this cross" and that he therefore ordered that the "sign of the cross" be depicted on all military banners.[20]

At verse 216, *Idem hominis natus, coeli qui in sede moratur* ("also the Son of Man, who is seated in heaven"), Marulus draws a cross on a socle into the left margin, but there is no explicit mention of the cross of Christ in the text. *Hominis natus* is the poetic version of *filius hominis*, and this initial verse is the paraphrase of John 3:13: *Filius hominis qui est in caelo*. It is not immediately clear why Marulus draws a cross at this point. However, the editor of Iuvencus's text, as the *editio princeps*, provided clues by printing the biblical cross-references *Nu. xxi. Io viii & xii* as marginal notes. They point, first, to the biblical book of Numbers, chapter 21, with the story of Moses raising the serpent: *Ut serpens olim uaste regionis i[n] oris [regionibus in desertis]* (line 217). Secondly, the editor refers to the Gospel of John, chapters 8 and 12. However, the foil is John 3 with Nicodemus's interview of Christ.[21] Christ says to him, "And just as Moses lifted up the serpent in the desert, so must the Son of Man be lifted up, so that everyone who believes in him may have eternal life" (vv. 14–15). The editor had referred to John 3 on the previous page where Nicodemus is being introduced. Evidently Marulus immediately recognizes the Christ typology contained in the image of Moses lifting up the serpent. "Typology" usually refers to a method of reading Christian significance into a person or event in the Old Testament by seeing them as types of Christ. Marulus does not need the explicit mention of the cross in order to see the christological implication of the verse. His proper reaction, therefore, is to draw the cross on a socle in the margin near the lines about the visual sign of Moses raising the serpent, which the poet has paraphrased in this way:

> As Moses raised the serpent
> with his own hands in the desert
> so must the Son of Man be lifted up so that everyone who looks at it

19. See MM, 190–91.

> *Aeternam capiat diuina in secula uitam*
> *Per dominum lucis Christum, qui in secula regnat.* (806–12, folio 86)

20. Lyra's *Postilla* in Marulus's *Biblia Latina*, vol. 4 reads as follows: *Et vidi alteru[m] angelum i[d est] imperatorem constantinu[m]* . . . ; f. 254.

21. Heinsdorff 2003, 169–83.

> will be healed from the snake bites
> as all who believe in him, will not die under the turbulence of the world,
> but will trample his enemy to death and will rise beyond the stars
> to receive the unassailable gift of life.²²

The "unassailable gift of life" (*donum inuiolabile uitae*) is eternal life with God "beyond the stars" (*trans sydera*). The next three lines represent the poetic rendering of John 3:16:

> For God so loved the world that he gave his only Son
> so that everyone who believes in him
> might not perish but might have eternal life.²³

Those biblical verses are marked by Marulus's vertical line in the margin. The Johannine expression *Filius suus unigenitus* ("His only Son") is rendered by Iuvencus with *unica proles*:

> For God so loved the world
> that his only Son descended onto the earth
> to give eternal life to those who are united with the Lord.²⁴

Proba (Second Half of the Fourth Century): The Hour of Christ's Crucifixion (Cento, f. 135)

In his copy of *Poetae Christiani veteres*, Marulus finds the following spelling: *Probae Falconiae* [sic] *centronis* [sic] *clarissimae foeminae excerptum e Maronis carminibus ad testimonium Veteris Novique Testamenti opusculum*. She is known as Faltonia Betitia Proba and her poem is usually called *Cento*

---

22. Translation:

> *Ut serpens olim uaste regionis i[n] oris [regionibus in desertis]*
> *Moseis manibus summo sublatur honore est*
> *Sic hominis natum tolli in sublime necesse est.*
> *Vt quicunque fidem mentis penetralibus altis*
> *Illius ad numen statuet, sub turbine secli Conculcet pedibus letum,*
> *& trans sydera surgens Sublimis capiet donum*
> *inuiolabile uitae.*

23. Vulgate: *sic enim dilexit Deus mundum ut Filium suum unigenitum daret ut omnis qui credit in eum non pereat sed habeat vitam aeternam*

24. Translation:

> *Nanque deus mundum tanto dilexit amore,*
> *Eius ut in terras descenderet unica proles,*
> *Credentes domino uitae iuncture perenni . . .*

Vergilianus de laudibus Christi.²⁵ She was the wife of Adalphius, the prefect of Rome in 351, as we learn from the short biography at the beginning of the volume. Also included is an explanation of what a *cento* (*zento*) is (f. 3-4), since her poem is composed in the form of a *cento* (*zento*), that is, a composition or patchwork created by piecing together lines from a well-known author. Marulus enters only the one note, *Cento*, into the margin (f. 3) along with the curly vertical line at the locus where the explanation of *cento* is given. Proba was well known in Marulus's time, as we may deduce from her biography by the contemporary Hermann Schedel (1440–1514) in his *Chronicle of the World* (*Nuremberg Chronicle*), saying that the "housewife" of the Roman senator composed this poem in such a fine way that the reader may very well believe that "Virgil was an evangelist."²⁶

Proba is, after all, also the only female writer of early orthodox Christianity who has an entire work still extant.²⁷

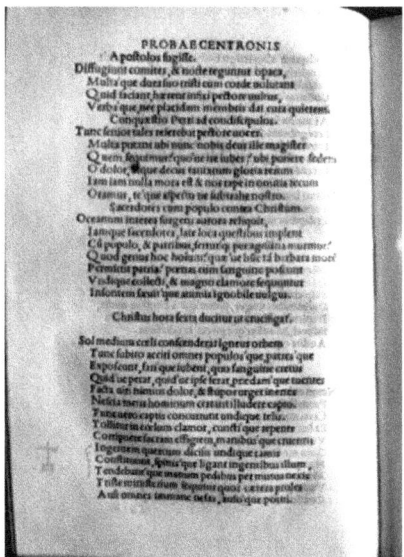

Fig. 7.2. Proba (f. 135), with a cross on a socle in the lower left margin.

25. On Proba, see Clark and Hatch 1981; Machaffie 2008; Ziolkowski and Putnam 2008, 475–80.

26. The German version on Proba in Schedel: "*Proba gar ein redlichs weib adelphi des römischen rathherren hawßfraw hat mit emsigem fleiss in den geticht virgilij des poeten alle die histori so im alten vnd newen gesetz bis zu sendung des hailigen gaists gelesen werden. also hüpschlich vnd zierlich zusamen gebracht. das der. der solcher zusamensetzung mit wol bericht.*" Schedel also included a picture of her on the same page with Saint Augustine and his mother Monica (f. CXXXVIr; see fig. 7.5).

27. See Clark and Hatch 1981, 98.

The poem, which may date from between 350 to 390, tells the history of salvation from creation to the life of Christ. As has been noted, there are no marginal notes of significance from Marulus's pen in most of the opus, but we do encounter his rare drawing of a cross on a socle with a short curly vertical line on folio 135, at lines 615–18. The "sacred symbol" (*sacram effigiem*) of line 615, which to Marulus is a reference to Christ's cross, must have triggered his drawing of the cross into the margin of the following verses:

> Resentment mixed with apathy urged on
> The idle men who watched his famous deeds—Man's mind is
> ignorant—and they vied among Themselves to mock their captive. Then in fact, Grabbing weapons from everywhere, they
> rushed him. Shouts rang to heaven, and all impulsively
> Laid hands upon the sacred symbol, and
> With bloody hands set up a massive oak,
> Its branches lopped away all around, and bound
> Him with great coils. Then they stretched his hands, Made
> one foot fixed upon the other—a sad attendance—The leaders
> whom the rest, the young men, followed.[28]

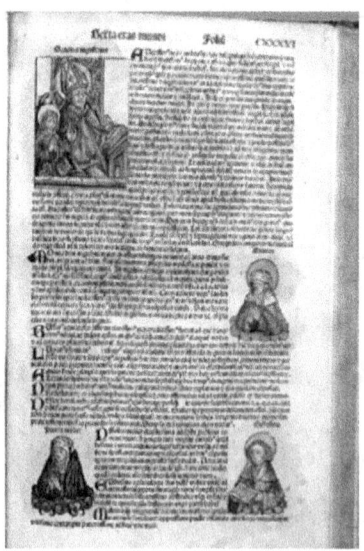

Fig. 7.3. Schedel's *Chronicle of the World* (f. 136), with Proba (without a halo) in the lower left corner, St. Augustine at the top of the page, St. Monica in the middle, and St. Eufrosina in the lower right corner.

28. Clark and Hatch 1981, 85.

There are a few instances in the Latin text of Marulus's edition that may be printing mistakes, but Marulus makes no reference or annotations to them: in 617, *spinis* ("with thorns") should be *spiris* ("with coils"); editors also prefer the relative pronoun *illum* instead of *ipsum*; in 618, it makes more sense to have the plural *manus* instead of the singular *manum* which is found in Marulus's text for the line: "Then they stretched his hands."

615 Corripuere sacram effigiem manibusque cruentis
616 Ingentem quercum dicisis undique ramis
617 Constituunt spinisque [spirisque] ligant ingentibus illum [ipsum]
618 Tendebantque manum [manus] pedibus per mutua nexis
619 Triste ministerium sequitur quos caetera proles
620 Ausi omnes immane nefas, ausoque potiti.

Marulus does not mark Proba's verse 623, on which later theologians have commented because it pertains to an angry, crucified Christ who vows to wreak vengeance on his enemies:

> Some day, for wrongs committed, you will pay
> With punishment unlike this one to me.[29]

Although, generally speaking, Proba contributed to the evangelization of her culture,[30] Marulus may have felt that her image of a vengeful Christ was not quite appropriate and therefore ignored these conspicuous words. Marulus's image of Christ is that of savior, not avenger. This may be a case in which the omission of a marginal note offers a clue to Marulus's orthodox Christology; it could have been, of course, that Marulus simply wasn't interested in those verses—for whatever reason.

Sedulius (Fifth Century): The Worldwide Significance of the Cross of Christ (Easter Song, bk. 4, f. 31)

Whereas the table of contents on folio 1 indicates the *Elegia* as that of Sedulius, the headline for the text itself says otherwise, attributing it to Turtius Ruffus (f. 35), a Roman consul in 495.[31] Marulus's abbreviations in Sedulius's *Carmen paschale* ("Easter Song"), familiar to us from his entries in his *Biblia Latina*,[32] include four *XCs* (Christograms, f. 14, 15, 23, and 31; references to

---

29. [623] *Post mihi non simili poena commissa luetis.*
30. See Meconi 2004.
31. See Springer 1988, 25.
32. See Posset 2010, 156; MM.

Christ) and the drawing of a cross on a socle which appears on folio 31 of the fourth book of the *Carmen paschale*.[33]

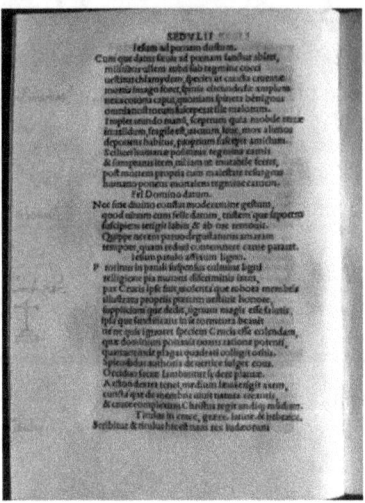

Fig. 7.4. Sedulius (f. 31) with a cross on a socle in the left margin.

The *Carmen paschale* came into existence at about 425 AD. It contains five books and two thousand lines of Latin hexameter. The poem is a versification of the Gospels in imitation of the earlier *Evangelica historia* of Iuvencus (c. 330). One may take issue with a modern interpreter's opinion that Sedulius's verses are "based on the account given in Matthew 27:27–51, supplemented by the details from Luke 23:39–43,"[34] because in fact Sedulius explicitly uses also John's Gospel, which alone notes the trilingual inscription on Christ's cross—"written in Hebrew, Latin, and Greek" (John 19:20). Sedulius is a much freer versifier of the Bible, however.

At the verse *Protinus in patuli suspensus culmine ligni* ("Then at once he was hung high on the spreading cross"), Marulus draws his cross on a socle (and his curly vertical line) in order to point out, in relation to the entire passage, the worldwide significance of the cross of Christ. The passage reads as follows:

> Then at once he was hung high on the spreading cross, Transforming the anger of the crisis by means of loving devotion. He himself was the peace of the cross and illuminating the violent

---

33. Sedulius's *Carmen paschale* has been translated by Sigerson 1922.
34. White 2000, 109.

> Forces with his own limbs he clothed the punishment with honor, Giving a sign that it was not a punishment but salvation,
> And sanctifying the tortures he suffered, he blessed them Everyone should know that the shape of the cross is to be revered For it bore our Lord in his triumph and by a powerful logic
> It brings together the four corners of the world.
> The radiant East shines forth from the creator's head, His holy feet are licked by the sun setting in the West,
> His right hand holds the North, his left supports the centre of the sky;
> The whole of Nature lives from the creator's limbs
> And Christ rules throughout the world, encompassed by the cross. (182–195)[35]

Sedulius continues his poem with the inscription on top of the cross (John 19:20). Marulus writes—as a reminder—the notion *Titulus* into the margin for the following verses:

> On it a heading also was inscribed: "This is the King of the Jews" So that nothing would lack divinity; for heaven arranged
> That this was recorded in Hebrew, in Latin and in Greek.
> Thus the one faith teaches us to call on the one King three times.
> Lots were thrown for the clothes they stripped from him
> So the sacred robe remaining whole might warn against schism from Christ. (196–201)[36]

In contrast to the *Easter Song*, there are no marginalia from Marulus's pen on Sedulius's *Hymnus de Christo succincte ab Incarnatione usque ad Ascensionem*. This is somewhat surprising for a text from which a man like Martin Luther in his old age quotes: "The blessed author of the world / Put on a lowly servant's form." Luther made this quotation from the second stanza thesis 36 of the disputation "On the Divinity and Humanity of Christ" (February 28, 1540), describing this as a saying of the "most Christian poet Sedulius."[37]

---

35. White 2000, 110.

36. White 2000, 110.

37. Thesis 36, *Sedulius poeta christianissimus canit: Beatus auctor seculi servile corpus induit*; WA 39.2:95, lines 11–12.

Caecilius Cyprianus Episcopus Carthaginensis (Pseudo-Cyprian; Fifth Century?): "The Tree of the Cross" (*De ligno crucis [versu heroico]*, f. 139–40v)

The Venetian edition of *Poetae Christiani veteres* from 1501 (*editio princeps*) in Marulus's library attributes the poem to Bishop Cyprian of Carthage (c. 200–258), following the eighth-century Benedictine monk and historian Paulus Diaconus (c. 720–799), but this attribution is false.[38] Other poems known under Cyprian's name are now, however, qualified as being by "Cyprian the Poet" or "Cyprian of Gaul."[39] The real author of "The Tree of the Cross" is unknown. In the past, the poem had been variously attributed also to Tertullian[40] or to Caius Marius Victorinus (fourth century, also known as the "African Victorinus" [*Victorinus Afer*]).[41] The poem should also not be confused with the similarly titled work by the thirteenth-century Franciscan friar Bonaventure, *De ligno vitae* ("The Tree of Life"). The poem under consideration here has been known also under the title *De Pascha* ("On Easter").

"The Tree of the Cross" is pseudepigraphic, a notion that need not be taken in a derogatory or offensive sense. From antiquity on, numerous works have been handed down to us under assumed names.

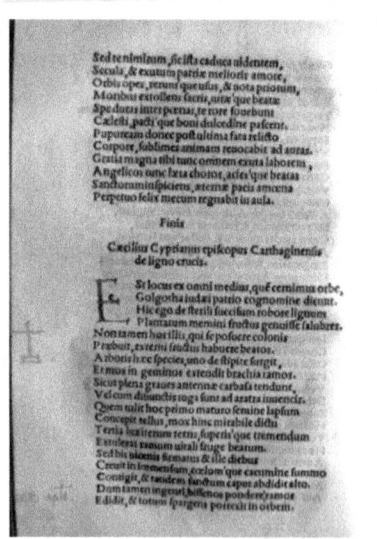

Fig. 7.5. Pseudo-Cyprian, f. 139, with a cross on a socle in the left margin.

38. See Roncoroni 1976; Schwind 1989.
39. See White 2000, 99.
40. See *Patrologia Latina* 2:1113–14.
41. White 2000, 136.

Pseudepigraphy then was a popular literary option. Textbooks contained samples of pseudepigraphy. In a collection of thirteen epistles under the name of Plato, for instance, not all are authentic. In the Old Testament, the books of Moses are pseudepigrapha. Not all psalms are written by David. There are letters under the name of Saint Paul that were not written by the apostle, such as a third letter to the Corinthians or the correspondence between Paul and Seneca.[42] In this context it is not surprising that poems were composed in the name of famous authors, such as "The Tree of the Cross" by Pseudo-Cyprian. Pseudepigraphical writings of that time were not meant to deceive.[43]

Regardless of whether it is pseudepigraphy or not, Marulus marks the poem because it relates to the mystery of the cross. The "Tree of Life" from Gen 2:9 gains its relevance through its symbolic alignment with the tree of the cross on which Christ died. Marulus liked this kind of typological thinking. The poem is the result of early Christian theology, which embraced the principle that everything revealed by God in the Old Testament is only made known to us because of its relevance to the coming event of salvation.[44] It is from this early Christian way of thinking that the Old Testament is understood as a single, vast parable in which the future hides itself. Simultaneously, though, the hidden mystery is made known to those who have understanding through faith. This idea is expressed in the last verse of Pseudo-Cyprian's poem: "This is the tree that is life to all who believe. Amen."

The poem[45] is important to Marulus, as he draws his cross on a socle into the margin at the beginning of the poem.

> There is a place, we believe, at the centre of the world, Called Golgotha by the Jews in their native tongue. Here was planted a tree cut from a barren stump:
> This tree, I remember hearing, produced wholesome fruits, But it did not bear these fruits for those who had settled there; It was foreigners who picked these lovely fruits.
> This is what the tree looked like: it rose from a single stem And then extended its arms into two branches[.] (1–8)

Marulus does not pick up on the contrast between those who "settled" there, that is, the Jews, and the "foreigners" (*externi*), the Christians of pagan

---

42. See Schelkle 1964, 121–23.

43. By making use of the names of renowned figures from the past, later writers were not primarily claiming literary authorship. They attempted to continue within an authoritative tradition; see Brashler 2008.

44. See Rahner 1963, 59–62 (with a brief mention of the poem of Pseudo-Cyprian).

45. White 2000, 137–39. The last few lines are inadvertently not translated.

origin. Only the next three lines are marked by Marulus's marginal curly vertical line. It is hard to tell what prompted him to do that. He may have simply liked the imagery familiar to him from living by the sea, namely the sail yards ("yardarms; *antennae*) or perhaps he just appreciated the poetry, which continues as follows:

> [And then extended its arms into two branches]
> Just like heavy yardarms on which billowing sails are stretched
> Or like the yoke beneath which two oxen are put to the plough.
> The shoot that sprung from the first ripe seed
> Germinated in the earth and then, miraculously
> On the third day it produced a branch once more,
> Terrifying to the earth and to those above, but rich in life-giving fruit. (8–14)

"On the third day" (*Tertia*) is a reference to the resurrection of Christ, when a new branch started to grow and "produce a branch rich in life-giving fruit" (*Extulerat ramum uitale fruge beatum*). However, those last three lines are not marked by Marulus's pen.

The poem continues with a description of the time and events after Easter, and Christ's ascension into heaven. The latter is poetically described in terms of Christ hiding his "sacred head on high." The twelve apostles are the "twelve branches" (*bisseni rami*, from Latin *bisextus*, two times six) that spread over the whole world. At this line, Marulus enters his note "Twelve Apostles" (*XII ap[osto]li*) in the margin. The tree with the "twelve branches" may be an allusion to and adaptation of the "tree of life that produces fruit twelve times a year" from Rev 22:2. When reading the book of Revelation in his *Biblia Latina*, Marulus was impressed by this image: he entered his Christogram (*XC*) in the margin (f. 267 [167]). The title of Pseudo-Cyprian's poem, and the entire poem itself, with the imagery of the tree by the running waters, may have been inspired not only by Rev 22 on the "life-giving water" and the "tree of life," but also by the vision of the "wonderful stream" from Ezek 47:1–12. The "wonderful stream" issues from the threshold of the temple in Jerusalem. Along its banks many trees are growing that bear fresh fruit forever:

> But over the next forty days it increased in strength,
> Growing into a huge tree which touched the heavens
> With its topmost branches and then hid its sacred head on high.
> In the mean time it produced twelve branches of enormous
> Weight and stretched forth, spreading them over the whole world:
> They were to bring nourishment and eternal life to all
> The nations and to teach that death can die. (15–21)

Marulus marks the following three verses with another curly vertical line in the left margin, and writes the word "Pentecost" in the right margin by the verse *Expletis etiam mox quinquaginta diebus* ("And soon fifty days had passed"). The translator Carolinne White rendered it incorrectly as "And then after a further fifty days had passed."[46] A better rendering takes this line not as an additional fifty days, but as the fifty days after Passover that leads to Pentecost with the coming of the Holy Spirit, as the poet speaks of the "breeze of the heavenly spirit":

> And soon fifty days had passed
> From its very top the tree caused a draught of divine nectar
> To flow into its branches, a breeze of the heaven spirit.
> All over the tree the leaves were dripping with sweet dew. (22–25)

For the following verse, which contains the Latin *fons* ("spring"), Marulus enters *bap*[*tismus*] ("baptism") in the right margin, as he interprets the poet's *fons* as a metaphor of the water of baptism with which "a variety of flowers" and "of colors" are being baptized, that is, persons from every nation and walk of life:

> And look! Beneath the branches' shady cover
> There was a spring, with waters bright and clear
> For there was nothing there to disturb the calm. Around it in the grass
> A variety of flowers shone forth in bright colors.
> Around this spring countless races and peoples gathered, Of different stock, sex, age and rank,
> Married and unmarried, widows, young married women, Babies, children and men, both young and old. (26–33)

When Marulus arrives at the next verses, he draws two curly vertical lines in the left margin concerning the following words about washing away the filth of the former, sinful life in the "holy spring" (*pius fons*). Those who wish to pick the fruit of the tree must cleanse themselves before they may eat of the fruit, that is, obtain salvation. Marulus then marks the following three verses with his curly vertical line:

> When they saw the branches here bending down, under the weight
> Of many sorts of fruit, they gleefully reached out with greedy hands
> To touch the fruits dripping with heavenly nectar. (34–36)

Marulus skips the next three Latin lines, which depict the contrast between the former life and the life redeemed in baptism (37–39). A second

---

46. White 2000, 137, line 22.

curly vertical line starts at the verse *Ergo diu circum spaciantes gramine molli* and extends to the two following verses:

> And so they strolled around on the soft grass for some time
> And looked up at the fruits hanging from the tall tree. If they are shells that fell from those branches
> And the sweet greenery dripping with plenty of nectar,
> Then they were overcome with a desire to pick the real fruit. (40–44)

The last two lines and the subsequent passage do not warrant any of Marulus's marginalia. The verses deal with those who have lapsed ("slipping back," *relapsi*) after having been baptized by the "holy waters" (*sanctos fontes*) and also deal with penance, which helps them "find their sick minds restored" (*Saepe quidem multi renovatis mentibus aegros restituere animos*). Here is the poetic version of the religious-historical vicissitudes of the early church (the quotation is given here to draw attention not only to what Marulus marked with marginalia, but also to what he did not find remarkable):

> And when their mouths first experienced the heavenly taste,
> Their minds were transformed and their greedy impulses Began to disappear; by the sweet taste they knew the man. We have seen that an unusual taste or poison of gall
> Mixed with honey causes annoyance in many:
> They rejected what tasted good because they were confused
> And did not like what they had eagerly grabbed at,
> Finally spitting out the taste of what they had for long drunk unwisely.
> But it often happens that many, once their thoughts are set to rights,
> Find their sick minds restored and achieve what they denied
> Was possible and so obtain the fruits of their labors. Many, too, having dared to touch the sacred waters, Have suddenly departed, slipping back again
> To roll around in the same mixture of mud and filth.
> But others, faithfully carrying the truth within them, receive it
> With their whole soul and store it deep in their hearts. (45–60)

Marulus's last curly vertical line in the left margin marks the following first three Latin verses about the seventh day, when those who can approach the "sacred springs" (*sacros fontes*) place themselves "by the waves" (*ad undas*):

> And so the seventh day sets those who can approach
> The sacred spring beside the waters they longed for,

And they dip their bodies that have been fasting. (61–63)

The English edition offers the following incomplete ending of the poem:

> Only so do they rid themselves of the filth of their thoughts And
> the stains of their former life, bringing back from death Souls
> that are pure and shining, destined for heaven's light. (64–66)

This edition omitted, presumably inadvertently, the last three Latin lines (67–69) that end with "Amen" and that speak of the "tree" that is "life to all who believe" (*Hoc lignum uita est* [not: that is the "tree of life"!]):

> From here we go to the branches and to the sweeter fruits of salvation
> From there through the branches of the tall tree toward heaven. This is
> the tree that is life to all who believe. Amen.[47]

Marulus may have had this poem in mind when he wrote about the triumph of the cross in his *Humility and Glory of Christ*. The fruit of this tree is nothing but "eternal life" for those who believe in Christ the Lord. "The cross thus is the tree of life to the one who understands."[48]

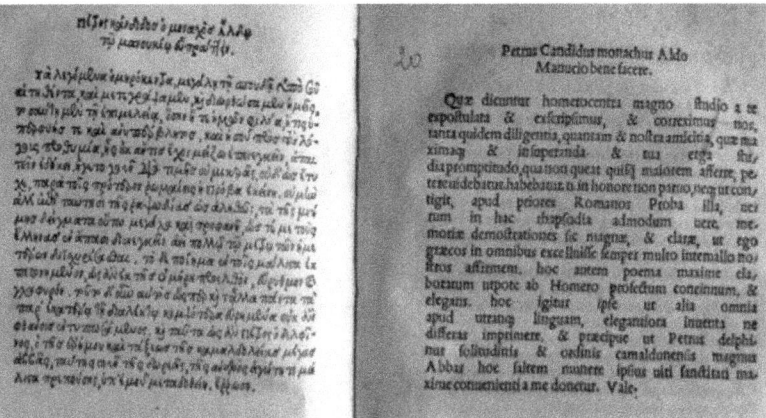

Fig. 7.6. Preface by Monk Petrus Candidus to Aldus Manutius, in Greek and Latin on facing pages (without any marginalia by Marulus).

---

47. My translation of the following Latin text:

    Hinc iter ad ramos, & dulcia poma salutis
    Inde iter ad caelum per ramos arboris altae.
    Hoc lignum uita est cunctis credentibus Amen. (67–69)

48. *Crux ergo lignum uitę est ei, qui apprehenderit illam*; *De humilitate*, p. 683.

CONCLUSION

Marulus's marginalia indicate that he was interested in the theological content of Christian poetry. He was selective in what he annotated. None of the Marian poems included in the edition he had at hand prompted him to enter any marginalia. Nor does the *anti-Turcica* poem by the poet laureate Zovenzonius seem to have impressed him, as there are no annotations on the respective pages. Marulus read much of the poetry Aldus Manutius had incorporated into his second volume of *Poetae*. Perhaps he read it all, but did not annotate everything. His marginalia emerge from a Christ-centered spiritual point of view, as he took his time to draw crosses on a socle in the margins of those poems that he apparently found to his liking.

Chapter 8

The Turks

Marulus on Christian-Muslim Relations

By Franz Posset and Bratislav Lučin with the assistance of Branko Jozić

BIOGRAPHY

Marko Marulić, or Marcus Marulus, to use his humanist name, was born on August 18, 1450 in Split, and died there on January 5, 1524.[1] He came from a noble family whose Croat surname was Pečenić or Pecinić; in the fifteenth century they had begun calling themselves Marulus or de Marulis. Split had been under the rule of the Republic of Venice since 1420 but by Marulus's time it was in imminent danger from the Turks. Little is known about Marulus's life, and even the little information that has reached us is sometimes unreliable: his *curriculum artis* is far better known than his *curriculum vitae*.

In the 1460s, Marulus attended the lay-led humanist school in his hometown, where his teachers were the Italian humanists Tydeus Acciarinus (Tideo Acciarini), Colla Firmianus (Nicola da Capua), and Hieronymus Genesius (Ienesius) Picentinus. Nothing is known about his further education, if he received any; the assumption that he studied in Padua cannot be

---

1. Božićević, *Vita Marci Maruli*, 30, 42.

confirmed. He may have had some training in law, because he performed municipal duties as examiner and authenticator of notarial documents, judge, plea bargainer, advocate in lawsuits, testifier, and prosecutor. In theology, he was most probably self-taught. From his works and from the list of books in his library, it is clear that he had a wide knowledge of the Bible and classical and patristic literature, and that he read the works of his contemporaries in Latin as well as in the Croatian and Italian vernaculars. In his forties, he gradually retired from public life and dedicated himself to study. He remained in Split, traveling occasionally to Venice (to trade) and perhaps to Rome (to celebrate the Jubilee year 1500). For about two years (c. 1509–11) he lived alone in Nečujam bay on the island of Šolta. When he was in his seventies the death of one his brothers, Valerius, compelled him to look after his family estate, but till then his life was mostly devoted to writing. He was buried in the Church of St. Francis in his hometown.

Marulus's view of Christian-Muslim relations can be understood only if the historical situation of Split around 1500 is taken into consideration. He must have been aware of the Ottoman threat from his early youth: the fall of Constantinople in 1453 was followed by the fall of Bosnia in 1463 and of Herzegovina in 1482; in 1493 the Croatian army was defeated at the Battle of Krbava Field. The unstoppable advance of the Turks at the end of the fifteenth century posed an imminent military danger to communities on the Adriatic, while the loss of their territories resulted in the decline of their economic and demographic potential: in 1467, 1468, and in 1469 the Ottoman incursions reached the hinterland of the Venetian-held towns of Zadar and Šibenik; the raids were repeated in 1471 and 1472, including into the hinterland of Split; and from this period, on attacks and plundering by Ottoman troops became a constant threat to Marulus's native city, both during his lifetime and for almost two centuries after his death.

The outbreak of the Second Ottoman-Venetian War (1499–1503) brought new hardships and intensified clashes between the Ottoman Empire and the Republic of Venice for control of the lands on the Aegean, Ionian, and the Adriatic Seas. Marulus was deeply concerned not only about the Ottoman advance in the vicinity of his hometown and in Dalmatia, but also about the fate of the region of Slavonia and the city of Zagreb.[2] In his seventy-first year he was shaken by the news that Belgrade had been captured.[3]

Marulus was a fervent reader of classical authors, and he became the center of what may be called the humanist *Sodalitas Spalatensis*. As a lay theologian and poet, he became one of the great figures of Renaissance

2. MR, 265.
3. MR, 97.

humanism and the preceptor of Croatia. In 1901, at the celebrations to mark the four-hundredth anniversary of his biblical and Virgilian epic *Iudit* (first published in Venice in 1521), he was given the honorary title "Father of Croatian Literature." The issue of whether this poem was a political allegory about his times remains highly controversial to this day.

He was also a strong advocate of the Catholic faith, with a Christ-centered spirituality,[4] and was heavily influenced by the *Devotio Moderna*, whose most influential text, *De imitatione Christi*, he translated into Croatian. He fits well into the historical context of late medieval "theology-for-piety". He was probably a self-taught theologian who constantly worked on his collection of excerpts from the Bible, classical authors and early Christian and humanist writers, known as his *Repertorium*.

Marulus's *Instruction on How to Lead a Virtuous Life Based on the Examples of the Saints* established his fame throughout Europe, as it was translated into Italian, German, Portuguese, French, and Czech. This work hints at the wars in Europe, but no direct mention is made of the Turks, or *Mahumetani* as he called them (*De institutione* 6.1). In his "sermon" of 1520–1521, titled *The Last Judgment of Christ*, he points out the Turkish threat and chastises the clergy for not doing enough to keep Christians from becoming *Mahumetani*.

Marulus's view of the Turks was shaped decisively by reports about the atrocities committed by the Ottomans in the Balkans. He became a voice for the victims, and the "existential fear" he expressed[5] permeates his entire work. At the time of the Second Ottoman-Venetian War, when the Venetian fleet was destroyed, he apparently wrote a short historical and philosophical tract in Italian about the Turkish threat, but the manuscript is lost. In a letter to Jerolim Cipiko (died ca. 1525) in 1501, detailed information is included about three hundred Turks defeating five hundred well-armed Croatian and Hungarian horsemen.[6] Following the death of the Croatian leader Žarko Dražojević (1438–1508) fighting the Turks, he wrote the *Epitaphium Xarci Draxoeuii*. Around 1517, he felt compelled to compose his "Lament of the City of Jerusalem." Identifying the Ottoman advance and wars among Christian nations as signs that the end of the world was near, Marulus issued a call to resist the *Mahumetani*, which was included in his lengthy sermon, *The Last Judgment of Christ*. He also composed an open letter to the pope (1522) about the calamities of his time, and included a call for Christian unity against the common enemy. In late November or early December of

4. Parlov 1997.
5. Novaković 1994.
6. MR, 264–65.

1523, he wrote a poem for the newly elected Pope Clement VII, hinting at the wounds caused by the Turkish attacks.

When speaking about Muslims, Marulus frequently uses the term *secta* ("sect," which he usually equates with *heresis*, "religious heresy"). Here he seems to be influenced by his reading of the late medieval biblical commentaries in his *Biblia Latina*, noting in the margin of his edition phrases such as *secta Machometi, secta Sarracenica, error Machometanorum, lex Machometi alcoranus* and the name Sergius, the monk who was believed to have taught Muḥammad.[7] When the commentator on the *Biblia Latina* mentions names of known heretics from church history, such as Arius and Pelagius, he also includes Muḥammad, which Marulus duly notes (he has a similar classification in his *Euangelistarium* 6.10), raising the possibility that he understood Islam as a heretical Christian sect. He certainly accepts the label of heretic for "Jews and Saracens," as is shown by the two notes he extracted from Nicholas of Lyra's comments on 1 Cor 15 in the *Biblia Latina*. However, in his own works Marulus views the Turks primarily as "damned pagans," unrelated to Christianity.

Marulus was a giant in Croatian literary circles, and many other authors in the sixteenth century were influenced by his works, particularly two who wrote on Islamic themes. The first was Brne Karnarutić (c. 1515–73) from Zadar, whose *Vazetje Sigeta grada* ("The Capture of the Town of Szigetvár"), written between 1568 and 1572, is the first Croatian historical epic. In it Karnarutić, with important themes borrowed from Marulus's *Judita*, describes the courageous defence of Szigetvár against the Ottomans in 1566 and the heroic death of Nikola Šubić Zrinski. The second, Petar Zoranić (1508–after 1569), who was from Zadar, is most important as the author of *Planine*,[8] the first Croatian language novel, which he wrote in 1538. In this he refers to wolves attacking from the east, in allusion to the danger of attacks on Croatia by the Ottomans.

MAIN SOURCES OF INFORMATION

Primary

Božićević, F. *Život Marka Marulića Splićanina* [*Vita Marci Maruli Spalatensis*]. Translated and edited by Bratislav Lučin. Split: Marulianum, 2007.
Glavičić, Branimir, and Bratislav Lučin, eds. *Marci Maruli Opera omnia*. Vols. 1–16 edited by Glavičić, vols. 17– edited by Lučin. Split: Književni Krug, 1988–.

---

7. See MM, Appendix V.
8. See Zoranić 1964.

Posset, F. *Marcus Marulus and the Biblia Latina of 1489: An Approach to His Biblical Hermeneutics*. Cologne: Böhlaus, 2013. Accompanied by a DVD of the entire *Biblia Latina* with Marulus's *marginalia*.

Secondary

Colloquia Maruliana, an annual publication devoted to Marulus and Croatian Renaissance humanism. http://hrcak.srce.hr/index.php?show=casopis&id_casopis=43&lang=en.

Banić-Pajnić, E. "Marulić, Marko." In *Encyclopedia of Renaissance Philosophy*, edited by M. Sgarbi. Cham: Springer International, 2014.

Béné, C. Études *maruliennes: Le rayonnement européen de l'oeuvre de Marc Marule de Split*. Zagreb: Erasmus Naklada; Split: Marulianum, 1998.

———. «Marc Marule de Split, un humaniste exemplaire.» *Réforme, Humanisme, Renaissance* 60 (2005) 51–56.

———. «Marule de Split (Marc) (1450–1524).» In *Centuriae Latinae: Cent une figures humanistes de la Renaissance aux Lumières*, edited by C. Nativel, 2:511–21. Geneva: Librairie Droz, 2006.

Borsetto, L., ed. *Italia-Slavia tra Quattro e Cinquecento: Marko Marulić umanista croato nel contesto storico-letterario dell'Italia e di Padova. Atti della Giornata di Studio tenutasi presso l'Università di Padova il 7 dicembre 2001*. Alessandria: Edizioni dell'Orso, 2004.

Budiša, D. "Humanism in Croatia." In *Renaissance Humanism: Foundations, Form and Legacy*, edited by A. Rabil Jr., 2:265–92. Philadelphia: University of Pennsylvania Press, 1988.

Dolibić, M., ed. *Marulić: Humaniste européen. Revue trimestrielle par l'Association Almae Matris Croaticae Alumni* (special issue) 1/2. Paris: L'Association Almae Matris Croaticae Alumni, 1997.

Erdmann, E. von. „Marko Marulić in den Religionskonflikten der Deutschen Länder des 16. Jahrhunderts." *CM* 20 (2011) 177–93.

Frangeš, I. *Geschichte der kroatischen Literatur: Von den Anfängen bis zur Gegenwart*. Cologne: Böhlau, 1995. See pp. 17–31, 32–66, 801–5.

Gálvez, F. J. J., trans. *Studia Croatica* 145. Buenos Aires, 2002. Studies on Marulus in Spanish, with Spanish translations of passages from Marulus's works.

Jelčić, D., ed. *Zbornik radova o Marku Maruliću: U povodu 550. obljetnice rođenja i 500. obljetnice njegove Judite 1450.-1501.-2001* [*Collected Papers on Marko Marulić: In Celebration of the 550th Anniversary of His Birth and the 500th Anniversary of the Birth of His Judita, 1450-1501-2001*]. Zagreb: Hazu, 2005.

Jozić, B., and B. Lučin, eds. *Bibliografija Marka Marulića*. Vol. 1, *Tiskana djela (1477–1997)* [*Bibliography of Marko Marulić. Vol. 1, Printed Works (1477–1997)*]. Split: Književni Krug, 1998.

Lučin, B., ed. *Dossier: Marko Marulić*. Special issue of *Most/The Bridge: A Journal of Croatian Literature* 1–4 (1999) 3–171. Selection of studies on Marulus in English translation.

———. *Iter Marulianum: Da Spalato a Venezia sulle tracce di Marko Marulić*. Rome: Viella, 2008.

———, ed. *Marko Marulić: 1450–1524*. Split: Hrvatsko-Njemačko Društvo, 2008. Croatian-German ed. translated by K. Jurčević. Spanish ed. translated by F. J. J. Gálvez, 2000.

———, ed. *The Marulić Reader*. Split: Književni Krug, Marulianum, 2007. With selected bibliography.

———. "Predgovor"; "Ljetopis Marka Marulića"; "Bibliografija: Izdanja djela Marka Marulića"; "Važnija literatura o Marku Maruliću." In *Hrvatski stihovi i proza*, edited by Bratislav Lučin, 9–101. Zagreb: Zagreb Matica Hrvatska, 2018.

Novaković, D. "Marulić and the Metaphysical Dimension of History." In *Epistola domini Marci Maruli Spalatensis ad Adrianum VI*, edited by Josip Bratulić, 43–52. Zagreb: Nacionalna i Sveučilišna Biblioteka; Split: Crkva u Svijetu, 1994.

Paolin, G. "Marulo, Marco (Marko Marulić, Marko Pečenić, Marcus Marulus Spalatensis o Dalmata)." In *Dizionario Biografico degli Italiani*, 71:406–8. Rome: Istituto della Enciclopedia Italiana, 2008.

Parlov, M. *Il mistero di Cristo: Modello di vita cristiana secondo Marko Marulic (1450–1524)*. Rome: Pontificia Universitas Gregoriana, 1997.

Paro, N. *Bibliografija Marka Marulića. Vol. 3, Radovi o Maruliću (1565–2000) [Bibliography of Marko Marulić. Vol. 3, Works on Marulić (1565–2000)]*. Biblioteka Marulianum 6. Split: Književni Krug, 2003.

Petrovich, M. B. "The Croatian Humanists: Cosmopolites or Patriots?" *Journal of Croatian Studies* 20 (1979) 17–36.

———. "Croatian Humanists and the Ottoman Peril." *Balkan Studies* 20 (1979) 257–73.

———. "Croatian Humanists and the Writing of History in the Fifteenth and Sixteenth Centuries." *Slavic Review* 37 (1978) 624–39.

Posset, F. "The Biblical Scholar in Cultural Context." In F. Posset, *Marcus Marulus and the Biblia Latina of 1489: An Approach to His Biblical Hermeneutics*, 20–40. Cologne: Böhlaus, 2013.

———. "Marulus, Marcus." In *Biographisch-Bibliographisches Kirchenlexikon*, 32:942–47. *Ergänzungen* 19. Nordhausen: Bautz, 2011. In German, with extensive bibliography.

———. "Marulus, Marcus." In *Encyclopedia of Christian Civilization*, edited by G. T. Kurian, 3:1435–36. Oxford: Oxford University Press, 2011.

Šimundža, D. *Marko Marulić, pjesnik i didaktičar*. Split: Književni Krug, Marulianum, 2017.

Slamnig, I. "Marko Marulić, Cosmopolitan and Patriot." In *Comparative Studies in Croatian Literature*, edite by M. Beker, 81–94. Zagreb: Zavod za znanost o književnosti Filozofskog Fakulteta, 1981.

Tijan, P. "Marulić, Marko.'" In *New Catholic Encyclopedia*, edited by B. L. Marthaler et al., 9:235–36. Washington, DC: Catholic University of America, 2003.

Tomasović, M. *Marco Marulić [Marcus Marulus]*. Translated from Italian by Charles Béné, translated from Croatian by Vera Miloš-Celin. Split: Književni Krug, 1966. http://www.studiacroatica.org/libros/tomasov/tomasov1.htm.

———. *Marko Marulić Marul: Monografija*. Zagreb: Erasmus Naklada; Split: Književni Krug, 1999. Croatian with summaries in English, French, German, and Italian.

———. *Marco Marulić Marulus*. Italian translation by D. Pušek. Lugano: Laghi di Plitvice, 1994.

———. "Marko Marulić Marulus: An Outstanding Contribution to European Humanism." In *Croatia and Europe II: Croatia in the Late Middle Ages and the Renaissance: A Cultural Survey*, edited by I. Supičić, 423-37. Zagreb: Skolska Knjiga, 2008.
Usmiani, M. A. "Marko Marulić (1450-1525)." *Harvard Slavic Studies* 3 (1957) 1-48.
Wallner, G. «Marcus Marulus Spalatensis humanista Croatus.» *Latinitas* 3 (2007) 277-84.

WORKS ON CHRISTIAN-MUSLIM RELATIONS

Molitva suprotiva Turkom ("A Prayer against the Turks")

Date: Between 1493 and probably 1500
Original language: Croatian

Description

This long prayer in the form of a poem of 172 lines was presumably written after the Croats were defeated at Krbava in 1493, and probably before 1500, when Marulus went on pilgrimage to Rome during the reign of Pope Alexander VI. It is addressed to "My almighty God," though it is more than a simple prayer since it includes a call to political action. The original Croatian text contains an acrostic with the first letter of each odd Croatian verse forming the Latin (!) phrase: *Solus Deus potest nos liberare de tribulatione inimicorum nostrorum Turcorum sua potentia infinita* ("God alone with his infinite power can free us from the tribulation of our enemies, the Turks").

This prayer may show some similarity in content to a prayer by the contemporary poet laureate from Trieste, Raphael Zouenzonius (Raffaele Zovenzoni, 1431-c.1485), titled *Ad Christum ut perdat Turcas* ("To Christ That He May Destroy the Turks"). Zouenzonius's prayer was the third of four poems included in the *Poetae Christiani veteres* (1502), a book in Marulus's possession. However, although Marulus entered numerous *marginalia* on other texts in that edition, he did not do so with respect to Zouenzonius's poems.

The patriotic prayer assumes an angry God, whose mercy the poet implores for the people suffering "at Turkish hands," from "Turkish might" and under the "pagan sword"; "pagans oppress us"; the Turks are "as angry as wild lions"; towns are robbed and burned, their populations captured and enslaved; girls and nuns are raped; boys are circumcised; Christian churches, crucifixes and chalices are desecrated; liturgical vestments are turned into kaftans; the Turks fight against Croats, Bosnians, Greeks, Romans, Serbs and Poles; those who do not convert to Islam are persecuted by those who disrespect "your holy faith"; the Christians are unable to resist them without divine assistance. May God "defeat all the Turks for their faithlessness"; they are the "damned ones."

> And you, who are crucified God, our Lord in heaven,
> You gave the Holy Cross to us, not to those who do not know you:
> Deliver us from sins and from the devil's hands;
> With your crucified limbs, gather the trusting folk.
> Do not let the pagans tread on us with their feet ...' (lines 155–59)

The conclusion is an invocation to the Virgin Mary asking her to intercede before her divine Son.

Significance

This is an important example of anti-Turcica literature. It (and other related texts by Marulus) differs from most other contemporary works concerning the Turkish threat, because Marulus did not write "from the detached perspective of the ... unthreatened analyst."[9] Marulus's prayer differs particularly from early German-Lutheran prayers against the Turks, as they compare the Turk to the pope.

Manuscripts

MS Zagreb, National and University Library: R 6634, f. 17r–20r. C. 1530. Title: Gospodin M. M. protiua Turchom, "Ser M. Marulus against the Turks."

Editions and Translations

Artl, I. M., ed. *Europa erlesen. Dubrovnik.* Klagenfurt: Celovec Wieser, 2001. German translation. Pp. 117–19.

Bogišić, R. *Die ältere kroatische lyrische Dichtung.* Zagreb: Društvo Knjiʐevnika Hrvatske, 1972. German translation. Pp. 18–19.

———, ed. *Leut i trublja. Antologija starije hrvatske poezije.* Zagreb: Skolska, 1971. Selections, pp. 33–34.

———, ed. *Vila Hrvatica. Hrvatsko pjesništvo humanizma i renesanse.* Zagreb: Alfa, 1998. Selections, pp. 30–32.

Bratulić, J., ed. *Hrvatska poezija humanizma i renesanse.* Vinkovci: Riječ, 2000. Selections, pp. 40–41.

---

9. Novaković 1994, 137.

Bratulić, J., et al., eds. *Mila si nam ti jedina. Hrvatsko rodoljubno pjesništvo od Bašćanske ploče do danas.* Zagreb: Alfa, 1998. Pp. 19–23.

Brešić, V., ed. *Krvatska: Lirika ratne 1991.* Zagreb: Hrvatsko Filološko Društvo, 1991. Extract, p. 2.

Car Matutinović, L., ed. *Hrvatski pjesnici.* Zagreb: Mozaik, 2005. Selections, pp. 25–26.

Franičević, M., ed. *Judita. Pjesme.* 2nd ed. Zagreb: Školska Knijga, 1976. Pp. 93–97.

Franičević, M., and H. Morović, eds. *Versi harvacki.* Split: Čakavski Sabor, 1979. Pp. 167–71.

Hrvatsko slovo 6/263 (2000) 15. English trans. by E. D. Goy; selections.

Juez Gálvez, F. J. "La caída de Constantinopla y los eslavos meridionales." *Nueva Roma* 19 (2003) 395–420. Spanish translation, selections, pp. 414–15.

———. "La recurrencia del tema Otomana en la literatura Croata de la edad moderna." *Bulletin d'Association Internationale d'Etudes du Sud-Est Européen*, Bucharest, 26–27 (1996–1997) 187–207. Spanish translation, selections, pp. 191–92.

Kolumbić, N., and P. Lucić, eds. *Vartal.* Split: Književni Krug, 1990. Pp. 222–26.

Kraljić, I. C., and S. Šajnović, trans. *Priere contre le Turc (Molitva suprotiva Turkom).* Bibliotheque Saint Libere, 2009. Croatian-French edition. http://www.liberius.net/article.php?id_article=200.

Kukuljević Sakcinski, I., ed. *Pjesme Marka Marulića.* Zagreb: Jugoslavenska Akademija Znanosti i Umjetnosti, 1869. First printed edition. Pp. 244–28.

Lőkös, I., ed. *Horvát irodalmi antológia.* Budapest: Eötvös József, 2004. Hungarian translation, selections, pp. 38–40.

———, trans. *Zsuzsánna. Jeruzsálem városának panasza. Imádság a török ellen.* Budapest: Eötvös József, 2007. Hungarian translation, pp. 53–56.

Lučin, B., ed. *Duhom do zvijezda.* Zagreb: Mozaik, 2001. Pp. 173–80.

———, ed. *Hrvatski stihovi i proza.* Zagreb: Zagreb Matica Hrvatska, 2018. Pp. 223–28.

———, ed. *The Marulić Reader.* Split: Književni Krug, Marulianum, 2007. Croatian-English edition. English trans. by M. Kovačićek, pp. 236–45.

Maroević, T., and M. Tomasović. *Versi harvacki.* Zagreb: Erasmus Naklada, 1996. Pp. 79–89.

Mihalić, S., and I. Kušan, eds. *La poésie croate des origines à nos jours.* Paris : Seghers, 1972. French translation by J. Matillon, selections, pp. 20–22.

Milićević, N., and A. Šoljan, eds. *Antologija hrvatske poezije od XIV stoljeća do naših dana*, Zagreb: Zora, 1966. Selections, pp. 33–35.

Pavešković, A., ed. *Judita.* Vinkovci: Riječ, 1997. Pp. 89–94.

———, ed. *Šturak i čemerika: Antologija hrvatskoga pjesništva do narodnoga preporoda.* Zagreb: Znange, 2010. Pp. 59–63.

Pavletić, V., ed. *100 pjesnika književnosti jugoslavenskih naroda.* Zagreb: Izdavačko Knjižarska Radna Organizacija Mladost, 1984. Pp. 3–6.

Petrač, B. *Od začetja Isusova. Izabrane duhovne pjesme.* Zagreb, 2001. Pp. 96–103.

Slamnig, I. ed. *Judita. Suzana. Pjesme.* Zagreb: Matica Hrvatske, 1970. Pp. 129–33.

Šmit, J., ed. *Antologija hrvaške poezije.* Ljubljana: Cankarjeva Založba, 1975. Slovenian translation, pp. 35–36.

Stamać, A., ed. *Antologija hrvatskoga pjesništva od davnina pa do naših dana.* Zagreb: Školska, 2007. Pp. 59–361.

Tomasović, M. ed. M. *Antologija. Izbor iz poezije i proze.* Zagreb: Konzor, 2000. Pp. 63–70.

Vončina, J., ed. *Pisni razlike*. In *Marci Maruli Opera omnia*, edited by B. Glavičić and B. Lučin, 148-52. Split: Književni Krug, 1988-.

Studies

Dukić, D. „Das Türkenbild in der kroatischen literarischen Kultur vom 15. bis zur Mitte des 19. Jahrhunderts." In *Osmanen und Islam in Südosteuropa*, edited by R. Lauer and H. G. Majer, 157-91. Berlin: De Gruyter, 2013. http://bib.irb.hr/prikazi-rad?rad=224477.

Paljetak, L. „Molitva suprotiva Turkom u kontekstu protuturskog otpora u Europi Marulićeva vremena i poslije njega." CM 11 (2002) 333-62. http://hrcak.srce.hr/index.php?show=clanak&id_clanak_jezik=12239. Includes summary in English.

Judita ("*Judith*")

Date: 1501
Original language: Chakavian (Croatian dialect)

Description

In 1501, Marulus commented on his epic *Judita*: "As I read this tale, it occurred to me to translate it into our tongue that those who knew no Italian or Latin books might understand it."[10] He revealed his poetic intentions by comparing the biblical story to a bunch of wheat, and his epic poem to a fruit tree in full blossom in spring. His poetic version in the vernacular contains several Turkish words, some of which appear more than once: *bar* ("multitude"), *bedev* ("mare"), *bičak* ("dagger"), *dolama* ("dolman"), *skender* (a kind of belt), *sultan, baša, subaša, vezir* ("vizier") and its adjectival form, *vezirski*. In order to convey the biblical story to his Croatian readership, the sophisticated religious teacher sometimes makes contemporaneous references: e.g., Judith is dressed and adorned like the ladies of Split in Renaissance times; the description of the armies may remind the reader of the Croatian and Hungarian cavalries.[11]

The epic (its title in full is *Libar Marka Marula Splićanina u kom se uzdarži istorija svete udovice Judit u versih harvacki složena, kako ona ubi vojvodu Oloferna po sridu vojske njegove i oslobodi puk izraelski od velike pogibili*; "The Book of Marko Marulić of Split Containing the History of the Holy Widow Judith, Written in Verses in Croatian, How She Killed the

---

10. MR, 209.
11. Lučin, in MR, 27.

General Holofernes in the Midst of His Army and Set the Israelitish People Free from Great Peril") was written in 1501, during the war between Venice and the Turks, but only came off the printing press in Venice two decades later; first in 1521, when a war was raging again, with reprints following in 1522 and 1523. The assumption is often made that Marulus composed the poem as an extended metaphor for events in his own homeland and hometown of Split—just as the biblical town of Betulia was threatened by the "great peril" (the Assyrian army led by Holofernes), so was Marulus's Split threatened by the Turks—but there is in fact not the slightest hint in Marulus's text to support that assumption. Only the 1522 edition, published by Bernardinus Benalius (Bernardino Benalio, c. 1458–1543), contains illustrations which may support this view: the title page shows two cavalry forces fighting each other. They are not identified by any banners, although the cavalrymen on the left are wearing turbans and most likely represent the Turks. The cavalry on the right would then represent the European forces.

Similar images appear at various points in the 1522 edition, but the battle scenes have no direct connection with the text of *Judita*. The woodcuts are those used in a 1516 Venetian edition of a text attributed to the medieval Cistercian abbot Joachim de Fiore (c. 1135–1202), *Expositio magni prophete Ioachim in librum Beati Cirilli de magnis tribulationibus & statu Sancte matris Ecclesie*, published by Lazaro Soardi (Laçarus de Soardis, c. 1450–c. 1517).[12] The military images in the 1522 edition show the following scenes which are taken from the 1516 *Expositio*:

1. A soldier steps on the French flag: *Expositio*, f. 30r = *Judita*, f. [a iv].
2. The Turkish flag flying high: *Expositio*, f. 35v (in commentary on Revelation 20, the reign of Satan) = *Judita*, f. b ii verso and again f. h.
3. Two cavalry forces (one Turkish, one European) fighting each other: *Expositio*, f. 24r = *Judita*, frontispiece, and again f. e ii verso.
4. Habsburg forces under the banner of the double-headed eagle defeat the fleeing forces of the pope: *Expositio*, f. 16r = *Judita*, f. h ii verso.

Significance

At a time when the Bible was not yet available in Croatian, Marulus appears to have wanted to familiarise his people with a story of courage from the Hebrew Scriptures in their own language. He had entered a few marginalia in the text of Judith in his *Biblia Latina* of 1489, including a note on the

12. Pelc 2006.

canonicity of the book (considered by non-Catholics as deuterocanonical). He obviously accepted it as canonical and transformed it into a biblical-Virgilian epic that is widely regarded as the cornerstone of Croatian language and literature. Marulus wanted to offer not only spiritual food, but also literary pleasure to his Croatian readers, and to prove his poetic abilities (see the letter to Jerolim Cipiko of July 19, 1501, in which he ventured to remark that, owing to his *Judita*, which he had just finished, his mother tongue would now also have its Dante).[13] The publisher of the 1522 edition added a significant twist: the book's title alone may have inspired the publisher to politicise and militarise the epic by adding woodcut illustrations showing battle scenes related to contemporary wars. If one assumes a non-political reading of the original text, the 1522 edition thus presents a decisive change in perspective and interpretation through its use of political iconography. The military scenes it incorporates illustrate not the biblical story of Judith but rather the wars of the early sixteenth century, utilising woodcuts that appear to have come into existence for an altogether different purpose and were created for a book published in 1516 that had nothing to do with the city of Split. They show city walls (perhaps of Jerusalem, for Fiore's text on p. 30), which, after the idea became current that Judith's Bethulia was a symbol of Split, may have been taken for the walls of Split. In 1522 Marulus's *Judita* appears to have been marketed not only for his elegant use of the Croatian language but as anti-Turcica propaganda, depicting contemporary wars and an imminent Turkish victory. The heraldic symbols shown on the flags depicted scattered on the ground in the images taken from the 1516 book represent the European nations. Only one standard is still flying high, which is identifiable as Turkish by the crescent moon. Only in this illustration and in that on the title page of the 1522 edition is the Turkish element presented directly to alert readers (even if they are not able to read the Croatian text) to an imminent Turkish victory. None of the other pictures make any specific reference to the Turks.

Questions remain: Did Marulus in his *Judita* make an intentional connection between the biblical story and Split? What is more legitimate: to interpret *Judita* as non-political, moral-catechetical, and theological, like his other works, such as the biblical poem *Suzana*, or *Davidias*, or *Evangelistarium* (the last was understood as a purely biblical work with "no spirit of dispute, or confused opinions, or enumerable purely human traditions," according to Sebastian Münster [1488–1552] in his letter *ad pium lectorem* at the end of the 1519 Basel edition; see below); or as a politicization and actualization of the biblical story, in line with Marulus's Croatian "Prayer against

---

13. MR, 266–67.

the Turks," which dates to roughly the same time? Does the morally and didactically minded author want primarily to actualise the biblical figure of "the holy widow Judith" and make it relevant, by way of a hagiography, to his intimidated Croatian readers? And if so, why would he not make any direct, or even implicit, reference to the contemporary political situation in Split?

Manuscripts

No early manuscripts are extant.
MS Zagreb, National and University Library: R 3642, 6 fasc. f. 1-85. Nineteenth-century transcription of the first printed edition by F. Kurelac (1811-74).

Editions and Translations

Béné, C., trans. *La Judith*. Zagreb: Most/Le Pont, 2002. French translation.
Bonifačić, A., ed. and trans. "Judith and Holofernes." In *The Anthology of Croat Verse 1450-1950*. Chicago; n.p., 1981. English translation, selections.
Borsetto, L., trans. *Giuditta. Libro di Marko Marulić Spalatino nel quale si contiene la storia della santa vedova Judit in versi croati composta come lei uccise il vojvoda Oloferne in mezzo al suo esercito e liberò il popolo di israele da gran pericolo*. Milan: Hefti, 2001. Italian translation with parallel Croatian text.
———, trans. "I libri di Marco Marulo di Spalato nei quali si contiene la storia della santa Giuditta in sei libri composta a gloria di Dio incominciano." CM 6 (1997) 133-48. Italian translation of the first canto.
Butler, T., ed. and trans. "Judita/Judith /The slaying of Holofernes by Judith. From Canto Five of *Judith*." In *Monumenta Serbo-Croatica: A Bilingual Anthology of Serbian and Croatian Texts from the 12th to 19th Century*. Ann Arbor, MI: Michigan Slavic, 1980. Pp. 230-35.
Cooper, H. R., Jr., ed. and trans. *Judith*. New York: Columbia University Press, 1991. English translation with parallel Croatian text.
Fališevac, D., ed. *Judita*. Zagreb: n.p., 1996.
Franičević, M., ed. *Judita. Pjesme*. 2nd ed. Zagreb: Školska Knijga, 1976. Pp. 15-90.
Franičević, M., and H. Morović, eds. *Versi harvacki*. Split: Čakavski Sabor, 1979. Pp. 67-141.
Grčić, M., ed. and trans. *Judit / Judita*. Zagreb: Matica Hrvatska, 2003. Modern Croatian translation with parallel facsimile of the 1521 edition.
———, trans. *Judita*. Zagreb: Mladost, 1983. Modern Croatian translation with parallel reprint of the edition by Slamnig (Zagreb, 1970).
———, ed. and trans. *Judita*. CD-ROM. Zagreb, 2001. Facsimiles of the 1521 and 1522 editions and modern Croatian translation.
Gulbinovič, J., et al., trans. *Judita*. Vilnius : Versus Aureus, 2007. Lithuanian translation.
"Judit." In *Linda patria nuestra. Poesia croata de ayer y de hoy*, edited by A. Blažeković, 14-15. Buenos Aires: n.p., 1996. Spanish translation, selections.

"Judita" = "Judith." In *Explorations in Time*, 3–9. Program for concert at Purcell Room, London, April 26, 2006. English translation based on H. Cooper Jr., selections with parallel Croation text.

"*Judita*, Selections." Contemporary Croatian translation by B. Lučin, French translation by L. Gordiani, English translation by J. Tyler Tuttle. In *Judith: Une histoire biblique de la Croatie renaissante*, 38–59. Paris: Alpha Productions. 2013. Booklet accompanying DVD and CD.

Juez Gálvez, F. J., trans. "Libro de Marko Marulić de Split en que se contiene la historia de la santa vidua Judit compuesta en versos a la croata." In *Marko Marulić (1450–1524)*, edited by B. Lučin, 82–88. Madrid: Ediciones Clásicas, 2000. Spanish translation, selections.

———, trans. "Libro de Marko Marulo de Split en que se contiene la historia de la santa vidua Judit compuesta en versos en croata cómo mató ella al general Holofernes en medio de sus huestes y liberó al pueblo de Israel de gran peligro." *Studia Croatica* 145 (2002) 44–104. Spanish translation, selections.

Kadić, A. "Marulić's *Judith*, Canto Five, Verses 165–240." *Journal of Croatian Studies* 27 (1986) 74–77. English translation.

Karpatsky, D., ed., L. Kubišta and I. Wenigová, trans. "Kniha Marka Marula Spliťana, v níž jest podána ve verších charvátských sepsaná historie, kterak svatá vdova Judita zabila vojvodu Holoferna prostřed jeho vojsk a zachránila lid izraelská od převeliké zkázy; Zpěv první" (1st book). In *Koráb korálový. Tisíc let charvátské poezie v dílé stovky básníků*, 130–38. Prague: Fori Prague, 2007. Czech translation.

Kiškyte, D., et al. "Istoria apie šventąją našlę Juditą, kroatiškom eilėm sudėta." CM 15 (2006) 215–40. Lithuanian translation of the dedicatory epistle and the first two cantos.

Kolumbić, N., trans. *Judita*. Split: Golden Marketing, 2007. Modern Croatian translation.

———. "Knjiga Marka Marula Splićanina u kojoj je sadržana priča o svetoj udovici Judit hrvatskim stihovima složena kako ona ubi vojvodu Holoferna posred vojske njegove i oslobodi narod izraelski od velike pogibelji." *Forum* 24 (1985) 1269–1328. Modern Croatian translation.

Kukuljević Sakcinski, I., ed. "Libar Marka Marula Splićanina, u kom se uzdrži istorija svete udovice Judit u versih hrvacki složena, kako ona ubi vojvodu Oloferna po sridu vojske njegove i oslobodi puk izraelski od velike pogibili." In *Pjesme Marka Marulića*, edited by I. Kukuljević Sakcinski, 1–72. Zagreb: Jugoslavenska Akademija Znanosti i Umjetnosti, 1869.

Kušar, M., ed. *Judita. Epska pjesma u šest pjevanja*. Zagreb: n.p., 1901.

Libar Marca Marula Splichianina V chom se usdarsi Istoria Sfete udouice Iudit u versih haruacchi slosena chacho ona ubi uoiuodu Olopherna Posridu uoische gnegoue i oslodobi puch israelschi od ueliche pogibili. Zagreb: n.p., 1950. Facsimile of the 1521 edition.

[*Libar*] *Marcha Marvla Splikyanina Vchomse, vzdarxi Isctoria Sfete vdouice Iudite u versih haruaschi sloxena: chacho ona vbi voy vodu Olopherna Posridu voysche gniegoue: I oslobodi puch israelschi od veliche pogibili*. Venice, 1627. Fifth edition, without war images.

Libar Marca Marvla Splichianina Vchomse vsdarsi Istoria Sfete vdouice Iudit u versih haruacchi slosena: chacho ona vbi voi vodu Olopherna Posridu voische gnegoue:

i olodobi puch israelischi od veliche pogibili, Venice, 1586. Fourth edition, with different illustrations.

Libar Marca Marula Splichianina V chom se usdarsi Istoria Sfete udouice Iudit u uersih haruacchi slosena chacho ona ubi uoiuodu Olopherna Posridu uoische gnegoue i oslodobi puch israelschi od ueliche pogibili. Venice, 1523. Third edition, without war images.

Libar Marca Marula Splichianina Uchom se vsdarsi Istoria Sfete vdouice Iudit u versih haruacchi slosena: chacho ona vbi voivodu Olopherna Posridu voische gnegoue: i oslodobi puch israelschi od veliche pogibili. Venice, 1522. Second edition, containing numerous war images. http://opak.crolib.hr/judita/pages/juditaooo1.html.

Libar Marca Marula Splichianina V chomse usdarsi Istoria Sfete udouice Iudit u uersih haruacchi slosena chacho ona ubi uoiuodu Olopherna Posridu uoische gnegoue i oslodobi puch israelschi od ueliche pogibili. Venice, 1521. Ffirst edition, without war images, but with some other woodcut illustrations. http://www.bulaja.com/Marulic/djela/judita/str1.htm.

Lökös, I., trans. "Horvát művek fordításaí (szemelvenyék) Spalatói Marko Marulić könyve, amely a szent életű Juditról szóló történetet tartalmazza, hat énekre osztva, az isten dicsőségére itt kezdődik: Első ének." In *Godišnja nagrada INE za promicanje hrvatske kulture u svijetu za 2002*, edited by Mijo Ivurek, 123–24. Zagreb: INA-Industrija Nafte, 2003. Hungarian translation, selections.

———, trans. *Judit. Spalatói Marko Marulić könyve, amely a szent életű özvegyről, Juditról szóló történetet tartalmazza horvát versekbe szedve: hogyan öli meg Holofernészt, a hadvezért, annak sergétől körülvéve, és szabadítja meg az izraeli népet a nagy pusztulástól*. Budapest: Eötvös József, 1999. Hungarian translation.

———, trans. "Juditnak, a szent özvegynek históriája horvát versekbe szedve." In *Horvát irodalmi antológia*, edited by I. Lökös, 38–45. Budapest: Eötvös József, 2004. Hungarian translation, selections.

———, trans. "Juditnak, a szent özvegynek históriája horvát versekbe szedve: Első ének." Új *Hevesi Napló: Heves megyei irodalom, társadalom, kultúra* 8/5 (1998) 11–17. Hungarian translation of the first canto.

Lökös. I. *Zrínyi eposzának horvát epikai elözményei*. Debrecen: Kossuth Egyetemi Kiadó, 1997. Hungarian translation, selections, pp. 48–70.

Lučin, B., ed. *Hrvatski stihovi i proza*. Zagreb: Zagreb Matica Hrvatska, 2018. Pp. 105–94.

———, ed. *Marko Marulić: 1450–1524*. Split: Hrvatsko-Njemačko Društvo, 2008. German translation by K. Jurčević, selections, pp. 64–72.

———, ed. *The Marulić Reader*. Split: Književni Krug, Marulianum, 2007. English translation by G. McMaster, pp. 208–35.

———, ed. *Duhom do zvijezda*. Zagreb: Mozaik, 2001. Pp. 31–137.

McMaster, G., trans. "The Book of Marko Marulić of Split Containing the History of the Holy Widow Judith Written in Verses in the Croatian Style How She Killed the General Holofernes in the Midst of His Army and Set the Israelitish People Free from Great Peril." In *Dossier*, 16–31.

Mihalić, S., and C. Zlobec, eds. *Antologija hrvaške poezije*. Ljubljana: Cankarjeva Založba, 1975. Slovenian translation by J. Šmit, selections, pp. 34–36.

Moguš, M., ed. *Judita*. Zagreb: Matica Hrvatska, 1998. With facsimile of the 1522 edition.

Moguš, M., ed. *Judita*. In *Marci Maruli Opera omnia*, vol. 1, edited by B. Glavičić.

Moguš, M., and M. Tomasović, eds. *Judita*. Zagreb: Skolska Knjiga, 1996.
Štefanić, V., ed. *Judita*. Zagreb: Zora, 1950. With illustrations from the 1522 edition.

Studies

Bassani, G. art. "Judit—Marko Marulič [sic]." In *Diccionario literario de obras y personajes de todos los tiempos y de todos los paises*, edited by Valentino Bompiani, 6:373. Barcelona, 1959.

Borsetto, L. "Per una introduzione alla *Judita* in Italiano." In *Italia-Slavia tra Quattro e Cinquecento. Marko Marulić umanista croato nel contesto storico-letterario dell'Italia e di Padova*, edited by L. Borsetto, 97–117. Alessandria: Edizioni dell'Orso, 2004.

———. "Storie di Giuditta in Europa tra Quattro e Cinquecento. Il cantare di Lucrezia Tornabuoni; il poema di Marko Marulić (*exordium* e *narratio*: prime ricognizioni)." In *Riscrivere gli Antichi, riscrivere i Moderni e altri studi di letteratura italiana e comparata tra Quattro e Ottocento*, 83–120. Alessandria: Edizioni dell'Orso, 2002. "Die Gestalt von Judith und Holofernes in der kroatischen und ungarischen Epik der Renaissance."

Dukić, D. *Sultanova djeca. Predodžbe Turaka u hrvatskoj književnosti ranog novovjekovlja*. Zadar: Thema, 2004. Pp. 46–49.

Gutsche, G. J. "Classical Antiquity in Marulić's *Judita*." *Slavic and East European Journal* 19 (1975) 310–21.

Heger, H. "À propos du titre de la *Judita* de Marulić." In *Poslanje filologa: zbornik radova povodom 70. rođendana Mirka Tomasovića*, edited by T. Bogdan and C. Pavlović, 235–49. Zagreb: FF, 2008.

Ivanišević, M. „Ikonografija drvoreza u starim izdanjima Marulićeve *Judite*" [„Iconography of the Woodcuts in the Old Editions of Marulić's *Judith*"]. *Mogućnosti* 49/10–12 (2002) 45–75.

Jelčić, D., ed. *Zbornik radova o Marku Maruliću; u povodu 550. obljetnice rođenja i 500. obljetnice njegove Judite 1450.-1501.-2001* ["Collected Papers on Marko Marulić; in Celebration of 550th Anniversary of His Birth and 500th Anniversary of the Birth of His Judit 1450–1501–2001"]. Zagreb: Hrvatska Akademija Znanosti i Umjetnosti, 2005. Contains, among others: D. Fališevac, "Judita Marka Marulića," 21–31; H. R. Cooper, "Judita i ja," 115–30; J. Vončina, "Marulićeva Judita u sazrijevanju jezikoslovne kroatistike," 163–74.

Jerkov, J. "Amor sacro e amor profano nei poemi croati di Marulić." *CM* 9 (2000) 219–25.

Jozić, B. "Marulićeva *Judita* kao *miles Christi*." *CM* 11 (2002) 187–205. With English summary, "Marulić's *Judith* as *miles Christi*." *CM* 11 (2002) contains numerous studies on *Judita*; see http://hrcak.srce.hr/index.php?show=toc&id_broj=304.

Juez Gálvez, F. J. "La caída de Constantinopla y los eslavos meridionales." *Nueva Roma* 19 (2003) 395–420. Pp. 410–18.

Kužić, K. "Nazivi oružja u *Juditi* i značenje drvoreza iz drugog izdanja" ["The Names of Weapons in *Judith* and the Meaning of the Woodcuts in the Second Edition"]. *Mogućnosti* 48/7–9 (2001) 58–73.

Livljanić, K. "The Agony of Judith: A Biblical Story from Medieval Dalmatia. Based on Judith by Marko Marulić." In *Explorations in Time*, 1–9. Program for concert at Purcell Room, London, April 26, 2006.

Lökös, I. "A Judit és Holofernész-téma a horvát és a magyar reneszáns epikában." *Studia Litteraria* 30 (1992) 19–45. With summary in German, Lökös, I. „Die Imitatio-Theorie der Renaissance und biblische Tradition in dem Epos *Judit* von Marko Marulić." In *Tusculum Slavicum*, edited by E. von Erdmann et al., 370–80. Zürich: Pano, 2005.

———. "Intertekstualnost u Marulićevoj Juditi." CM 13 (2004) 57–66. With English summary, "ntertextuality in Marulić's Judith."

Mecky Zaragoza, G. "Virgo und Virago. Zwei frühneuzeitliche Judith-Figuren im Vergleich." *Daphnis: Zeitschrift für Mittlere Deutsche Literatur und Kultur der Frühen Neuzeit (1400–1750)* 31 (2002) 107–26.

Moguš, M. *Rječnik Marulićeve Judite*. Zagreb: Institut za Hrvatski Jezik i Jezikoslovlje, 2001.

Pelc, M. "Podrijetlo drvoreza Marulićeve *Judite* (1521–1523)" ["The Origin of the Woodcuts in Marulić's *Judita* (1521–23)"]. *Mogućnosti* 56/4-6 (2006) 1–12. Pelc proves that Marulus is not the creator of the woodcuts. The book from which the pictures are borrowed is titled *Expositio in Librum Beati Cirilli de tribulationibus et statu Sancte matris Ecclesie*. Venice: Joachim de Flore, 1516.

Pšihistal, R. "Treba li Marulićeva *Judita* alegorijsko tumačenje?" CM 11 (2002) 154–86. With English summary, "Does Marulić's *Judith* need an allegorical interpretation?"

Skok, P. "O stilu Marulićeve *Judite*" ["On the Style of Marulić's *Judith*"]. In *Zbornik u proslavu petstogodišnjice rođenja Marka Marulića: 1450–1950*, edited by J. Badalić and N. Majnarić, 165–241. Zagreb: Jugoslavenska Akademija Znanosti i Umjetnosti, 1950. For words of Turkish origin in *Judita*, see p. 172.

Tomasović, M. "*Judita*: A Biblical, Humanist and Renaissance Epic." In *Dossier*, 107–14.

Qual Maraviglia se 'l Furor Turchesco ("What Wonder If the Turkish Fury")

Date: 1501
Original language: Italian

Description

This is one of only two known sonnets from a group that Marulus mentions in his letter to Jerolim Cipiko of November 2, 1501.[14] It may be considered a summary of his lost treatise in Italian on the oppression of the Christians by the infidels, mentioned in a letter to Jerolim Cipiko of July 19, 1501.[15] The Turkish fury bears down on the Christian people. Referring to the

---

14. MR, 270–71.
15. MR, 263–65.

metaphors in Dante's *Inferno* I:33–60 and to Rom 2:24, Marulus laments that the name of God is reviled and asserts that if this is not corrected the wrath of God the Father will not abate.

Significance

In explaining the causes of the persecutions of Christians by the Turks, Marulus uses an interesting reversal: negative characteristics usually connected with the Turks are here applied to the Christians—it is they who are rapacious, cunning, arrogant, greedy, etc. This reversal of attributes is both strengthened and complicated by the use of animal metaphors, some of which are applied in a traditional way to represent negative moral characteristics in general, but some of which might also have political connotations.[16] The main sin of the Christians, however, seems to be blasphemy. The only way for them to obtain God's help against the persecutors is through moral improvement. In his sonnets Marulus admonishes Christians for their sinful actions and irresponsibility.

Manuscripts

MS Zagreb, Archive of the Croatian Academy of Sciences and Arts: I a 64, f. 46v–47r (c. 1530).

Editions and Translations

Deanović, M. "Due sonetti inediti di Marco Marulo." *Giornale storico della letteratura italiana* 108/234 (1936) 216–24. Pp. 217–18.
Juez Gálvez, F. J., trans. "Éstos son los males que nos oprimen." *Nueva Roma* 19 (2003) 416–18. Spanish translation, selections, p. 413.
Hekman, J., ed. *Split 1999: Dossier*. Zagreb: Matica Hrvatska, 2005. Croatian translation by M. Tomasović, p. 236.
Lučin, B., ed. *Duhom do zvijezda*. Zagreb: Mozaik, 2001. Croatian translation by M. Tomasović, p. 464.
Milošević M., trans. *Mogućnosti* 38/11–12 (1991) 942–43. Italian with Croatian translation.
———. "Sedam nepoznatih pisama Marka Marulića" ["Seven Unpublished Letters of Marcus Marulus"]. CM 1 (1992) 5–31. Italian with Croatian translation, pp. 14–15.
Tomasović, M., ed. *Antologija. Izbor iz poezije i proze*. Zagreb: Konzor, 2000. Croation translation, p. 161.

---

16. See Posset 2008b.

———. "Marulić o sonetu." CM 9 (2000) 371-80. Italian with Croatian translation by M. Milošević and M. Tomasović, pp. 376-78.
———. *Prepjevni primjeri*. Zagreb: Ceres, 2000. Italian with Croatian translation, pp. 75-77.
Scotti, G. "Marco Marulo—Marulić sotto una diversa luce." *La Battana* 118 (1995) 107-18. P. 117.

Studies

Deanović, M. "Due sonetti inediti di Marco Marulo." *Giornale Storico della Letteratura Italiana* 108/234 (1936) 216-24.
Milošević, M. "Sedam nepoznatih pisama Marka Marulića" ["Seven Unpublished Letters of Marko Marulić"]. CM 1 (1992) 5-31. With English summary, pp. 165-66.
Posset, F. "The Mouse, the Frog, and the Unidentified Flying Object: Metaphors for 'Empires' in the Latin Works of the Croatian Humanist Marcus Marulus and of the German Humanist Ulrich von Hutten." CM 17 (2008) 125-48.
Tomasović, M. "Marulić o sonetu." CM 9 (1992) 371-80. With Italian summary.
———. "Marulić sonetima opominje 'kršćanski puk' zbog grešnih čina i neodgovornosti." In *Split 1999: Dossier*, edited by J. Hekman, 234-36. Zagreb: Matica Hrvatska, 2006.
———. "Marulićevi talijanski soneti." In *Prepjevni primjeri*, 69-79. Zagreb: Ceres, 2000.

De Humilitate et Gloria Christi
("On the Humility and Glory of Christ")

Date: 1506
Original language: Latin

Description

This is one of Marcus Marulus's major theological works; it comprises three books: *Liber euangelicus*, *Liber propheticus*, and *Liber gloriosus*. The work alternates between fragments of sermon writing, exegetical deliberations, and political digressions. Written in cultivated Latin, it contains numerous figurative interpretations of biblical passages.[17]

In book 1, Marulus includes a section on heresies; this includes the heresies of the early church,[18] but not the *Machumetana heresis*, about which he writes in his *Evangelistarium*. In book 2, he refers twice to the

17. MR, 16.
18. OO, 9:426.

"Mohammedans." First, within the section on the apostles, he says that one should read the lives of the martyrs and see that the church of Christ suffered from attacks by heretics; Christian cities and kingdoms are occupied and forced into servitude by the henchmen of the "Mohammedan depravity" (*a Machumetanę prauitatis sectatoribus*[19]). Second, within the section on *Communio*, he inserts a passage on Luke 22:31–32, about Christ's prayer for Peter's faith and his command that Peter should strengthen the faith of his brethren, whom Marulus interprets to be the universal church. The infidels rage; they persecute the church; occupy Christian cities, land, and kingdoms; and control the entire world, but the religion of Christ will stand tall on earth as Peter's faith in Christ will persevere to the end. Then Israel, too, will convert to Christ and be saved. Although the Muslims may dominate all the nations of the earth, the faith in Christ will be victorious; Marulus cites 1 John 5:4: "our faith that conquers the world." At this point, he speaks of the Turks and likens them to the pagan Roman Empire: neither the Romans nor the Turks will be able to destroy faith in Christ, since Christ's prayer for Peter is more powerful, and so the Christian faithful should remain confident.[20]

Significance

Marulus reveals a typically hostile attitude towards the Turks and confidence—maybe in defiance of the facts—that Christianity will win in the end. His comments show the scale of the threat from the Turks, and the extent of Christian desperation.

Editions and Translations

De humilitate et gloria Christi Marci Marvli opvs. Venice, 1519. http://books.google.ca/books?id=iVMRwcmcXHUC.
Dell'humilta et della gloria di Christo libri. Venice, 1595. http://books.google.hr/books?id=eRhSAAAAcAAJ.Italian translation by Gioseffo Alchaini.
Glavičić, B., ed. *Marci Maruli Opera omnia*, vol. 9. Latin-Croatian edition.

Studies

Glavičić, B. «Sudbina Marulićeva djela *De humilitate et gloria Christi*.» Radovi (Razdio Filoloških Znanosti, Sveučilište u Splitu, Filozofski Fakultet Zadar) 29/19 (1990)

---

19. OO, 9:554.
20. OO, 9:579.

167–74. With summary in English, «The Fate of Marulić's Work *De humilitate et gloria Christi*.»

Runje, P. «O nekim izdanjima *Quinquaginta parabolae* i *De humilitate et gloria Christi* Marka Marulića.» CM 2 (1993) 9–12. With summary in Italian, «Intorno alle edizioni sconosciute delle *Quinquaginta parabolae* e del *De humilitate et gloria Christi* di Marko Marulić,» pp. 120–21.

Evangelistarium

Date: approximately 1515
Original language: Latin

Description

The *Evangelistarium* is about seven hundred pages long, filling two volumes (4 and 5) of *Opera omnia*. It is the first major result of Marulus's scriptural studies, and he published his first version in "seven books," probably based on his study of the *Biblia Latina cum comento*, which he had purchased after 1489. The *Evangelistarium* is an impressive treatise on practical Christian morality based upon the three theological virtues of faith, hope, and love. However, it is not simply a book on morality, even though its declared priority is ethics. It is also a general theological work and a guide for readers of Scripture.[21]

Probably as a result of his study of the biblical commentaries contained in his 1489 *Biblia*, Marulus observes in his *Evangelistarium* that in his time not a few Christians are converting to Islam. He mentions the *Machumetani* again, along with other historical heresies such as Arianism and also with those in the church who dare to contradict the "Catholic truth" (*Catholica veritas*), and he explicitly uses the very rare expression *Machumetana heresis* ("Mohammadan heresy"), and also calls Turks *infideles Turci*.[22]

Significance

The *Evangelistarium* is regarded today as Marulus's "most important moral and theological work."[23] Its remarkable success is primarily indicated by the fact that soon after its first publication in Venice it was also printed elsewhere. Its corrector and editor in Basel, the German humanist and

---

21. Jovanović 2003.
22. OO, 5:605–6, 671.
23. MR, 14.

Franciscan friar Sebastian Münster, later a Lutheran,[24] says of it: "There is no spirit of dispute, or confused opinions, or enumerable purely human traditions. You will hear what is fitting for a truly evangelical work [*opus vere evangelicum*]: only the voice of God, of our Saviour Jesus Christ, apostle, and prophet, and the pure truth" (*Frater Sebastianus Munsterus ... ad pium lectorem*, p. [399]).

Later editions underscore the effect of the work. The editions of 1529 and 1532 in Cologne played a role in theological debate when the Reformation was being introduced in the city.[25] In the eighteenth century, the memory of these Cologne editions was kept alive by Johann Albert Fabricius, who listed the *Evangelistarium* in his *Bibliotheca Latina Mediae et Infimae Aetatis* (Hamburg, 1736, p. 138) as a work about "hope, faith, and charity" (in this sequence!). It was translated in full or in part into Italian, Spanish, French and Flemish (extract). Altogether, it was printed about fifteen times, in Venice, Basel, Cologne, Paris, and Antwerp.

King Henry VIII of England owned a copy of the 1529 edition, and with the exception of his Psalter it is the most heavily annotated book known from his library.

Editions and Translations

Baccherius, P. *Hortvlvs precationvm. Dat is, Het hofken der bedinghen* ... Louvain, 1566. Extract in Flemish, f. 40–40v.

Euangelistarium Marci Maruli Spalatensis, opus vere euangelicum, sub fidei, spei &charitatis titulis in VII. libros partitum. Paris, 1545. http://www.google.hr/books?id=DYffH0ATbuAC.

Evangelistarium M. Maruli Spalatensis, opus vere euangelicum, sub fidei, spei et charitatis titulis in VII. libros partitum. Cologne, 1541. http://reader.digitale-sammlungen.de/ resolve/display/bsb10205563.html.

Evangelistarium M. Maruli Spalatensis, opus vere euangelicum, sub fidei, spei & charitatis titulis in septem libros partitum. Cologne: G. Hittorp, 1532. http://daten.digitale-sammlungen.de/~db/0003/ bsb00034888/images/.

Evangelistarium M. Maruli Spalatensis, opus vere euangelicum, sub fidei, spei & charitatis titulis in septem libros partitum, Cologne: P. Quentell, 1532. http://daten.digitale-sammlungen.de/~db/0002/bsb00028370/images/.

Evangelistarium Marci Maruli Spalatensis viri disertissimi, opus vere euangelicum cultissimoque adornatum sermone, sub fidei, spei & charitatis titulus. Cologne: F. Birckmann, 1529. For different title page see *Bibliografija*, no. 33.

Evangelistarium Marci Maruli Spalatensis viri disertissimi, opus vere euangelicum cultissimoque adornatum sermone, sub fidei, spei & charitatis titulus, in septem

---

24. Raupp 1994.
25. Erdmann 2011.

partitum libros. Cologne: F. Birckmann, 1529. For different title page see *Bibliografija*, no. 34.

Evangelistarium M. Maruli Spalatensis opus uere euangelicum, sub fidei, spei & charitatis titulis in septem libros partitum. Cologne: G. Hitorpius, 1529. For different title page see *Bibliografija*, no. 35.

Evangelistarium M. Maruli Spalatensis uiri disertissimi, opus uere euangelicum, cultissimoque adornatum sermone sub fidei, spei & charitatis titulis, in VII. partitum libros. Cologne: G. Hitorpius, 1529. For different title page see *Bibliografija*, no. 36.[26]

Evangelistarium Marci Maruli Spalatensis viri disertissimi, opus uere euangelicum, cultissimoque adornatum sermone, sub fidei, spei & charitatis titulis, in septem partitum libros. Basel, 1519. http://books.google.hr/books?id=-ANRAAAAcAAJ.

Fernandez de Reuenga, B., trans. *Evangelistario de Marco Marulo Spalatense.* Madrid, 1655. Spanish translation. http://books.google.hr/books?id=8Us1jL98ZwQC.

Garet, J. et al. *De la vraye presence du corps de Jesus-Christ au s. sacrement de l'autel . . .* Paris, 1599. Extract in French, f. 293v–294v.

Glavičić, B., ed. *Marci Maruli Opera omnia,* vols. 4 and 5. Latin-Croatian edition, translation by B. Glavičić.

M. Maruli Evangelistarium, opus vere euangelicum, sub fidei, spei & charitatis titulis, in septem libros partitum. Cologne, 1556. http://daten.digitale-sammlungen. de/~db/0001/bsb00016192 /images/index.html.

Marci Maruli Spalatensis Evangelistarium. Venice, 1516. http://reader.digitale-sammlungen. de/resolve/display/bsb10198513.html. The earliest extant print, an improved version of an earlier unknown one.

Opus vere euangelicum, de fide, spe & charitate. In *Operum M. Maruli Spalatensis tomus posterior.* Antwerp, 1601. http://books.google.hr/books?id=y2KD4mYA_2AC.

Razzi, S., trans. *Evangelistario di Marco Marulo Spalatense.* Florence, 1571. Italian translation.

Studies

Béné, C. "Henry VIII et Thomas More, lecteurs de Marulić." CM 5 (1996) 87–106.

———. "L'*Evangelistarium,* maître-livre de Marulić." CM 12 (2003) 5–22.

Cattaneo, R. "La base senecana della dottrina dei benefici nell' *Evangelistario* di Marko Marulić." CM 24 (2015) 115–44.

Clarke, A. "Henry VIII and Marko Marulić's *Evangelistarium.*" CM 20 (2011) 167–75.

Erdmann, E. von. "Marko Marulić in den Religionskonflikten der Deutschen Länder des 16. Jahrhunderts." CM 20 (2011) 177–93.

Jovanović, N. "Paratekst i *loci Biblici* kao put od stila do tumačenja Marulićeva *Evandelistara.*" CM 12 (2003) 23–45. With English summary, "From Style to Interpretation: Paratext and *Loci Biblici* in the *Evangelistarium* by Marko Marulić."

Jovanović, N., and H. Šoškić, eds. "Editio notarum Henrici regis in Maruli *Evangelistario.*" CM 25 (2016) 157–227.

Jozić, B. "Marci Maruli *Evangelistarium—vetera & nova*: uz petstoljetnicu izdanja (1516-2016)." CM 26 (2017) 207–37. With English summary, "Marci Maruli

---

26. The four different editions that were published in 1529 have different title pages; further information on these can be found in Jozić and Lučin 1998, 44–46.

Evangelistarium—vetera & nova: Marking the Fifth Centenary of the Edition (1516–2016)."

Juez Gálvez, F. J. "El *Evangelistarium* en Espana y el *Evangelistario* espanol de 1655." CM 19 (2009) 249–68.

Leschinkohl, F. "Le rôle historique de l'*Evangelistarium* et de l'*Institutio* au XVIe siècle." *Cahiers Croates* 1/1–2 (1997) 81–86.

Leschinkohl, F. "Marko Marulić u njemačkim knjižnicama." CM 3 (1994) 99–126. With English summary, "Marko Marulić in German Libraries."

Leschinkohl, F. "Povijesna uloga *Evanđelistara* i *Institucije* u 16. stoljeću." CM 4 (1995) 81–102. With English summary, "The Historical Role of the *Evangelistarium* and the *De Institutione* in the Sixteenth Century."

Lukač, S. "Marulićev *Evanđelistar* (Coloniae, 1529) iz mađarskog Gyöngyösa." CM 12 (2003) 255–60. With English summary, "The Marulić *Evangelistary* from Gyöngöys in Hungary."

Martinović, I. "Marulićev etički nauk o miru." *Prilozi za istraživanje hrvatske filozofske baštine* 51–52 (2000) 17–57. With English summary, "Marko Marulić's Ethical Doctrine on Peace."

Runje, P. "O ranim izdanjima *Evanđelistara* i *Institucije*." CM 3 (1994) 93–98. With English summary, "On the Early Editions of the *Evangelistarium* and the *De Institutione* by Marko Marulić."

Tuženje grada Jerozolima moleći papu da skupi gospodu karstjansku ter da ga oslobodi od ruk poganskih "Lament of the City of Jerusalem, Begging the Pope to Assemble Christian Nobles and Deliver It from Pagan Hands."

Date: approximately 1516–1517
Original language: Croatian

Description

This work was written after the occupation of Syria and neighbouring territories by the Turks in 1516–1517, although it was first printed only in 1869. It comprises 128 lines. Although there is an early Christian poem on this subject (*Elegia in Hierusalem*) in the 1501 edition of *Poetae Christiani veteres*, which was in Marulus's possession, there are no traces of any marginalia from his pen to indicate that he had actually read it.

Marulus's poem is a passionate plea calling for help from the European powers: the captured city of Jerusalem addresses the "Holy Father" and enumerates the Western rulers and states that he should call for a crusade. In the final line, the Turkish ruler is referred to as *car* (in Croatian, South Slavic)—"czar"/"tsar."

Significance

The call goes out to the unnamed "Holy Father." Another call for help was to be issued by Marulus in 1522 as an "open letter" to Pope Hadrian VI, and yet another in 1523, an epistle to Pope Clement VII in the form of a poem.[27] The Holy Father is to gather the Christian peoples together in order to liberate Jerusalem from "pagan hands." The Turks are called the "damned people" and "pagan beast" (Revelation 17); they are worse than "those who put Christ on the cross." Marulus's advocacy of papal leadership proves his Roman Catholic position in anti-Turcica literature, distinct from the anti-papal German-Lutheran attitude of the time and the refusal to call upon the pope.

Manuscripts

MS Zagreb, Archives of the Croatian Academy of Arts and Sciences: "Vartal" Petra Lucija, IV.a.31, f. 62v–64v (late sixteenth century).
MS Zagreb, National and University Library: R 6634, f. 20r–22r (c. 1530).
MS Zagreb, National and University Library: "Splitska pjesmarica trogirskoga kaptola" ["Split poetic miscellany of the Trogir chapter"], no shelfmark, f. 55r–57v (late sixteenth or early seventeenth century).

Editions and Translations

Franičević, M., and H. Morović, eds. *Versi harvacki*. Split: Čakavski Sabor, 1979. Pp. 172–75.
Glavičić, B., ed. *Marci Maruli Opera omnia*, vol. 2. Pp. 144–47.
Kukuljević Sakcinski, I., ed. *Pjesme Marka Marulića*, Zagreb: Jugoslavenska Akademija Znanosti i Umjetnosti, 1869. Pp. 241–44.
Lökös, I., trans. *Zsuzsánna. Jeruzsálem városának panasza. Imádság a török ellen.* Budapest: Eötvös, 2007. Hungarian translation, pp. 49–52.
Lucić, P. *Vartal*. Edited by N. Kolumbić. Split: Književni Krug, 1990. Pp. 175–78.
Lučin, B., ed. *Duhom do zvijezda*. Zagreb: Mozaik, 2001. Pp. 181–86.
———, ed. *Hrvatski stihovi i proza*. Zagreb: Zagreb Matica Hrvatska, 2018. Pp. 229–33.
———, ed. *The Marulić Reader*. Split: Književni Krug, Marulianum, 2007. Croatian-English edition, English translation by M. Kovačiček, pp. 246–53.
Maroević, T., and M. Tomasović, eds. *Plavca nova*. Zagreb: n.p., 1971. Pp. 117–19.
Petrač, B., ed. *Od začetja Isusova*. Zagreb: n.p., 2001. Pp. 89–95.
Šajnović, S., and I. C. Kraljić, trans. *Plainte de la ville de Jérusalem suppliant le Pape de réunir les seigneurs chrétiens pour la délivrer des mains des infideles*. Bibliotheque Saint Libere, 2009.
Slamnig, I., ed. *Judita. Suzana. Pjesme*. Zagreb: Matica Hrvatske, 1970. Pp. 134–37.

---

27. OO, 17:101.

Zaninović, A. "Marulićeva pjesma Tužen'je grada Hjerozolima." *Vjesnik za Arheologiju i Historiju Dalmatinsku 1924-1925*, supplement 2 (1925) 7-11.

Studies

Dukić, D. "Das Türkenbild in der kroatischen literarischen Kultur vom 15. bis zur Mitte des 19. Jahrhunderts." In *Osmanen und Islam in Südosteuropa*, edited by R. Lauer and H.G. Majer, 157-91. Berlin: De Gruyter, 2013.

———. *Sultanova djeca. Predodžbe Turaka u hrvatskoj književnosti ranog novovjekovlja*. Zadar: Thema, 2004. Pp. 245-53.

Zaninović, A. "Marulićeva pjesma Tužen'je grada Hjerozolima." *Vjesnik za Arheologiju i Historiju Dalmatinsku 1924-1925*, supplement 2 (1925) 1-6.

De Gallis et Hispanis inter se bellantibus ("On the French and the Spanish Fighting One Another")

Date: approximately 1521
Original language: Latin

Description

This is a short poem of only twelve lines, featuring France and Spain as hatefully warring nations who should instead join forces against Muḥammad, who is enraged against the Christians. In his commentary on the poem, Novaković suggests that it might have been written "ca. 1521?"[28]

Significance

France and Spain are singled out as battling against each other instead of uniting against the common enemy, the Turks. The two nations are guilty of not making lasting peace with each other while the enemy "has conquered almost the entire world". In his sermon about the Last Judgment of Christ of 1520-21, Marulus again pleads with the rulers of France and Spain, and also of Italy, to make peace in order to be able to resist the *Mahumetani*.[29]

---

28. OO, 17:164.
29. OO, 11:231.

Manuscripts

MS Glasgow, University Library: Hunter 334 / U. 8.2, f. CVIv (c. 1524–1550)

Editions and Translations

Lučin, B., ed. *Duhom do zvijezda*. Zagreb: Mozaik, 2001. Croatian translation by D. Novaković, p. 453.
Lučin, B. *Marko Marulić: 1450–1524*. Madrid: Ediciones Clásicas, 2000. Spanish translation by F. J. Juez Gálvez, p. 71.
Lučin, B., ed. *The Marulić Reader*. Split: Marulianum, 2007. Latin-English edition, translation by M. Kovačićek, pp. 144–45.
Lučin, B., ed. *Marci Maruli Opera omnia*, vol. 17. Latin-Croatian edition, translation by D. Novaković, pp. 164–65 (no. 95).
McMaster, G., and M. Kovačićek. "Latin Poems / Marko Marulić." *Most / The Bridge Literary Magazine* 1–4 (1999) 85. English translation.
Novaković, D., ed. "Marci Maruli epigrammata." CM 6 (1997) 37–77. First edition, p. 41.
Novaković, D., ed. and trans. *Marko Marulić. Glasgowski stihovi*. Zagreb: Matica Hrvatska, 1999. Latin-Croatian edition, pp. 22–23.
No studies.

Epistola domini Marci Maruli Spalatensis ad Adrianum VI. Pont. Max. ("The Epistle of Master Marko Marulić of Split to Pope Hadrian VI")

Date: April 3, 1522
Original language: Latin

Description

The open letter (its title in full is *Epistola domini Marci Maruli Spalatensis ad Adrianum VI. Pont. Max. de calamitatibus occurrentibus et exhortatio ad communem omnium Christianorum unionem et pacem*, "The Epistle of Master Marko Marulić of Split to Pope Hadrian VI about Present Misfortunes and a Call to Union and Peace of All Christians") comprises nine pages in *Opera omnia*, plus a few lines (including the dedicatory epistle to Father Dominik Buća [Dominicus Buchia] and a prayer for the pope at the end). The dedicatory epistle is dated April 3, 1522, while the date of publication (in the colophon) is April 30, 1522.

The name of the new pope does not appear until the very end of the letter, raising the question of whether Marulus had written it at an earlier stage rather than as a response to the election of Hadrian VI. He may well have, because the prayer for the pope that he includes here is virtually identical with the prayer he had written for Pope Leo X,[30] and also because he sent the letter as early as spring 1522, when the new pope had not yet arrived in Rome from Spain.

The open letter is another significant work of anti-Turcica literature. The first marginal note in the original edition reads: *Pax Maumethana cum Christianis* ("Muhammadan peace with the Christians"), referring to the Venetians, the rulers of Split, and their so-called friendship with Sultan Bayezid II. Marulus says that this peace cannot be called a real friendship, since an opponent of Christ cannot be a friend of Christians. With such differences in faith, laws, and customs, the only friendship is a feigned friendship (*amicitia simulata*). The Turks are the most impious nation of all the Antichrists; they represent the barbaric *Maumethana perfidia*, the denial of Christ, and the worship of Muhammad. They are a ravaging wolf, the Muhammadan beast, the infidel tyrant, and the common enemy.

Marulus calls upon Hadrian to unite the Christian nations against the Ottoman armies' attacks because it is the pope, and not the Holy Roman Emperor or the Doge of Venice, who should be the leader in defending Europe. In this he opposes, whether consciously or not, the views of the German nationalists Ulrich von Hutten (1488–1523) and Martin Luther (1483–1546) that the pope should not be involved in such affairs.

Marulus employs Aesop's fable of the Mouse and the Frog, representing the Holy Roman Empire and the Republic of Venice. Ulrich von Hutten, spokesman for the movement of a "church without Rome," called for the financial support that was given to the papacy to be given instead to the emperor for the war against the Turks.[31] Taking an opposing view, Marulus uses the fable to warn against the threat from the Bird of Prey ("the barbarian foe," the Turks) to both the Frog and the Mouse (the Christian nations of Europe).[32]

Significance

The Turkish threat was usually perceived at that time as a result of the wrath of God, and in this open letter the wrath of God is said to be caused by the sinful disunity of Europe and the Christian nations fighting against each other. Although it cannot be assumed that the letter was actually read by the

30. OO, 17:93.
31. Wheelis 1977, 122.
32. Posset 2008b.

pope,[33] or that there was any immediate response, Hadrian VI did make the issue of Christian unity the topic of his first speech at the consistory held on September 1, 1522, immediately after his coronation. Shortly afterwards, he wrote to Emperor Charles V and warned of the disunity that actually offered much greater assistance to the Turkish tyrant than an army of thousands of soldiers. Marulus was convinced of this very point and called for the pope's involvement.

Editions and Translations

Andrassy, V., trans. "The Epistle of Marko Marulić of Split to Pope Adrian VI about Present Misfortunes and a Call to Union and Peace of all Christians." In *Dossier*, 46–51.

Andrassy, V., trans. "Epistola domini Marci Maruli Spalatensis ad Adrianum VI. pontificem maximum de calamitatibus occurrentibus et exhortatio ad communem omnium Christianorum unionem et pacem" = "Epistle of Lord Marko Marulić of Split to Pope Adrian VI about Present Misfortunes and a Call to Union and Peace of All Christians." In *The Marulić Reader*, edited by B. Lučin, 90–109. Split: Književni Krug, Marulianum, 2007. Latin edition with English translation.

Bratulić, J., ed. *Epistola ad Adrianum VI. P. M. = Poslanica Papi Hadrijanu VI. = Epistle to Pope Adrian VI. 1522.* Zagreb: Nacionalna i Sveučilišna Biblioteka; Split: Crkva u Svijetu, 1994. Trilingual edition, in Latin, with Croatian translation by V. Gligo, V. Gortan, and D. Novaković, and English translation by V. Andrassy, with a separate booklet containing the facsimile edition of the Latin edition of 1522.

Cattaneo, R., trans. "Epistola di don Marco Marulo da Spalato al Sommo Pontefice Adriano VI." CM 22 (2013) 150–57. Italian translation.

Epistola domini Marci Maruli Spalatensis ad Adrianum. VI. Pont. Max. Rome, 1522. http://mek.oszk.hu/03600/03625. First edition.

"Epistola domini Marci Maruli Spalatensis ad Adrianum VI. pontificem maximum de calamitatibus occurrentibus et exhortatio ad comunem omnium Christianorum unionem et pacem" = "Lettre de messire Marcus Marulus de Split à Adrien VI. souverain Pontife au sujet des malheurs qui se produisent et exhortation à l'union et à la paix de tous les chretiens" = "The Epistle of Marko Marulić of Split to Pope Adrian VI about present misfortunes and a call to union and peace of all Christians." In *Epistola*, by I. Malec. Luxembourg, 2009. Booklet accompanying the CD with the recording of Malec's cantata. French translation by G. Lafon, English translation by V. Andrassy, selections.

Gligo, V., trans. "Poslanica Papi Hadrijanu VI." *Zadarska smotra* 3–4 (2001) 220–21. Croatian translation, selections. Reprinted in *Marko Marulić, europski humanist: 1450–1524*, edited by B. Glavičić. Zadar: Matica Hrvatska, 2001.

Gligo, V., and V. Gortan, trans. "Pismo papi Hadrijanu VI o nevoljama koje nahrupljuju i poticaj za opće jedinstvo i mir svih kršćana." In *Govori protiv Turaka*, edited

---

33. However, see the latest research by Branko Jozić as mentioned in the Preface above (subchapter 'Research Continues').

by V. Gligo, 165-78. Split: Logos, 1983. Facsimile of the 1522 edition. Croatian translation, pp. 449-62.

Gligo, V., V. Gortan, and D. Novaković, trans. "Epistola domini Marci Maruli Spalatensis ad Adrianum VI. Pont. Max. de calamitatibus occurrentibus et exhortatio ad communem omnium Christianorum unionem et pacem." In *Marci Maruli Opera omnia*, vol. 17, edited by B. Lučin, 245-65. Latin-Croatian edition.

Gortan, V., and V. Vratović, eds. *Hrvatski latinisti = Croatici auctores qui Latine scripserunt*. Zagreb: Matica Hrvatska, 1969. Latin-Croatian edition, translation by V. Gortan, selections, vol. 1, pp. 308-13.

Hrvatska Revija = La Revista Croata 1 (1951) 20-21. Croatian translation, selections.

Juez Gálvez, F. J., trans. "Epistola al papa Adriano VI." In *Marko Marulić: 1450-1524*, edited by B. Lučin, 60-62. Madrid: Ediciones Clásicas, 2000. Spanish translation, selections.

Juez Gálvez, F. J., trans. "Epístola del señor Marko Marulić de Split al papa Adriano VI." *Studia Croatica* 145 (2002) 75-84. Spanish translation.

Juez Gálvez, F. J., trans. "Éstos son los males que nos oprimen." *Nueva Roma* 19 (2003) 416-18. Spanish translation, selections.

Kraljić, I. C., trans. "Lettre du Seigneur Marko Marulić de Split au Souverain Pontife Adrien VI au sujet des désastres actuels, et exhortation à l'union de tous les chrétiens et à la paix." Bibliotheque Saint Libere, 2010. French translation.

Lafon, G., trans. "Au Souverain Pontife Adrien VI. Marko Marulić de Split s'adresse en toute humilité en l'implorant." *Cahiers Croates* 2/5-6 (1998) 135-53. French translation.

Lafon, G., trans. "Epistola domini Marci Maruli Spalatensis ad Adrianum VI. pontificem maximum de calamitatibus occurrentibus et exhortatio ad communem omnium christianorum unionem et pacem" = "Lettre de Messire Marcus Marulus de Split à Adrien VI. souverain pontife au sujet des malheurs qui se produisent et exhortation à l'union et à la paix de tous les chretiens." In *Programme du concert d'ouverture Luxembourg et Grande Région, Capitale européenne de la Culture 2007*, 10-15. Luxembourg, 2006. Latin edition with French translation, selections.

Lafon, G., trans. "Epistola domini Marci Maruli Spalatensis ad Adrianum VI. pontificem maximum de calamitatibus occurrentibus et exhortatio ad communem omnium Christianorum unionem et pacem" = "Lettre de Messire Marcus Marulus de Split à Adrien VI. souverain pontife au sujet des malheurs qui se produisent et exhortation à l'union et à la paix de tous les chrétiens." In *Epistola. Cantate pour solistes, choeur & grand orchestre; texte de Marko Marulić*, by I. Malec. Paris, 2006. French translation, selections, p. 4.

Lučin, B., ed. *Duhom do zvijezda*. Zagreb: Mozaik, 2001. Croatian translation by V. Gligo, V. Gortan, and D. Novaković, pp. 331-43.

Mirth, K., trans. "Epistola domini Marci Maruli Spalatensis ad Adrianum VI. pont. max. de calamitatibus occurrentibus et exhortatio ad communem omnium christianorum unionem et pacem, Roma 1522." *CM* 13 (2004) 203-4. Spanish translation, selections.

Novaković, D., ed. *Hrvatski latinisti. Razdoblje humanizma*. Zagreb: n.p., 1997. Croatian translation by V. Gligo and V. Gortan, selections, pp. 66-71.

Pivčević, E., trans. "Letter from Marko Marulić to Pope Adrian VI." *British-Croatian Review* 4 (1977) 10-12. English translation, selections.

Tomasović, M., and T. Maroević, eds. *Plavca nova.* Split: n.p., 1971. Croatian translation, selections, pp. 160-61.

Studies

Cattaneo, R. "L'*Epistola a papa Adriano VI* di Marco Marulić in Italiano. Versione e nota traduttologica." CM 22 (2013) 145-49.

Cattaneo, R. "O stilu i kulturnom značenju Marulićeve *Poslanice papi Adrijanu VI.*" CM 17 (2008) 91-115. With summary in Italian, "Sullo stile e la rilevanza culturale dell'Epistola a Papa Adriano VI di Marco Marulić," pp. 116-24.

Gligo, V. "Marko Marulić Splićanin, Pismo papi Hadrijanu VI o nevoljama koje nahrupljuju i poticaj za opće jedinstvo i mir svih kršćana." In *Govori protiv Turaka,* edited by V. Gligo, 141-63. Split: Logos, 1983.

Jovanović, N. "Antiturcica iterata—ponovni pogled na hrvatsku renesansnu protutursku književnost." CM 25 (2016) 101-148. With English summary, "Antiturcica iterata—Another Look at Croatian Anti-Turkish Writings during the Renaissance."

Jovanović, N. "Croatian Anti-Turkish Writings during the Renaissance." In *Christian-Muslim Relations: A Bibliographical History,* vol. 7, *Central and Eastern Europe, Asia, Africa and South America (1500-1600),* edited by D. Thomas and J. Chesworth, 491-515. Leiden: Brill, 2015.

Jozić, B. "Nepoznato pismo pape Hadrijana VI. Marku Maruliću." CM 25 (2016) 149-56. With English summary, "An Unknown Letter of Pope Adrian VI to Marko Marulić."

Marijanović, S. "Poslanice Marka Marulića i Stjepana Brodarića papi Hadrijanu VI. (s osvrtom na temu 'suprotiva Turkom' sjevernohrvatskih humanista." CM 12 (2003) 85-93. With Englishh summary, "The Epistles of Marko Marulić and Stjepan Brodarić to Pope Adrian VI (with Reference to the 'Against the Turks' Theme of the Northern Croatian Humanists)."

Novaković, D. "Marko Marulić and the Metaphysical Dimension of History." In *Epistola domini Marci Maruli Spalatensis ad Adrianum VI,* edited by Josip Bratulić, 43-52. Zagreb: Nacionalna i Sveučilišna Biblioteka; Split: Crkva u Svijetu, 1994.

Paić, I. *Sloboda i strah. Hermeneutika predziđa—ogled o iskustvu svijesti hrvatskoga narodnog opstanka.* Zagreb: Hrvatska Sveučilišna Naklada, 1997. Pp. 179-80.

Pivčević, E. "Letter from Marko Marulić to Pope Adrian VI." *British-Croatian Review* 4 (1977) 10.

Posset, F. "The Mouse, the Frog, and the Unidentified Flying Object: Metaphors for 'Empires' in the Latin Works of the Croatian Humanist Marcus Marulus and of the German Humanist Ulrich von Hutten." CM 17 (2008) 125-48.

———. "Open Letter of a Croatian Lay Theologian to a 'German' Pope: Marko Marulić to Adrian VI." CM 18 (2009) 5-27.

In discordiam principum Christianorum
("Against the Discord among Christian Rulers")

Date: unknown; about 1522

Original language: Latin

Description

This work, only twelve lines long, may have been written at about the same time as the 1522 open letter to Pope Hadrian VI, because it also uses Aesop's fable of the Mouse and the Frog, which are both threatened by the Bird of Prey, their common enemy. Like the letter, it is against the disunity of the nations in Europe who wage wars against one other instead of against the Turks, their "barbarian enemy."

Significance

Marulus's advocacy of papal leadership against the Turks here, as in his other writings, proves once more his distinct Roman Catholic position among authors writing about the Turkish threat at the time.

Manuscripts

MS Glasgow, University Library: Hunter 334 / U. 8.2, f. CVIv–CVIIr (c. 1524–1550)

Editions and Translations

Hekman, J., ed. *Split 1999: Dossier*. Zagreb: Matica Hrvatska, 2006. Croatian translation by D. Novaković, p. 242.
Lučin, B., ed. *Marci Maruli Opera omnia*, vol. 17. Latin-Croatian edition, translation by D. Novaković, pp. 164–67 (no. 96).
Lučin, B. *Marko Marulić: 1450–1524*. Split: Hrvatsko-Njemačko Društvo, 2008. Croatian translation by D. Novaković, German translation by K. Jurčević, p. 53.
Lučin, B., ed. *The Marulić Reader*. Split: Književni Krug, Marulianum, 2007. Croatian-English edition, English translation by M. Kovačićek, pp. 144–47.
McMaster, G., and M. Kovačićek. "Latin Poems / Marko Marulić." *Most / The Bridge Literary Magazine* 1–4 (1999) 85. English translation.
Novaković, D., ed. "Marci Marvli epigrammata." CM 6 (1997) 37–77. First edition, p. 42.
Novaković, D., ed. and trans. *Marco Marulić. Glasgowski stihovi*. Zagreb: Matica Hrvatska, 1999. Pp. 24–25.

Studies

Posset, F. "The Mouse, the Frog, and the Unidentified Flying Object: Metaphors for 'Empires' in the Latin Works of the Croatian Humanist Marcus Marulus and of the German Humanist Ulrich von Hutten." CM 17 (2008) 125-48.

Ad Clementem VII. Pontificem Maximum ("To Clement VII, Supreme Pontiff")

Date: after November 19, 1523
Original language: Latin

Description

This is a congratulatory poem of thirty-two lines which does not appear to have actually been sent to the newly elected Pope Clement VII (in office November 19, 1523 to 1534), who was "probably the most disastrous of all the popes" (Leopold von Ranke).

Marulus employs a play on words based on the pope's family name, Medici, and the Latin *medicus* ("physician"), as he had done before in his poem for the previous Medici pope, Leo X, cousin of Clement VII. Marulus again expresses his hope that the new pope will unite Europe against the Turkish threat. This is the pope's task. The poem is thus similar to the open letter to Pope Hadrian and to the "Lament of the City of Jerusalem." It also includes a catalogue of Turkish atrocities that is reminiscent of the "Prayer against the Turks," while the hint that some Christians even resort to converting to Islam (*Maumetica sacra sequuntur*) repeats what is said in *De ultimo Christi iudicio* (*Nonne nostra ętate plurimos nouimus a fide discessisse et ex Christianis Mahumetanos factos?*).[34]

Significance

This is Marulus's last known piece in the anti-Turcica genre and, as far as we know, the very last thing he wrote (he died only a month and a half after the pope's election, on January 5, 1524). The poem calls for the unity of the Christian nations against the Turkish threat; the underlying thought in the poem is *Nomen est omen*: the Medici name, "so venerable to us," is a good omen for those who are oppressed by war. The Medici pope should be like

---

34. OO, 11:235.

a physician, who with his medicine would be able to heal any wounds that "the perfidious barbarian inflicts on us," referring to the Ottomans, who were attacking Marulus's home region. The poem testifies to the author's impulse for literary engagement in the public appeal for anti-Turkish resistance, as well as to his undying hope that the saving and uniting impetus might come from the pope—a hope he retained up to the very last moments of his life.

Manuscripts

MS Glasgow, University Library: Hunter 334 / U. 8.2, f. CXXr–CXXv (c. 1524–1550)

Editions and Translations

Lučin, B., ed. *Duhom do zvijezda*. Zagreb: Mozaik, 2001. Croatian translation by D. Novaković, pp. 454–55.

Lučin, B., ed. *Marko Marulić: 1450–1524*. Split: Hrvatsko-Njemačko Društvo, 2008. Croatian-German edition, German translation by K. Jurčević, p. 53.

Lučin, B., ed. *Marci Maruli Opera omnia*, vol. 17. Latin-Croatian edition, translation by D. Novaković, p. 170 (no. 101).

Novaković, D., ed. "Marci Marvli epigrammata." CM 6 (1997) 37–77. First edition, pp. 66–67.

Novaković, D., ed. *Marko Marulić, Glasgowski stihovi*. Zagreb: Matica Hrvatska, 1999. Latin-Croatian edition, pp. 106–9.

No studies.

In Place of a Conclusion

IN MARULUS'S HOMETOWN OF Split there is a Franciscan monastery (St. Anthony) whose church is dedicated to the Assumption of the Blessed Virgin Mary. This church is not to be confused with the church of his burial place, St. Francis, in a different part of the city. This church in the neighborhood of Poljud, near the sports stadium, houses an extraordinary painting which is displayed on the northern wall of the church (not an "altarpiece"). The Immaculate Virgin Mary is shown in a lecture hall being surrounded by numerous, presumably mostly Christian theologians, who apparently talk about the immaculate conception of the Virgin. They show their messages on scrolls which they hold in front of them.

We do not know whether Marulus, our "Advocate of the Evangelical Truth," ever saw the original painting which Nikola Bralić (Braccio) created between 1515 and 1518, i.e., during Marulus's lifetime. What is extraordinary about it is that the artist included Mohammed, who is featured with his scroll and, being placed in the foreground, it is clearly legible. Mohammed points to a quotation from the Koran which is given in Latin, including the source reference to the *Coranus*, i.e., the Koran, book 5:

> *Nullus est, ex Adam, quem non tenuerit Satan, pręter Mariam et Filium eius.*
> "No one descended from Adam has not been touched by Satan, except Mary and her Son."

The present picture which is on display in the church is, however, a copy made in 1727 by the Split architect and painter Mihovil Luposignoli of the Baroque period.[1]

---

1. Tolan 2016, 115. I am grateful to B. Lućin for making me aware of this book.

According to legend the painting saved the church from destruction by the Ottoman army because of the depiction of Mohammed. The city of Split, with this church and its painting, now lost, from the early sixteenth century represents the bulwark of Western Christianity against advances of armies of the Ottoman Turks.

Fig. 8.1. Painting by Mihovil Luposignoli (1727).

IN PLACE OF A CONCLUSION 185

Fig. 8.2. Detail from lower right corner of the painting.

Bibliography

Akkerman, Fokke, Gerda Huisman, and Arjo Vanderjagt, eds. *Wessel Gansfort (1419–1489) and Northern Humanism*. Leiden: Brill, 1993.

Albrecht, Edelgard. *Das Türkenbild in der ragusanisch-dalmatinischen Literatur des XVI. Jahrhunderts*. Bern: Peter Lang, 1965.

Andrassy, Vera, trans. "Epistola domini Marci Maruli Spalatensis ad Adrianum VI. pontificem maximum de calamitatibus occurrentibus et exhortatio ad communem omnium Christianorum unionem et pacem" ["Epistle of Lord Marko Marulić of Split to Pope Adrian VI about present misfortunes and a call to union and peace of all Christians"]. In *The Marulić Reader*, edited by Bratislav Lučin, 90–109. Split: Književni Krug, 2007.

Augustijn, Cornelis. *Humanismus*. Translated into German by Hinrich Stoevesandt. Die Kirche in ihrer Geschichte. Ein Handbuch 2. Göttingen: Vandenhoeck & Ruprecht, 2003.

Awerbuch, Marianne. "Imperium. Zum Bedeutungswandel des Wortes im staatsrechtlichen und politischen Bewußtsein der Römer." *Archiv für Begriffsgeschichte* 25 (1981) 162–84.

Babcock, William S. *The Book of Rules of Tyconius*. Atlanta: Scholars, 1989.

Backer, Augustin de. *Essai bibliographique sur le livre De imitatione Christi*. L. Liège: Grandmont-Donders, 1864.

Becker, Kenneth Michael. *From the Treasure-House of Scripture: An Analysis of Scriptural Sources in De Imitatione Christi*. Brepols: Turnhout, 2002.

Béné, Charles. *La reception des oeuvres de Marulić dans les provinces du Nord*. Split: Književni Krug, 1995.

———. "Les Pères de l'Église et la réception des auteurs classiques." In *Die Rezeption der Antike. Zum Problem der Kontinuität zwischen Mittelalter und Renaissance*, edited by August Buck, 41–53. Hamburg: Ernst Hauswedell, 1981.

———. *Sudbina Jedne Pjesme* [*Destin d'un Poème; Destiny of a Poem*]: *Carmen de Doctrina Domini Nostri Iesu Christi Pendentis in Cruce Marci Maruli*. Split: Književni Krug; Zagreb: Nacionalna i Sveučilišna Biblioteka,1994.

Benecke, Gerhard. *Society and Politics in Germany 1500–1750*. London: Routledge, 2006.

Bernstein, Eckhard. "Humanistische Intelligenz und kirchliche Reformen." In *Die Literatur im Übergang vom Mittelalter zur Neuzeit*, edited by Werner Röcke and Marina Münkler, 176–79. Munich: Carl Hanser, 2004.

Beutel, Albrecht. "Predigt." In *Das Luther-Lexikon*, edited by Volker Leppin and Gury Schneider-Ludorff, 559. Regensburg: Bückle & Böhm, 2014.

Biasiori, Lucio. "Before the Inquisitor: A Thousand Ways of Being Lutheran." In *Luther: A Christian between Reforms and Modernity (1517–2017)*, edited by Alberto Melloni, 1:509–26. Berlin: de Gruyter, 2017.

Biemer, Günter. "Laientheologe im Mittelalter, Ramon Lull (1232–1315/116)." *Katechetische Blätter* 114 (1989) 145–48.

Bietenholz, Peter G., and Thomas B. Deutscher, eds. *Contemporaries of Erasmus: A Biographical Register of the Renaissance and Reformation*. 3 vols. Toronto: University of Toronto Press, 1985–1987.

Bigane, John E. *Faith, Christ or Peter: Matthew 16:18 in Sixteenth Century Roman Catholic Exegesis*. Washington, DC: University Press of America, 1981.

Bihlmeyer, Karl, and Hermann Tüchle. *Kirchengeschichte*. 3 vols. Paderborn: Schöningh, 1960.

Bisaha, Nancy. *Creating East and West. Renaissance Humanists and the Ottoman Turks*. Philadelphia: University of Pennsylvania Press, 2004.

Bleibrunner, Hans, ed. *Das Leben des heiligen Wolfgang nach dem Holzschnittbuch des Johann Weyssenburger aus dem Jahre 1515*. Regensburg: Pustet, 1967.

Böcking, Eduard, ed. *Ulrichs von Hutten Schriften*. Leipzig: Teubner, 1862.

Boehmer, Heinrich. *Martin Luther: Road to Reformation*. New York: Meridian, 1957.

Bohnstedt, John W. *The Infidel Scourge of God: The Turkish Menace as Seen by German Pamphleteers of the Reformation Era*. Philadelphia: American Philosophical Society, 1968.

Botley, Paul. *Latin Translation in the Renaissance: The Theory and Practice of Leonardo Bruni, Giannozzo Manetti and Erasmus*. Cambridge: Cambridge University Press, 2004.

Božićević, Frane. *Život Marka Marulića Splićanina* [*Vita Marci Maruli Spalatensis*]. Translated and edited by Bratislav Lučin. Split: Marulianum, 2007.

Brashler, James. "Pseudepigraphy." In *The New Westminster Dictionary of Church History*, edited by Robert Benedetto et al., 1:542. Louisville: Westminster John Knox, 2008.

Brecht, Martin. "Luther und die Türken." In *Europa und die Türken in der Renaissance*, edited by Bodo Guthmüller und Wilhelm Kühlmann, 9–27. Frühe Neuzeit 54. Tübingen: Max Niemeyer, 2000.

British Museum. *Catalogue of Printed Books: Luther (Martin)*. London: W. Clowes, 1894.

Bubrin, Vladimir. "Renaissance to the East: Western Scholarship's Blind Spot or Justified Neglect?" CM 22 (2013) 161–82.

Budiša, Dražen. "Humanism in Croatia." In *Renaissance Humanism: Foundations, Forms, and Legacy*, edited by Albert Rabil Jr., 2:265–92. Philadelphia: University of Pennsylvania Press, 1991.

Bunte, Wolfgang. *Rabbinische Traditionen bei Nikolaus von Lyra: Ein Beitrag zur Schriftauslegung des Spätmittelalters*. Frankfurt: Peter Lang, 1994.

Burckhardt, Jacob. *The Civilization of the Renaissance in Italy*. London: Phaidon, 1995.

Burns James H., and Thomas M. Izbicki, eds. *Conciliarism and Papalism*. Cambridge: Cambridge University Press, 1997.

Cahn, Walter. "Architecture and Exegesis: Richard of St.-Victor's Ezekiel Commentary and Its Illustrations." *The Art Bulletin* 76 (1994) 53-68.

Cattaneo, Ruggero. "Sullo stile e la rilevanza culturale dell' Epistola a Papa Adriano VI di Marco Marulić." CM 17 (2008) 91-124.

Chamberlin, E. R. *The Bad Popes*. New York: Dorset, 1969.

Chen, Sheryl Frances. "Bernard's Prayer Before the Crucifix that Embraced Him: Cistercians and Devotion to the Wounds of Christ." *Cistercian Studies Quarterly* 29 (1994) 23-54.

Clark, Elizabeth A., and Diane F. Hatch. *The Golden Bough, the Oaken Cross: The Virgilian Cento of Faltonia Betitia Proba*. Chico, CA: Scholars, 1981.

Colloquia Maruliana IX: Atti del Convegno Internazionale Marco Marulic, poeta Croato e Umanista Cattolico: Una Proposta per l'Europa del Terzo Millennio, 26-29 Novembre 1998, Spalato, 19-20 Aprile 1999. Rome: Pontificium consilium de cultura; Split: Knjizevni Krug, 2000.

Cooper, Henry R., Jr., trans. and ed. *Judita*. Boulder, CO: East European Monographs, 1991.

Coudert, Allison P., and Jeffrey S. Shoulson, eds. *Hebraica Veritas? Christian Hebraists and the Study of Judaism in Early Modern Europe*. Philadelphia: University of Pennsylvania Press, 2004.

Cronia, Arturo. "Marko Marulic: Ein Vertreter und Deuter der christlichen Renaissance in Dalmatien." Translated by O. Hietsch. *Wiener Slavistisches Jahrbuch* 3 (1953) 5-21.

Cytowska, Maria. "Erasme et les Turcs." *Eos: Commentarii Societatis Philologiae Polonorum* 62 (1974) 311-21.

Dall'Asta, Matthias, and Gerald Dörner, eds. *Johannes Reuchlin Briefwechsel*. 4 vols. Stuttgart-Bad Cannstatt: Frommann-Holzboog, 2000-11.

Daly, Lloyd W. "Guillelmus Brito and His Works." *The Library Chronicle* 32 (1966) 1-17.

De Simone, Daniel, ed. *A Heavenly Craft: The Woodcut in Early Printed Books*. New York: George Braziller, in association with the Library of Congress, 2004.

De Smet, Rudolf, ed. *Les humanistes et leur bibliothèque: Actes du colloque international: Bruxelles, 26-28 août 1999 [Humanists and Their Libraries: Proceedings of the International Conference]*. Travaux de l'Institut interuniversitaire pour l'étude de la renaissance et de l'humanisme 13. Leuven: Peeters, 2002.

Delgado, Mariano. "Patterns in the Reception of Luther in the Hispanic World." In *Luther: A Christian between Reforms and Modernity (1517-2017)*, edited by Alberto Melloni, 3:1261-62. Berlin: de Gruyter, 2017.

Denk, J. "Pseudo-Laktanz' 'Carmen de passione Domini'—das Machwerk eines italienischen Humanisten aus dem 15. Jahrhundert?" *Theologische Revue* 5 (1906) 382-83.

Dickens, A. G. *Reformation and Society in Sixteenth-Century Europe*. London: Harcourt, Brace, 1966.

Diller, Aubrey, Leendert G. Westerink, and Henry D. Saffrey. *Bibliotheca graeca manuscripta cardinalis Dominici Grimani (1461-1523)*. Venice, Edizioni della Laguna, 2003.

Dingel, Irene. "Luther und Europa." In *Luther Handbuch*, edited by Albrecht Beutel, 240-52. Tübingen: Mohr Siebeck, 2017.

D'Onofrio, Giulio. *History of Theology II: The Middle Ages*. Translated by Matthew J. O'Connell. Collegeville, MN: Liturgical Press, 2008.

Egg, Erich, and Wolfgang Pfaundler, eds. *Kaiser Maximilian I und Tirol*. Innsbruck, Vienna, Munich: Tyrolia, 1969.

Eire, Carlos M. N. "Vives, Juan Luis." In *New Westminster Dictionary of Church History*, edited by Robert Benedetto et al., 1:669. Louisville: Westminster John Knox, 2008.

Erdmann, Elisabeth von. "Marcus Marulus Spalatensis—Marko Marulić aus Split (1450–1524). Zu einem Forschungsprojekt in Split, Zadar und Zagreb." *Südost-Forschungen. Internationale Zeitschrift für Geschichte, Kultur und Landeskunde Südosteuropas* 58 (1999) 313–20.

———. „Marko Marulić in den Religionskonflikten der Deutschen Länder des 16. Jahrhunderts." CM 20 (2011) 177–93.

———. "Marko Marulićs Werke in der deutschen Kultur." CM 18 (2009) 357–64.

———. "Zur Poetik von Marko Marulić (I): Der geistige Schriftsinn: Allegorie und Typologie." CM 9 (2000) 315–26.

Fata, Márta, and Anton Schindling, eds. *Luther und die Evangelisch-Lutherischen in Ungarn und Siebenbürgen vom 16. Jahrhundert bis 1918*. Münster: Aschendorff, 2017.

Fine, John V. A., Jr. *When Ethnicity Did Not Matter in the Balkans: A Study of Identity in Pre-Nationalist Croatia, Dalmatia, and Slavonia in the Medieval and Early Modern Periods*. Ann Arbor: University of Michigan Press, 2006.

Fischer-Galati, Stephen A. *Ottoman Imperialism and German Protestantism, 1521–1555*. Cambridge, MA: Harvard University Press, 1959; reprint, New York: Octagon, 1972.

Fontaine, Jacques. "Dominus lucis. Un titre singulier du Christ dans le dernier vers du Iuvencus." In *Mémorial André-Jean Festugière: Antiquité païenne et chrétienne*, edited by Enzo Lucchesi and Henry D. Saffrey, 131–41. Cahiers d'Orientalisme 10. Geneva: Cramer, 1984.

Francisco, Adam S. "Martin Luther." In *Christian-Muslim Relations: A Bibliographic History*, vol. 7, *Central and Eastern Europe, Asia, Africa and South America (1500–1600)*, edited by David Thomas et al., 225–34. Leiden: Brill, 2015.

Franolić, Branko. *A Historical Outline of Literary Croatian*. Zagreb and London: Erasmus, 2008.

Freudenberger, Theobald. "Die Bibliothek des Kardinals Domenico Grimani," *Historisches Jahrbuch* 56 (1936) 15–45.

Friedrich, Udo. "Johannes Reuchlin am Heidelberger Hof. Poeta—orator—paedagogus." In *Reuchlin und die politischen Kräfte seiner Zeit*, edited by Stefan Rhein, 163–85. Sigmaringen: Thorbecke, 1998.

Froehlich, Karlfried. "Saint Peter, Papal Primacy, and the Exegetical Tradition, 1150–1300." In *The Religious Roles of the Papacy: Ideals and Realities 1150–1300*, edited by Christopher Ryan, 3–44. Toronto: Pontifical Institute of Medieval Studies, 1989.

Fuller, Foss. *The Brotherhood of the Common Life and Its Influence*. Albany, NY: SUNY Press, 1995.

Ganzer, Klaus, and Bruno Steimer, eds. *Lexikon der Reformationszeit*. Freiburg: Herder, 2002.

Garin, Eugenio, ed. *Renaissance Characters*. Translated by Lydia G. Cochrane. Chicago: University of Chicago Press, 1991.

Geiger, Ari. "A Student and an Opponent: Nicholas of Lyra and His Jewish Sources." In *Nicholas de Lyre, Franciscain du XIVe siècle, Exégète et théologien*, edited by Gilbert Dahan, 167–203. Paris: Institut d'Études Augustiniennes, 2011.
Gennadius of Marseilles, and Jerome. *Lives of Illustrious Men*. Translated by E. C. Richardson. In *Nicene and Post-Nicene Fathers* 2, edited by Philip Schaff and Henry Wace, 3:385–402. Grand Rapids: Eerdmans, 1953.
Gibbs, Laura, trans. *Aesop's Fables*. Oxford: Oxford University Press, 2002. Available at http://mythfolklore.net/aesopica/oxford/index.htm.
Gillert, Karl, ed. *Der Briefwechsel des Conradus Mutianus*. 2 vols. Halle: O. Hendel, 1890.
Gligo, Vedran, ed. *Govori protiv Turaka / Orationes contra Turcas*. Split: Logos, 1983.
Glavičić, Branimir, trans. and ed. *Latinska manja djela*. Split: Knjizevni Krug, 1992.
———, ed. *Repertorium*. 3 vols. Split: Književni Krug, 1998–2000.
Glavičić, Branimir, and Bratislav Lučin, eds. *Marci Maruli Opera omnia*. Vols. 1–16 edited by B. Glavičić, vols. 17– edited by B. Lučin. Split: Književni Krug, 1988–.
Gleason, Elizabeth G. *Gasparo Contarini: Venice, Rome, and Reform*. University of California Press, 1993.
Gloning, Marian. "Konrad Reuter, Abt von Kaisheim 1509–1540." *Studien und Mitteilungen zur Geschichte des Benediktinerordens und seiner Zweige*, Neue Folge, 2 (1912) 450–92.
Göllner, Carl. *Turcica: Die europäischen Türkendrucke des XVI. Jahrhunderts*. 3 vols. Bucarest: Editura Academiei, 1961–78.
Gortan, Veljko, and Vladimir Vratović. "The Basic Characteristics of Croatian Latinity." *Humanistica Lovaniensia* 20 (1971) 37–67.
Gow, Andrew Colin. *The Red Jews: Antisemitism in an Apocalyptic Age, 1200–1600*. Leiden: Brill, 1995.
Grosse, Sven. *Heilsungewissheit und Scrupulositas im späten Mittelalter: Studien zu Johannes Gerson und Gattungen der Frömmigkeitstheologie seiner Zeit*. Tübingen: Mohr Siebeck, 1994.
Guthmüller, Bodo, and Wilhelm Kühlmann, eds. *Europa und die Türken in der Renaissance*. Tübingen: Niemeyer, 2000.
Hagen, Kenneth. "A Ride on the *Quadriga* with Luther." *Luther-Bulletin* 13 (2004) 5–24.
Hagen, Kenneth. *The Word Does Everything: Key Concepts of Luther on Testament, Scripture, Vocation, Cross, and Worm. Also on Method and on Catholicism. Collection of Essays*. Milwaukee: Marquette University Press, 2016.
Hailperin, Herman. *Rashi and the Christian Scholars*. Pittsburg: University of Pittsburg Press, 1963.
Hamm, Berndt. *Frömmigkeitstheologie am Anfang des 16. Jahrhunderts. Studien zu Johannes von Paltz und seinem Umkreis*. Tübingen: Mohr/Siebeck, 1982.
———. "Hieronymus-Begeisterung und Augustinismus vor der Reformation: Beobachtungen zur Beziehung zwischen Humanismus und Frömmigkeitstheologie (am Beispiel Nürnbergs)." In *Augustine, the Harvest, and Theology (1300–1650): Essays Dedicated to Heiko Augustinus Oberman in Honor of his Sixtieth Birthday*, edited by Kenneth Hagen, 127–235. Leiden: Brill, 1990.
Hans-Jörg Köhler, ed. *Flugschriften als Massenmedium der Reformationszeit*. Stuttgart: Klett-Cotta, 1981.
Heger, Henrik, and Janine Matillon. *Les croates et la civilisation du livre*. Paris: Presses de l'Université de Paris-Sorbonne, 1986.

Heinsdorff, Cornel. *Christus, Nikodemus und die Samaritanerin bei Iuvencus: Mit einem Anhang zur lateinischen Evangelienvorlage.* Berlin: de Gruyter, 2003.

Hekman, J., ed. *Split 1999: Dossier.* Zagreb: Matica Hrvatska, 2005.

Helmrath, Johannes. "Pius II." In *Dictionary of Popes and the Papacy*, edited by Bruno Steimer and Michael G. Parker, translated by Brian McNeil and Peter Heinigg. New York: Crossroad, 2001.

Hernán, Enrique García. "Ignatius: The Anti-Lutheran Reformer." In *Luther: A Christian between Reforms and Modernity (1517-2017)*, edited by Alberto Melloni, 1:536-37. Berlin: de Gruyter, 2017.

Hervieux, Léopold. *Les fabulistes latins depuis le siècle d'Auguste jusqu'à la fin du Moyen-Age (1893-1899).* Vol. 2, *Phèdre et ses anciens imitateurs directs et indirects.* Hildesheim: G. Olms, 1970.

Herzog, Reinhart. *Die Bibelepik der lateinischen Spätantike: Formgeschichte einer erbaulichen Gattung.* Munich: Fink, 1975.

Hobbs, R. Gerald. "Hebraica Veritas and Traditio Apostolica: Saint Paul and the Interpretation of the Psalms in the Sixteenth Century." In *The Bible in the Sixteenth Century*, edited by David Steinmetz, 83-99. Durham, NC: Duke University Press, 1990.

Hocks, Else. *Der letzte deutsche Papst: Adrian VI. 1522-1523.* Freiburg: Herder, 1939.

Horvat, Marijana and Sanja Perić Gavrančić. "Observations on the Lexis of Marulić's *Naslidovan'je (Imitation)*—from Latin Original to Croatian Translation." CM 19 (2010) 235-35.

Housley, Norman. "A Necessary Evil? Erasmus, the Crusade, and War against the Turks." In *The Crusades and Their Sources: Essays Presented to Bernard Hamilton*, edited by John France and William G. Zajac, 259-79. Aldershot: Ashgate, 1998.

Husner, Fritz. "Die Bibliothek des Erasmus." In *Gedenkschrift zum 400 Todestag des Erasmus von Rotterdam*, 228-59. Basel: Braus-Riggenbach, 1936.

Iserloh, Erwin. *The Theses Were Not Posted: Luther between Reform and Reformation.* Toronto: Saunders of Toronto, 1966; Boston: Beacon, 1968.

Jerome, and Gennadius of Marseilles. *On Illustrious Men.* Translated by T. P. Halton. Washington, DC: Catholic University of America Press, 2000.

Jovanović, Neven, ed. *Carmina Latina amicorum Maruli.* CM 15 (2006) 175-97.

———. "Paratekst i *loci Biblici* kao put od stila do tumačenja Marulićeva *Evanđelistara*." CM 12 (2003) 23-45.

Jozić, Branko. "The Biographical Elements in Marulić's Epistolary Texts." English summary. CM 17 (2008) 156.

———. "Marulić and the Dualist Temptation." CM 18 (2009) 239-48.

———. "An Unknown Letter of Pope Adrian VI to Marko Marulić." English summary. CM 25 (2016) 149-156.

Jozić, Branko, and Bratislav Lučin, eds. *Pet stoljeća Marulićeva Evanđelistara (1516-2016).* Split: Marulianum, 2016.

———. *Bibliografija Marka Marulića.* Split: Književni Krug, 1998.

Junghans, Helmar. *Der junge Luther und die Humanisten.* Weimar: Böhlaus, 1984; Göttingen: Vandenhoeck & Ruprecht, 1985.

———. "Der nationale Humanismus bei Ulrich von Hutten und Martin Luther." In *Spätmittelalter, Luthers Reformation, Kirche in Sachsen. Ausgewählte Aufsätze*, edited by Michael Beyer and Günther Wartenberg, 67-90. Leipzig: Evangelische Verlagsanstalt, 2001.

———. "Plädoyer für 'Wildwuchs der Reformation' als Metapher." In *Spätmittelalter, Luthers Reformation, Kirche in Sachsen. Ausgewählte Aufsätze*, edited by Michael Beyer and Günther Wartenberg, 261–67. Leipzig: Evangelische Verlagsanstalt, 2001.

Jurišić, Hrvatin Gabrijel. "A Time for Re-Examination." In *Epistola domini Marci Maruli Spalatensis ad Adrianum VI*, edited by Josip Bratulić. Zagreb: Nacionalna i Sveučilišna Biblioteka; Split: Crkva u Svijetu, 1994.

Kartschoke, Dieter. *Bibeldichtung. Studien zur Geschichte der epischen Bibelparaphrase von Iuvencus bis Otfried von Weissenburg*. Munich: Fink, 1975.

Kaufmann, Thomas. "Luther und die reformatorische Bewegung in Deutschland." In *Luther Handbuch*, edited by Albrecht Beutel. Tübingen: Mohr Siebeck, 2017.

Kečkemet, Duško. *The Place of Jews in the History of the City of Split*. Condensed English version by Živko Vekarić. 3rd ed. Lipanj: n.p., 2000.

Keil, Gundolff, and Marianne Halbleib. "Biobibliographisches zu Paulus Ricius." *Würzburger medizinhistorische Mitteilungen* 7 (1989) 233–36.

Kleinhans, Arduinus. "De vita et operibus Petri Galatini, O.F.M. Scientiarum Biblicarum Cultoris (c. 1460–1540)." *Antonianum* 1 (1926) 145–79.

Klepper, Deeana Copeland. *The Insight of Unbelievers: Nicholas of Lyra and Christian Reading of Jewish Text in the Later Middle Ages*. Philadelphia: University of Pennsylvania Press, 2007.

Knjizevni Krug Split, ed. Œuvres complètes de Marko *Marulic / Marci Maruli Opera omnia*. Split: Cercle littéraire de Split, 1984–.

Kock, Thomas. *Die Buchkultur der Devotio Moderna: Handschriftenproduktion, Literaturversorgung und Bibliotheksaufbau im Zeitalter des Medienwechsels*. Frankfurt: Peter Lang, 2002.

Kohler, Alfred, ed. *Quellen zur Geschichte Karls V*. Darmstadt: Wissenschaftliche Buchgesellschaft, 1990.

Köhler, Hans-Jörg, ed. *Flugschriften als Massenmedium der Reformationszeit*. Stuttgart: Klett-Cotta, 1981.

Köpf, Ulrich, ed. *Theologen des Mittelalters: Eine Einführung* Darmstadt: Wissenschaftliche Buchgesellschaft, 2002.

———. *Martin Luther: Der Reformator und sein Werk*. Stuttgart: Reclam, 2015.

Krause, Carl. *Der Briefwechsel des Mutianus Rufus*. Kassel: A Freyschmidt, 1885.

Kreitzer, Beth. "The Lutheran Sermon." In *Preachers and People in the Reformations and Early Modern Period*, edited by Larissa Taylor, 35-63. Leiden: Brill, 2001.

Krey, Philip D. W. "Döring, Matthias." In *The New Westminster Dictionary of Church History*, edited by Robert Benedetto et al., 1:205. Louisville: Westminster John Knox, 2008.

———. "Paul of Burgos." In *The New Westminster Dictionary of Church History*, edited by Robert Benedetto et al., 1:501. Louisville: Westminster John Knox, 2008.

Kristeller, Paul Oskar. *Renaissance Thought: The Classic, Scholastic, and Humanistic Strains*. New York: Harper, 1961.

Kück, E., ed. *Die Schriften Hartmuths von Cronberg*. Halle: Niemeyer, 1899.

Kühlmann, Wilhelm. "Der Poet und das Reich—Politische, kontextuelle und ästhetische Dimensionen der humanistischen Türkenlyrik in Deutschland." In *Europa und die Türken in der Renaissance*, edited by Bodo Guthmüller and Wilhelm Kühlmann, 193–248. Tübingen: Niemeyer, 2000.

Künzle, Pius, ed. *Heinrich Seuses Horologium Sapientiae*. Fribourg: Universitätsverlag, 1977.
Labowsky, Lotte. *Bessarion's Library and the Biblioteca Marciana: Six Early Inventories*. Rome: Edizioni di storia e letteratura, 1979.
Landsberg, John. *A Letter from Jesus Christ*. Translated and edited by John Griffiths. Gill's Spiritual Classics. New York: Crossroad, 1981.
Leschinkohl, Franz. "Marko Marulić in the Germanophone Part of Europe—Switzerland." [Marulićeva djela na njemačkom jezičnom području u Europi: Švicarska.] CM 10 (2001) 257–66.
Liepold, Antonio. *Wider den Erbfeind christlichen Glaubens: Die Rolle des niederen Adels in den Türkenkriegen des 16. Jahrhunderts*. Frankfurt: Lang, 1998.
Lourdeau, W., and D. Verhelst, eds. *The Concept of Heresy in the Middle Ages (11th–13th C.): Proceedings of the International Conference, Louvain, May 13–16, 1973*. Leuven: Leuven University Press; Hague: M. Nijhoff, 1976.
Lučin, Bratislav. "Erasmus and the Croats in the Fifteenth and Sixteenth Centuries." *Erasmus of Rotterdam Society Yearbook* 24 (2004), 89–114.
———, ed. *The Marulić Reader*. Split: Književni Krug, Marulianum, 2007.
———. "Od uskarsa Isusova." CM 1 (1992) 95–114.
———. "*Studia humanitatis* u Marulićevoj knjižnici." CM 6 (1997) 170–201.
Lučin, Bratislav, and Darko Novaković, eds. *Latinski stihovi*. Vol. 15 of Split: Književni Krug, 2005.
Ludwig, Pastor. *The History of the Popes, from the Close of the Middle Ages: Drawn from the Secret Archives of the Vatican and Other Original Sources*. London: Routledge and Kegan Paul, 1898–.
Luther, Martin. *D. Martin Luthers Werke: Kritische Gesamtausgabe*. Weimar, Böhlau: 1883–.
Machaffie, Barbara J. "Proba." In *The New Westminster Dictionary of Church History*, edited by Robert Benedetto et al., 1:537. Louisville: Westminster John Knox, 2008.
Marcovich, Miroslav, ed. *M. Marvli Delmatae Davidias*. Leiden: Brill, 2006.
Marijanović, Stanislav. "The Epistles of Marko Marulić and Stjepan Brodarić to Pope Adrian VI." CM 12 (2003) 84–92.
Markwald, Rudolf K. *A Mystic's Passion: The Spirituality of Johannes von Staupitz in His 1520 Lenten Sermons. Translation and Commentary*. New York: Peter Lang, 1990.
McMaster, Graham, trans. "To Pope Leo X." In *The Marulić Reader*, edited by Bratislav Lučin, 144–45. Split: Književni Krug, 2007.
Meconi, David Vincent. "The Christian Cento and the Evangelization of Christian Culture." *Logos: A Journal of Catholic Thought and Culture* 7 (2004) 109–132.
Miller, Edward Waite. *Wessel Gansfort*. Vol. 1, *Life and Writings*; vol. 2, *Principal Works*. Translated by Jared Waterbury Scudder. New York: Putnam's, 1917.
Miller, Gregory J. "Fighting Like a Christian: The Ottoman Advance and the Development of Luther's Doctrine of Just War." In *Caritas et Reformatio: Essays on Church and Society in Honor of Carter Lindberg*, edited by David M. Whitford, 41–57. St. Louis: Concordia, 2002.
———. "Luther and the Turks." In *Luther: A Christian between Reforms and Modernity (1517–2017)*, edited by Alberto Melloni, 2:649–61. Berlin: de Gruyter, 2017.
———. "Luther on the Turks and Islam." In *Harvesting Martin Luther's Reflection on Theology, Ethics, and the Church*, edited by Timothy J. Wengert, 185–203. Grand Rapids: Eerdmans, 2004.

Nicholas, David. *The Transformation of Europe, 1300–1600*. New York: Oxford University Press, 1999.
Nobilis Domini Marci Maruli Testamentum. CM 13 (2005) 28–71.
Novaković, Darko. "La Davidiade di Marulić e gli epici protomedievali latini." CM 9 (2000) 205–17.
———. "Marulić and the Metaphysical Dimension of History." In *Epistola domini Marci Maruli Spalatensis ad Adrianum VI*, edited by Josip Bratulić, 43–52. Zagreb: Nacionalna i Sveučilišna Biblioteka; Split: Crkva u Svijetu, 1994.
———. "A New Marulić: Vita divi Hieronymi." CM 3 (1994) 5–24.
Olson, Oliver K. "Matthias Flacius Illyricus, 1520–1575." In *Shapers of Religious Traditions in Germany, Switzerland, and Poland, 1560–1600*, edited by Jill Raitt, 1–17. New Haven, CT: Yale University Press, 1981.
———. *Matthias Flacius and the Survival of Luther's Reform*. Wiesbaden: Harrassowitz, 2002.
Oswald, Josef. "Die Gedichte des Abtes Wolfgang Marius von Aldersbach." *Ostbairische Grenzmarken: Passauer Jahrbuch für Geschichte, Kunst und Volkskunde* (1964/65) 310–19.
Ott, Joachim, and Martin Treu, eds. *Luthers Thesenanschlag—Faktum oder Fiktion*. Leipzig: Evangelische Verlagsanstalt, 2008.
Pandžić, Zvonko. "'Magnificat Anima Mea Dominum': Croatian Translation und Exegesis of Marko Marulić." *Anafora: Journal of Literary Studies* 6 (2019) 7–80.
———. *Nepoznata proza Marka Marulića*. Zagreb: Tusculanae Editiones, 2009.
Parlov, Mladen. *Il mistero di Cristo: Modello di vita cristiana secondo Marco Marulić (1450–1524)*. Rome: Pontificia Universitas Gregoriana, 1997.
———. "Još jedna knjiga iz Marulićeve biblioteke." CM 9 (2000) 305–13.
———. "Marulićevo poimanje otajstva Crkve." CM 10 (2001) 167–86.
———. *Propagator fidei. S Marulom na putu*. Split: Crkva u svijetu, 2012.
Paulus, Nikolaus. "Wolfgang Mayer, ein baierischer Cisterzienser des 16. Jahrhunderts." *Historisches Jahrbuch* 15 (1894) 575–88.
Pelc, Milan. "Podrijetlo drvoreza Marulićeve *Judite* (1521–1523)." *Mogućnosti* 56/4–6 (2006) 1–12.
Pfleger, Luzian. "Nicolaus Salicetus, ein gelehrter elsässischer Cistercienserabt des 15. Jahrhunderts." *Studien und Mitteilungen aus dem Benediktiner und dem Cistercienser-Orden* 22 (1901) 588–97.
Pirie, Valérie. *The Triple Crown: An Account of the Papal Conclaves from the Fifteenth Century to the Present Day*. London: Sidgwick and Jackson, 1935.
Posner, Johann. *Der deutsche Papst Adrian VI*. Recklinghausen: Paulus, 1962.
Posset, Franz. "Affektive Christozentrik. Luther und Bernhard." *Geist & Leben: Zeitschrift für christliche Spiritualität* 89 (2016) 283–90 (Posset 2016a).
———. "Benedictus Chelidonius O.S.B. (c. 1460–1521), a Forgotten Monastic Humanist of the Renaissance." *The American Benedictine Review* 53 (2002) 430–32.
———. "A Cistercian Monk as Editor of the Carmen of the Croatian Humanist Marcus Marulus (died 1524): The German Humanist Henricus Urbanus, O. Cist. (died 1538)." *Cistercian Studies* 39 (2004) 399–419.
———. "Contarini, Gasparo." In *New Westminster Dictionary of Church History*, edited by Robert Benedetto et al., 1:169. Louisville: Westminster John Knox, 2008 (Posset 2008a).

———. "The Crucified Embraces Saint Bernard: The Beginnings of the *Amplexus Bernardi*." Cistercian Studies Quarterly 33 (1998) 289–314.

———. *Die zweifältige Erkenntnis: Geistliche Lesungen zum Thema Selbsterkenntnis und Gotteserkenntnis nach Bernhard von Clairvaux*. Nordhausen: Traugott Bautz, 2003 (Posset 2003a).

———. *The Front-Runner of the Catholic Reformation: The Life and Works of Johann von Staupitz*. Aldershot: Ashgate, 2003 (Posset 2003b).

———. "'The Hebrews Drink from the Source, the Greeks from the Rills and the Latin People from the Puddle'—Some Observations on Luther's Table Talk of August 9th, 1532." In *Ad Fontes Witebergenses: Select Proceedings of "Lutheranism and the Classics III: Lutherans Read History": Concordia Theological Seminary, Ft. Wayne, Indiana, October 2–3, 2014*, eds James A. Kellerman, E. J. Hutchinson, and Joshua J. Hayes, 249–62. Minneapolis: Lutheran, 2017 (Posset 2017a).

———. "The Illustrated *Biblia Cum Comento* from the Library of the Father of Croatian Literature, with samples of his Marginalia." CM 19 (2010) 141–61.

———. "Ispiratori e sostenitori di Lutero. Dal maestro Johann von Staupitz ai circoli di Norimberga e Augusta." In *Luther: A Christian between Reforms and Modernity (1517–2017)*, edited by Alberto Melloni. English and German ed.: Berlin: de Gruyter, 2017. Italian ed.: Bologna: Il Mulino, 2017 (Posset 2017b).

———. *Johann Reuchlin (1455–1522): A Theological Biography*. Berlin: de Gruyter, 2015 (Posset 2015a).

———. "Johann von Staupitz (c. 1465–1524) and Martin Luther (1483–1546): Two German Augustinians at Work for the Renewal of 'Preaching and Religious Formation.'" In *Lutero, La Riforma, Sant'Agostino, L'Ordine Agostiniano*, by Christian Danz et al., 33–56. Lugano: Nerbini, 2018.

———. "Johannes von Staupitz's Influence on Martin Luther." In *Oxford Research Encyclopedia of Religion*, edited by John Barton. Oxford: Oxford University Press, 2016 (Posset 2016b). https://oxfordre.com/religion/view/10.1093/acrefore/9780199340378.001.0001/acrefore-9780199340378-e-371.

———. *Marcus Marulus and the Biblia Latin of 1489: An Approach to His Biblical Hermeneutics*. Cologne: Böhlaus, 2013.

———. "Marko Marulić." In *The Encyclopedia of Christian Civilization*, edited by George Kurian, 1435–36. Oxford: Blackwell, 2011 (Posset 2011a).

———. "Marulus, Marcus." In *Biographisch-Bibliographisches Kirchenlexikon*, edited by Friedrich Wilhelm Bautz and Traugott Bautz, 32:942–47. Nordhausen: Bautz, 2011 (Posset 2011b).

———. "The Mouse, the Frog, and the Unidentified Flying Object: Metaphors for 'Empires' in the Latin Works of the Croatian Humanist Marcus Marulus and of the German Humanist Ulrich von Hutten." CM 17 (2008) 125–48 (Posset 2008b).

———. "Open Letter of a Croatian Lay Theologian to a 'German' Pope: Marko Marulić to Adrian VI." CM 18 (2009) 5–27.

———. "Polyglot Humanism in Germany circa 1520 as Luther's Milieu and Matrix: The Evidence of the 'Rectorate Page' of Crotus Rubeanus." *Renaissance and Reformation* 27 (2003) 5–33 (Posset 2003c).

———. *The Real Luther: A Friar at Erfurt and Wittenberg: Exploring Luther's Life with Melanchthon as Guide*. Saint Louis: Concordia, 2011 (Posset 2011c).

———. *Renaissance Monks: Monastic Humanism in Six Biographical Sketches*. Leiden: Brill, 2005.

———. "The 'Rock': Marcus Marulus' Theological Patrimony Concerning the Interpretation of "You Are Peter and upon This Rock I Will Build My Church." *CM* 23 (2014) 213–31.

———. "Rock and Recognition: Martin Luther's Catholic Interpretation of 'You Are Peter and on This rock I Will Build My Church' (Mt 16:18) and the Friendly Criticism from the Point of View of the 'Hebrew Truth' by His Confrère, Caspar Amman, Doctor of the Sacred Page." In *Ad fontes Lutheri: Toward the Recovery of the Real Luther. Essays in Honor of Kenneth Hagen's Sixty-Fifth Birthday*, edited by Timothy Maschke, Franz Posset, and Joan Skocir, 214–52. Milwaukee: Marquette University Press, 2001.

———. "*Sola Scriptura*—Martin Luther's Invention? Commemorating the 500th Anniversary of the Printed Edition of the Constitutions of the Order of St. Augustine in Nuremberg in 1504–1506." *Augustiniana* 56 (2006) 123–27.

———. "A Trio of Augustinian Reformers: Johann von Staupitz, Martin Luther and Wenceslaus Linck during the early Reformation (1517–1524)." *Analecta Augustiniana* 80 (2017) 47–72 (Possset 2017c).

———. *Unser Martin. Martin Luther aus der Sicht katholischer Sympathisanten*. Münster: Aschendorff, 2015 (Posset 2015b).

———. "Vom Sumpf und den Bächen zurück den Quellen." In *Anwälte der Freiheit!: Humanisten und Reformatoren im Dialog: Begleitband zur Ausstellung im Reuchlinhaus Pforzheim, 20. September bis 8. November 2015*, edited by Matthias Dall'Asta, 159–65. Heidelberg: Winter, 2015 (Posset 2015c).

Posset, Franz, and Bratislav Lučin. "Marko Marulić, Marko Pecinić, Marcus Marulus." In *Christian-Muslim Relations: A Bibliographic History*, vol. 7, *Central and Eastern Europe, Asia, Africa and South America (1500–1600)*, edited by David Thomas et al., 90–124. Leiden: Brill, 2015.

Praga, Giuseppe. "I maestri a Spalato nel Quattrocento." *Annuario del R. Istituto tecnico Francesco Rismondo* 11 (1933–) 3–18.

Rabe, Horst. *Reich und Glaubensspaltung: Deutschland, 1500–1600* Munich: Beck, 1989.

Rädle, Fidel. "Bibeldichtung. Mittellateinische Literatur." In *Lexikon des Mittelalters*, edited by Robert Auty et al., 2:75–77. Munich: Deutscher Taschenbuch, 2003.

Raeder, Siegfried. *Das Hebräische bei Luther, untersucht bis zum Ende der ersten Psalmenvorlesung*. Tübingen: Mohr, 1961.

———. *Die Benutzung des masoretischen Textes bei Luther in der Zeit zwischen der ersten und zweiten Psalmenvorlesung (1515–1518)*. Tübingen: Mohr, 1967.

Rahner, Hugo. *Greek Myths and Christian Mystery*. Translated by B. Battershaw. London: Burns & Oates, 1963.

Ramminger, Johann. "Marulus as a Neo-Latin Writer." *CM* 20 (2010) 123–38.

Raupp, Werner. "Münster, Sebastian." In *Biographisch-Bibliographisches Kirchenlexikon*, edited by Friedrich Wilhelm Bautz and Traugott Bautz, 6:316–26. Herzberg: Bautz, 1993.

Rehberg, Andreas, ed. *Ablasskampagnen des Spätmittelalters: Luthers Thesen von 1517 im Kontext*. Berlin: de Gruyter, 2017.

Reuchlin, Johannes. *Johannes Reuchlin: Briefwechsel*. Edited by Heidelberger Akademie der Wissenschaften in cooperation with the city of Pforzheim. Stuttgart-Bad Cannstatt: Frommann-Holzboog, 1999–2013.

Rex, Richard. "Luther among the Humanists." In *Martin Luther: A Christian between Reforms and Modernity (1517–2017)*, edited by Alberto Melloni, vol. 1. Berlin: de Gruyter, 2017.

Rice, Eugene F., Jr. *Saint Jerome in the Renaissance*. Baltimore: Johns Hopkins University Press, 1985.

Ridderbos, Bernhard. *Saint and Symbol: Images of Saint Jerome in Early Italian Art*. Translated by P. de Waard-Dekking. Groningen: Bouma's Boekhuis, 1984.

Roberts, Michael. *Biblical Epic and Rhetorical Paraphrase in Late Antiquity*. Liverpool: Francis Cairns, 1985.

Robinson, James Harvey, ed. *Readings in Modern European History*. Vol. 2. Boston and New York: Ginn, 1904.

Roling, Bernd. "Mediatoris fungi munere: Synkretismus im Werk des Paolo Ricci." In *Christliche Kabbala*, edited by Wilhelm Schmidt-Biggemann, 77–100. Ostfildern: Thorbecke, 2003.

Roncoroni, Angelo. "Ps.-Cipriano, De ligno crucis. Testo e osservazioni." *Rivista di storia e letteratura religiosa* 20 (1976) 380–90.

Rosenau, Helen. "The Architecture of Nicolaus de Lyra's Temple Illustrations and the Jewish Tradition." *Journal of Jewish Studies* 25 (1974) 294–304.

Rummel, Erika. *The Case against Johann Reuchlin: Religious and Social Controversy in Sixteenth-Century Germany*. Toronto: University of Toronto Press, 2002.

———, ed. *A Companion to Biblical Humanism and Scholasticism in the Age of Erasmus*. Leiden: Brill, 2008.

———. *Erasmus' Annotations on the New Testament: From Philologist to Theologian*. Toronto: University of Toronto Press, 1986.

Runje, Petar. "On the Early Editions of the Evangelistarium and the De institutione by Marko Marulić." *CM* 3 (1994) 93–98.

Rupprich, Hans, ed. *Der Briefwechsel des Konrad Celtis*. Munich: C. H. Beck, 1934.

Russell, Paul A. *Lay Theology in the Reformation: Popular Pamphleteers in Southwest Germany, 1521–1525*. Cambridge: Cambridge University Press, 1986.

Sabellicus, Marcus Antonius. *Ab orbe condito: Repertorium*. Edited by Branimir Glavičić. Split: Književni Krug, 2000.

Šanjek, Franjo. "Marulić and the Spiritual Movements of Humanism and the Reform." Translated by Nella Popović. In *Dossier: Marko Marulić*, edited by Bratislav Lučin. Special issue of *Most/The Bridge: A Journal of Croatian Literature* 1–4 (1999) 133–39.

Schedel, Hartmann, and Stephan Füssel. *Chronicle of the World: The Complete and Annotated Nuremberg Chronicle of 1493*. Cologne: Taschen, 2001.

Schelkle, Karl Hermann. *Das Neue Testament: Seine literarische und theologische Geschichte*. Kevelaer: Butzon and Bercker, 1964.

Schneider-Lastin, Wolfram. *Johann von Staupitz: Salzburger Predigten 1512: Eine textkritische Edition*. Tübingen: Universität Tübingen Neuphilologische Fakultät, 1990.

Schwaiger, Georg. "Hadrian VI." In *Dictionary of Popes and the Papacy*, edited by Bruno Steimer and Michael G. Parker, 54. New York: Crossroad, 2001.

———. "Leo X." In *Dictionary of Popes and the Papacy*, edited by Bruno Steimer and Michael G. Parker, 88–89. New York: Crossroad, 2001.

Schwind, Johannes. "Das pseudo-cyprianische Carmen de Pascha seu de Ligno Crucis." In *Ars et Ecclesia: Festschrift für Franz J. Ronig*, edited by Hans-Walter Stork, Christoph Gerhardt, and Alois Thomas, 79–95. Trier: Paulinus, 1989.

Schwoebel, Robert. *The Shadow of the Crescent: The Renaissance Image of the Turk (1453–1517)*. Nieuwkoop: B. de Graaf, 1967.

Seiler, Stefan. "Altes Testament." In *Das Luther-Lexikon*, edited by Volker Leppin and Gury Schneider-Ludorff, 56. Regensburg: Bückle & Böhm, 2014.

Shaw, Christine. *Julius II: The Warrior Pope*. Cambridge, MA: Blackwell, 1993.

Sicherl, Martin. "Zwei Briefe Johannes Cunos an den Bischof von Basel, Christoph von Utenheim." *Basler Zeitschrift für Geschichte und Altertumskunde* 77 (1977) 45–55.

Siebert, Susanne. "Ricius, Paul." In *Biographisch-Bibliographisches Kirchenlexikon*, edited by Friedrich Wilhelm Bautz and Traugott Bautz, 8:255–56. Herzberg: Bautz, 1994.

Sigerson, George. *The Easter Song: Being the First Epic of Christendom, by Sedulius, the First Scholar-Saint of Eirinn; with Introduction, Verse Translation and Appendices Including a Schedule of Milton's 'Debts'*. Dublin and London: Talbot, 1922. Reprint, Kessinger, 2007.

Simoncelli, Paolo, *Evangelismo italiano del Cinquecento: Questione religiose e nicodemismo politico* (Italia e Europa). Rome: Instituto Storico Italiano per Peta Moderna e Contemporanea, 1979.

Škunca, Stanko Josip. "Toma Niger Mrčić." *Radovi Zavoda za povijesne znanosti HAZU u Zadru* 43 (2001).

Smith, Lesly. "Nicholas of Lyra and Old Testament Interpretation." In *Hebrew Bible/Old Testament: The History of Its Interpretation*, edited by Magne Sæbø, Göttingen: Vandenhoeck and Ruprecht, 2008.

Springer, Carl P. E. "The Biblical Epic in Late Antiquity and the Early Modern Period: The Poetics of Tradition." In *Antiquity Renewed: Late Classical and Early Modern Themes*, edited by Z. von Martes and V. M. Schmidt, 103–26. Leuven: Peeters, 2003.

———. *The Gospel as Epic in Late Antiquity: The Paschale Carmen of Sedulius*, Leiden: Brill, 1988.

Tamani, Giuliano. "La Bibliothèque Hébraïque du Cardinal Domenico Grimani." In *Actes du XXIXe Congrès International des Orientalists: Études hébraïque*, edited by Georges Vajda, 10–45. Paris: L'Asiathèque, 1975.

Thomas, David, and John Chesworth, eds. *Christian-Muslim Relations: A Bibliographical History*. Leiden: Brill, 2015.

Tolan, John V. "Islam in the Mirror of Our Phantasms." In *Islam and Public Controversy in Europe*, edited by Nilüfer Göle, 113–22. 2014. Reprint, New York: Routledge, 2016.

Tomasović, Mirko. *Marko Marulić [Marcus Marulus]*. Translated from Italian by Charles Béné, translated from Croatian by Vera Miloš-Celin. Split: Književni Krug, 1996.

———. "Marko Marulić Marul." In *Epistola domini Marci Maruli Spalatensis ad Adrianum VI*, edited by Josip Bratulić. Zagreb: Nacionalna i Sveučilišna Biblioteka; Split: Crkva u Svijetu, 1994.

Tracy, James D. *Balkan Wars: Habsburg Croatia, Ottoman Bosnia, and Venetian Dalmatia, 1499–1617*. Lanham, MD: Rowman & Littlefield, 2016.

Turrentine, Herbert C. "Hans Weiditz's 'Emperor Maximilian at Mass': An Intriguing Liturgical Scene in the Chapel of Annakirche in Augsburg." *Explorations in Renaissance Culture* 27 (2001) 21–30.

Usmiani, Mirko A. "Marko Marulić (1450–1525)." *Harvard Slavic Studies* 3 (1957) 1–48.

Van Engen, John, trans. *Devotio Moderna: Basic Writings.* Mahwah, NJ: Paulist, 1988.

———. *Sisters and Brothers of the Common Life. The Devotio Moderna and the World of the Later Middle Ages.* Philadelphia: University of Pennsylvania Press, 2008.

Vanderjagt, Arjo. "Wessel Gansfort (1419–1489) and Rudolph Agricola (144?–1485): Piety and Hebrew." In *Frömmigkeit, Theologie, Frömmigkeitstheologie: Contributions to European Church History: Festschrift für Berndt Hamm zum 60. Geburtstag,* edited by Gudrun Litz, Heidrun Munzert, and Roland Liebenberg, 159–72. Studies in the History of Christian traditions 124. Leiden: Brill, 2005.

Vasoli, Cesare. "The Crisis of Late Humanism and Expectations of Reform in Italy at the End of the Fifteenth and Beginning of the Sixteenth Centuries." In *History of Theology III: The Renaissance,* edited by Giulio D'Onofrio, translated by Matthew J. O'Connell, 371–457. Collegeville, MN: Liturgical Press, 1998.

———. "The Mature Stage of Humanist Theology in Italy." In *History of Theology III: The Renaissance,* edited by Giulio D'Onofrio, translated by Matthew J. O'Connell, 188–247. Collegeville, MN: Liturgical Press, 1998.

"Verona." In *Catholic Encyclopedia,* vol. 5. *Catholic Online* digital ed. https://www.catholic.org/encyclopedia/view.php?id=11990.

Vives, Juan Luis. *Joannis Ludovici Vivis Valentini Opera Omnia.* 8 vols. London: Gregg, 1964.

Waley, Daniel, and Peter Denley. *Late Medieval Europe 1250–1520.* 3rd ed. London: Longman, 2001.

Weber, Robertus, ed. *Biblia sacra iuxta vulgatam editionem.* Stuttgart: Deutsche Bibelgesellschaft, 1994.

Wehrli, Max. "Sacra Poesis: Bibelepik als europäische Tradition." In *Formen mittelalterlicher Erzählung. Aufsätze,* 51–71. Zurich: Atlantis, 1969.

Wheelis, Sam. "Ulrich von Hutten: Representative of Patriotic Humanism." In *The Renaissance and Reformation in Germany: An Introduction,* edited by Gerhart Hoffmeister, 111–27. New York: F. Ungar, 1977.

White, Carolinne. *Early Christian Latin Poets.* London: Routledge, 2000.

Wiesflecker, Hermann. *Kaiser Maximilian I: Das Reich, Österreich und Europa an der Wende zur Neuzeit.* Vienna: Verlag für Geschichte und Politik, 1986.

Worstbrock, Franz J. "Aus Gedichtsammlungen des Wolfgang Marius." *Zeitschrift für bayerische Landesgeschichte* 44 (1981) 491–504.

Ziolkowski, Jan M., and Michael C. J. Putnam. *The Virgilian Tradition: The First Fifteen Hundred Years.* New Haven, CT: Yale University Press, 2008.

Zoranić Petar. *Planine.* Edited by Franjo Švelec, Juraj Baraković. Pet Stoljeća Hrvatske Književnosti 8. Zagreb: Matica Hrvatska, 1964.

Index of Personal Names

NB: the data given for popes and emperors usually refer to their time in office.

Acciarini, Tideo (humanist, 1430–1490), 33, 34, 149
Adalphius (husband of Proba), 137
Adam (biblical figure), 183
Adrian VI (pope, 1522–1523), xii, xiii, xxv, xxvii-xxx, 43, 55, 56, 61–67, 69–72, 74, 76, 82, 84, 173, 175–177, 180, 181
Adrian Florensz Boeyens see Adrian VI
Aesop (author), 40–45, 50, 56, 58, 62, 69, 176, 180
Ahaz (biblical figure), 107
Alcuin (Anglo-Saxon cleric, c. 735–804), 134
Aldhelm (poet, abbot, c. 639–709), 134
Alexander VI (pope, 1492–1503), 67, 79, 155
Alvise, Giovanni and Alberto (editors, 15th century), 40
Ambrose (frater, letter-carrier for Jerome), 96
Andreis see Andronicus
Andronicus, Tranquillus (nobleman, 1490–1571), 45, 48
Aquinas, Thomas (Dominican friar, c. 1225–1274), 111
Arator (subdeacon, poet, sixth century), 110, 131, 132
Arius (heretic, died 337), 152

Augustine of Hippo (church father, 354–430), xxiv, 10, 82, 118, 138

Backere, Pieter de (Petrus Bacherius, Dominican friar, 1517–1601), x
Barbaro, Francesco (senator, c. 1398–1454), 89
Bayezid II (sultan, reigned from 1389–1402), 176
Bayle, Pierre (author, 1647–1706), x
Bede (Anglo-Saxon monk, 673–735), 134
Begnius, Simon (bishop, 1460–1536), 74
Benalius, Bernardinus (publisher, c. 1458–1543), 159
Benko, Damir (reviewer), xiii
Béné, Charles (classical philologist, 1919–2005), xi, 39
Benedict of Nursia (saint, c. 480-c. 547), 34
Benedict XVI (pope emeritus), 113
Berchorius, Petrus (Benedictine monk, 1290–1362), 125
Berislavić, Petar (viceroy, reined 1513–1520), 73
Bernard of Clairvaux (Cistercian abbot, 1090–1153), xi, 36, 111, 126

Bernardinus de Vitalibus (printer, 16th century), 34, 70
Bessarion of Nicaea, John (bishop, cardinal, 1403–1472), 88
Billy, Jacques de (Christian moralist, 1535–1581), x
Bomberg, Daniel (printer, 1483–1553), 91
Bonaventure (Franciscan friar , c. 1221–1274), 37, 111, 142,
Borgia, Rodrigo (cardinal, c. 1431–1503), 67
Borromeo, Charles (saint, 1538–1584), x
Borsetto, Luciana (professor of comparative literature, 1949-), xi
Bošković, Ivan J. (Literary Circle, 1953-), xiv
Braccio see Bralić
Bralić, Nikola (artist, 16th century), 183
Brant, Sebastian (humanist, 1457–1521), 42
Brito, William (Franciscan friar, Bible scholar, c. 1230–1300), 94, 95
Brodarić, Stjepan (orator, c. 1480–1539), 84
Bubrin, Vladimir (Slavist), xvii
Buća see Buchia
Buchia, Dominicus (Dominican friar, c. 1480-c.1560), xxvii, 57, 70, 175
Burgos, Paul of (Hebraist, bishop, c. 1350–1435), 95, 96, 103, 108, 112, 121, 124

Caecilius see Pseudo-Cyprian
Cajetan, Thomas de Vio (cardinal, 1469–1534), 49
Canappus see Knappe
Candidus, Petrus (Benedictine monk, humanist, 1399–1477) , 147
Canisius, Peter (saint, 1521–1597), x
Carpus (biblical figure), 111
Catherine of Aragon (wife of Henry VIII, 1485–1536), 83
Cattaneo, Ruggero (philologist, 1975-), xi
Catullus (poet, 84–54 BC), ix

Caxton, William (printer, 15th century), 41, 42
Celtis, Conrad (humanist, 1459–1508), 32
Charles V (emperor, 1519–1556), x, xxviii, 48, 54, 65, 72, 76, 177
Chasteigner, Henri-Louis de la Rocheposay (author, 1577–1651), xxviii
Chelidonius, Benedictus (Benedictine monk, c. 1460–1521), 28–31
Cippico see Cipiko
Cipiko, Jerolim (lawyer, died c. 1525), 151, 160, 165
Clement VII (pope, 1523–1534), xxv, 61, 152, 173, 181
Constantine (emperor, 306–337), 109, 134, 135
Contarini, Gasparo (cardinal, 1483–1542), 81, 83
Crotus Rubeanus (author, c. 1480–1545), 44
Croy, Guillaume de (cardinal, 1498–1521), 82
Cusanus, Nicolaus (cardinal, 1401–1464), 88
Cyprianus see Pseudo-Cyprian

Damasus (pope, c. 305–384), 132, 133
Dante Alighieri (writer, 1265–1321), 160, 166
Dantyszek, Jan (Dantiscus, diplomat, 1485–1548), x
David (biblical figure), xxx, 59, 91, 110, 143
Dobrica de Albertis (Marulus's Italian mother), 33
Döring, Matthias (Franciscan friar, Bible scholar, c. 1400–1469), 95, 96, 124
Drach, Peter (printer, 1455–1504), 99
Dražojević, Žarko (Croatian leader, 1438–1508), 151
Dürer, Albrecht (artist, 1471–1528), 29, 47, 49

Esop see Aesop

INDEX OF PERSONAL NAMES   203

Erasmus of Rotterdam (humanist, c. 1466–1536), ix, xii, xxii, xxx, 25, 52, 68, 82, 87, 88, 90, 117
Erdmann, Elisabeth von (Slavist, 1956-), xi
Eufrosina (saint, 410–470), 138
Evans, G.R. (theologian), xiii
Eysengrein, Guilielmus (author, 1543–1584), 116

Fabricius, Johann Albert, author, 18th century), 170
Felix de Prato (Hebraist, Augustinian friar, c. 1460–1559), 91
Ferdinand I (king, emperor, 1503–1564), 48, 80
Firmianus Colla (humanist, 15th century), 149
Fortunatus, Venantius (poet, c. 540–600), 133
Fowler, John (editor, 1537–1578/79), x
Francis (pope), 113
Francis I (king, 1594–1547), 48
Francis de Sales (saint, 1567–1622), x
Francis Xavier (saint, 1506–1552), x, xxix, 9, 36
Francisco de Quevedo y Villegas (author, 1580–1645), x
Frankopan, Krsto (embassador, 1482–1527), 84
Froben, Johannes (printer, c. 1460–1527), 25, 82, 88

Galatinus, Petrus (Franciscan friar, 1460–1540), 52
Galba (emperor, 3 BC–69 AD), 111
Gálvez, Francisco Javier Juéz (philologist, 1962-), xi
Gansfort, Wessel (lay theologian, 1419–1489), 78, 79, 116, 117
Garin, Eugenio (philosopher, historian, 1909–2004), 77
Gennadius (author, fifth century), 131
Gerson, Jean (theologian, 1363–1429), 115
Graf, Vrs (Urs Graf, artist, c. 1485–1528), 7

Gregory the Great (church father, c. 540–604), 123
Grimani, Antonio (doge, reigned 1521–1523), 47
Grimani, Dominico (cardinal, 1461–1523), 88
Grüninger, Johann (printer, 1455–1531), 28
Guarinus Veronensis (philosopher, 1374–1460), 89
Gymnicus, Ioannes (printer, active 1520–1544), 34

Hadrian (pope) see Adrian
Haselberg, Johann (pamphleteer, active 1515–1538), 54
Henry VIII (king (1491–1547), x, xxix, 18, 19, 48, 170
Hercules (mythological figure), xxx, 35, 86
Hieronymus de Papalibus (friend of Marulus, 16th century), 131
Holofernes (biblical figure), 159
Hopfer, Daniel (artist, 1470–1536), 55
Howard, Philip (saint, translator, 1557–1595), x, 38
Hutten, Ulrich von (humanist, 1488–1523), 40, 43–50, 58, 61, 62, 79, 176

Jacobus de Pforzheim (Wolff; printer, died 1518), 42
Jerome (church father, c. 347–419), xxix, 4, 5, 34, 94, 96, 105, 107, 110, 118–120, 125–127, 131, 133
Jerome of Padua (author, 15th century), 28
Joab (biblical figure), 59
Joachim de Fiore (Cistercian abbot, c. 1135–1202), 159
Johannes de Ragusa (Dominican friar, c. 1390–1443), 60, 87
John the Baptist (biblical figure), 118
John (evangelist), 17, 135, 140
John of Landsberg see Lanspergius
John Paul II (pope, 1920–2005), xxiv, 10, 27, 115

INDEX OF PERSONAL NAMES

Josephus, Flavius (historian, first century), 92
Jozić, Branko (staff member at Marulianum, 1960-), x, xxvi, 116, 149
Judith (biblical figure), x, xi, xxv, xxvi, xxx, 35, 158–161
Julius II (pope, 1503–1513), 48, 52, 73
Juvencus (Iuvencus, Spanish nobleman, priest, poet, fourth century), 110, 131–136, 140

Karnarutić, Brne (author, c. 1515–1573), 152
Knappe, Hans (printer, active c. 1500), xxiii, xxiv, 32
Koberger, Anton (printer, 1445–1513), 96
Krause, Carl (historian, 19th century), 31
Kronberg, Hartmut von (Lutheran knight, 1488–1549), 61

Lactantius (poet, died c. 320), 28, 37, 132, 133
Lang, Matthew (cardinal, 1468–1540), 80
Langendorff see Petri
Lanspergius, Johannes (Carthusian monk, 1489–1539), 38
Lascaris, Constantine (Grecian, died c. 1500), 34
Louis XII (king, reigned 1498–1515), 48
Leo X (pope, 1513–1521), xxviii, 34, 48, 52, 53, 56, 68, 71–75, 84, 91, 176, 181
Leschinkohl, Franz (historian of printing, 1920–2012), xxi
Liberale da Verona (painter, c. 1445–1526), 41
Liechtenstein, Peter (printer, active 1497–1528), 91
Locatellus, Bonetus (priest, printer, active 1485–1510), 93, 94
Lökös, István (professor of comparative literature, 1933-), xi
Loredan, Leonardo (doge, reigned 1501–1521), 47

Lucensis, Franciscus (priest, printer 16th century), 32
Lučin, Bratislav (director of Marulianum, 1956-), xiv, xv, xvii, xxi, xxvi, 149
Luis de Granada (Dominican friar, 1504–1588), x
Lullus, Raimundus (lay theologian, 1232–1316), 77
Luposignoli, Mihovil (architect, painter, 1693–1750), 183, 184
Luther, Martin (Augustinian friar, reformer, 1483–1546), xi, xxii–xxv, xxviii, 1–15, 20–26, 43, 44, 56, 60, 76, 77, 79, 92, 127, 141, 176
Lyra, Nicholas de (Franciscan friar, Bible scholar, c. 1270–1349), 5, 6, 93–95, 104, 105, 108, 110–112, 121–126, 135, 152

Mancinus, Dominicus (author, 15th century), 29
Manetti, Giannozzo (lay theologian, 1396–1459), 77, 78
Mantuanus, Baptista (Carmelite friar, humanist, poet, 15th century), 29
Manutius, Aldus (printer, 1449–1515), 28, 131, 147, 148
Marius, Bolfgangus (Cistercian abbot, 1469–1544), 29, 30
Martiniacus, Franciscus (poet, c. 1480–1527), 70
Mary (Virgin, biblical figure), 156, 183
Matthew (evangelist), 124, 128, 140
Maximilian I (king, emperor, reigned 1493–1519), 44–48, 80
Melanchthon, Philip (humanist, reformer, 1497–1560), 80, 92
Miller, Johann (printer, 16th century), 45, 48
Mohammed see Muhammad
Monica (saint), 139
More see Morus
Morus, Thomas (lawyer, saint, 1477/1478–1535), x, xxix, 18, 82

INDEX OF PERSONAL NAMES 205

Moses (biblical figure), 133, 135, 143
Muhammad (prophet, c. 570–632), 57, 60, 152, 174, 176, 183, 184
Münster, Sebastian (Franciscan friar, Lutheran, 1488–1552), x, xxix, 20, 34, 92, 160, 170
Müntzer, Thomas (priest, revolutionary, c. 1489–1525), 56
Mutianus Rufus, Conrad (humanist, c. 1470–1526), xii, 31–32

Neralić, Jadranka (historian), xiii
Nicholas V (pope, 1447–1455), 78
Nicodemus (biblical figure), 135
Niger, Thomas (diplomat, c. 1460–1531), xxviii, 73, 74, 76
Novaković, Darko (philosopher, 1953-), 174

Odo of Cheriton (author, died 1247), 44
Origen (theologian, c. 185-c. 254), 77, 125, 127

Palazzi, Giovanni (author, c. 1646-c.1703), xxviii
Parlov, Madlen (theologian), 116, 131
Pandžić, Basil Stephen (Franciscan friar, 1918–2018), 1
Pandžić, Zvonko (classical philologist, 1956-), xiii, xvii, xxviii
Pasquino (name of a statue in Rome), 68, 73
Paul (apostle), 16, 17, 109–111, 132, 143
Paul III (pope, 1534–1549), 81
Paulinus (bishop, c. 352–431), 96
Paulus Diaconus (Benedictine monk, c. 720–799), 142
Pečenić or Pecinić (Marulus's Croatian family name), xxix, 33, 149
Pelagius (heretic, 360–420), 152
Peter (Simon, son of Jonah, apostle), xxvi, 11, 113, 118, 121, 124, 126, 128, 168
Petrarca, Francesco (Petrarch; humanist, 1304–1374), 87
Petri, Adam (printer, 1454–1527), 2, 7, 9, 12, 20, 22, 24, 26, 32
Petronius (author, 27–66 AD), ix

Peutinger, Conrad (jurist, 1465–1547), x
Philip (elector of the Palatinate, 1448–1508), 79
Picentinus, Hieronymus Genesius (humanist, 15th century), 33, 91, 149
Piccolomini, Enea Silvio (humanist, Pope Pius II, 1458–1464), 67
Pius II see Piccolomini
Plato (philosopher, c. 430–348 BC), 143
Plutarch (philosopher, 46 BC-c. 119 AD), 69
Poggio Bracciolini, Giovanni Francesco (humanist, 1380–1459), 89
Posedarski, Stjepan (humanist, prince, 15th/16th century), 74
Possevino, Antonio (author, active c. 1600), xxvii, xxviii
Proba, Faltonia Betitia (poetess, fourth century), 131, 136–139
Pseudo-Bernard, 28, 36
Pseudo-Cyprian (bishop, poet, fifth century), 132, 142–144
Pseudo-Lactantius, 132
Ptolemy (geographer, c. 100-c. 170), 70

Ranke, Leopold von (historian, 1795–1886), 181
Rashi, Solomo ben Isaac (rabbi, Hebraist, 1040–1105), 95
Reuchlin, Johann (humanist, 1455–1522), xi, xxiii, 5, 17, 30, 78–80, 87, 88, 90, 119
Reuter, Conrad (Cistercian abbot, 16th century), 29, 30
Ricci see Ricius
Ricius, Paulus (physician, lay theologian, c. 1480-c. 1541), 80, 81
Rio, Baldassare del (papal chamber servant, archdeacon, 16th century), 74
Ritz von Sprinzenstein see Ricius
Romulus (mythological figure), 51
Rufus see Mutianus

INDEX OF PERSONAL NAMES

Rumpler, Angelus (Benedictine abbot, c. 1460–1513), 29

Sacon, Jacob (printer, 16th century), 125
Saint-Charles, Louis Jacob de (Carmelite friar, lexicologist, 1608–1670), xxviii
Salicetus, Nicolaus (Cistercian, humanist, died c. 1494), 28, 36
Sallust (historian, 86 BC-35 BC), 59, 69
Šanjek, Franjo (historian, 1939-), 116
Sarah (biblical figure), 109
Schedel, Hartmann (author of Chronicle of the World, 1440–1514), 41, 42, 137, 138
Schwandtner, Johann Georg (historian, 1716–1791), x
Scilurus (Skilurus, king, second century), 69
Scotus Eriugena, John (theologian, c. 800-c. 850), 77, 111
Scotus, Octavianus (publisher, 15th century), 93
Sedulius, Coelius (poet, fifth century), 110, 131, 132, 139–141
Selim I (sultan, reigned 1512–1520), 52, 53, 56
Seneca (philosopher, died 65 AD), 143
Sergius (heretical monk, legendary teacher of Muhammad), 152
Severus, Sulpicius (author, 363–425), 131
Shimei (biblical figure), 59
Sigismund (king, 1506–1548), 74
Skarga, Piotr (counter-reformer, 1536–1612), x
Soardi, Lazaro (publisher, c. 1450-c. 1517), 159
Soleyma(n) see Sulayman
Solomo (biblical figure), 59
Soncino, Gershom (printer, died 1534), 17
Špoljarić, Luka (historian, 1983-), xiii
Springer, Carl P.E. (classical philologist), 130
Staupitz, Johann von (Augustinian friar, later Benedictine abbot, c. 1465–1524), xi, 3, 10–12, 15, 92

Steinhöwel, Heinrich (humanist, died 1478), 42
Stojković see Johannes de Ragusa
Stuchs, Johannes (printer, 16th century), 48
Sulayman I (sultan, 1494–1566), 54, 56
Suso, Henry (spiritual author, c. 1300–1366), 3

Tertullian (lay theologian, c. 160-c. 220), 77, 142
Thayer, Anne (church historian), xiii
Thomas à Kempis (spiritual author, 1380–1471), xxix, 3, 34, 115
Tiphernus, Gregorius (poet, 1414-c. 1462), 132
Tobit (biblical figure), 106, 109
Tomasović, Mirko (author, 1938–2017), xxi
Tracy, James D. (historian), xxv
Trunte, Nicolina (Slavist, 1948-), xiii
Turtius Ruffus (Roman consul, fifth century), 139
Tyconius (Bible scholar, died c. 400), 93

Urbanus, Henricus (Cisterican monk, c. 1470-c. 1539), xii, xxiv, 27, 28, 30–33, 35, 36, 39

Valdaura, Marguerite (wife of Vives), 82
Valerius (Marulus's brother), 150
Valerius Maximus (Roman author, died c. 50), 35
Valla, Lorenzo (humanist, Bible scholar, 1407–1457), 41, 89
Victorinus, Caius Marius (poet, fourth century), 142
Virgil (poet, 70–19 BC), 67, 131, 133, 137
Vitellius, Erasmus (bishop, 1460–1522), 74
Vives, Ioannes Ludovicus (humanist, theologian, 1492–1540), 82, 83
Vuyrsung, Marcus (printer, 16th century), 48

Walter of England (author of fables, c. 1160–1205), 51
Weiditz, Hans (artist, c. 1495- c. 1536), 45–47, 79
Weyssenburger, Johann (priest, printer, died c. 1535), 29
White, Carolinne (Latinist, translator), 145
Wirsung see Vuyrsung
Wolff (printer) see Jacobus de Pforzheim

Yôhô-ken, Paulo (Japanese translator, 1510–1599), xxix, 9

Zane, Bernardo (archbishop of Split, c. 1450–1527), 4, 73
Zell, C. (printer, died 1590), 55
Zoranić, Petar (author, 1508- after 1569), 152
Zovenzonius, Raphael (poet laureate, 1431-c.1485), 132, 133, 148, 155
Zrinski, Nicola Šubić (Croatian leader, 16th century), 152
Zwingli, Ulrich (reformer, 1484–1531), 77.

Index of Biblical References

OLD TESTAMENT

Genesis
19	106, 109
22	6, 112

Numbers
21	135

Joshua
	110

2 Samuel
16:5	59
19:16	59

1 Kings
2:5–9	59

2 Kings
20:11	107

Tobit
	106, 109
3:21	110

Maccabees
	96

Psalms
Seven Penitential Psalms	5, 70, 90
22	91
71:16	108

Canticle (Song of Songs)
	93
8	108

Ecclesiasticus
	xxvii

Isaiah
	96
38:7–8	101, 107
66	108

Jeremiah
31:12	17

Ezekiel
33:6	81

40	122
47:1–12	96, 100, 144

Daniel

	96

Habakkuk

	13, 14, 104
3	13, 109

Zechariah

	103, 108
9	109
14:20–21	108, 109

NEW TESTAMENT

Matthew

12:25	59
16	xiii, xxvi, 11, 12, 113, 117, 118, 120–123, 125, 128, 129
25	17
27:27–51	140

Luke

22:31–32	168
23:39–43	140

John

1:42	126
3:13	135
3:16	136
4:14	17
5	109
8	135
12	135
19:20	140, 141

Romans

2:24	166

1 Corinthians

15	152

Galatians

2	126
5:7	12

Ephesians

6:17	86

1 Thessalonians

4:15–18	16

2 Timothy

4:13	110, 111

Hebrews

11	109

2 Peter

1:20	86

1 John

5:4	168

Revelation

	144
7	105, 109
17	173
20	159
22:2	144